To the memory of Kent Gerecke (1937–1992)

Cities Without Citizens

Cities Without Citizens
Modernity of the City as a Corporation

Engin F. Isin

BLACK ROSE BOOKS

Montréal/New York

BLACK ROSE BOOKS No. V173
Hardcover ISBN: 1-895431-27-1
Paperback ISBN: 1-895431-26-3
Library of Congress Catalog No. 92-70622

Canadian Cataloguing in Publication Data

Isin, Engin Fahri, 1959-
Cities without citizens

ISBN: 1-895431-27-1 (bound) — ISBN: 1-895431-26-3 (pbk.)

1. Municipal government—Canada. 2. Municipal government—Comparative studies. I. Title.

HT113.I85 1992   320.8'5'0971   C92-090134-4

Cover Illustration: Robert Darrel

Mailing Address

BLACK ROSE BOOKS
C.P. 1258
Succ. Place du Parc
Montréal, Québec
H2W 2R3 Canada

BLACK ROSE BOOKS
340 Nagel Drive
Cheektowaga, New York
14225 USA

A publication of the Institute of Policy Alternatives of Montréal (IPAM)

Printed in Canada

CONTENTS

PREFACE

FOR us moderns it is hard to imagine ourselves as citizens of cities. We are citizens of nations. But, in the history of Western civilization, citizenship originated as membership in the city as an institution. Both the Greek and Roman practices of citizenship were inextricably associated with cities—*polis* and *civitas*. Yet neither the Greek *polis* nor the Roman *civitas* was organized as a corporation. It was throughout the medieval centuries that this association evolved into a unique practice of cities as corporations: sworn association of citizens *as a whole*. Between the twelfth and fourteenth centuries, the Italian city republics, German Hansa cities, French communes, and English boroughs evolved into powerful cities as sworn associations of citizens. Until the fifteenth century in English and European legal systems, a citizen was defined as an inhabitant of a city entitled to the rights and privileges of a 'freeman'. After the fifteenth century, however, the citizen became the subject of the emerging European States, and in the nineteenth century a citizen was a member of a national State. Along with these changes, the definition and status of the corporation underwent profound changes. Until the fifteenth century the city was autonomous; it then became a subordinate entity created by the State. And in the last two centuries, in the modern era, citizenship no longer has been associated with cities but with nations. Although our language is still infused with the older tradition—we often call city-dwellers 'citizens'—citizenship no longer has a formal association with the city.

By portraying modern cities as cities without citizens, I want to draw attention to the fact that citizenship is no longer associated with cities. City-dwellers as a whole are not vested with any rights, powers or privileges. The remarkable contrast between medieval and modern cities as corporations is that, in the late-medieval centuries, citizens secured collective rights (citizens were *collectively* the city) while in modernity citizens are *individuals* with rights and obligations derived from the nation. Accordingly, modern cities are corporations created as legal entities *distinct from their inhabitants*. This means that it is the legal corporation that is vested with rights and obligations, not the citizens. By contrast, there was no distinction between the rights of the corporation and rights of citizens in medieval cities.

How did cities evolve from being autonomous corporations of citizen associations to modern corporations without citizens? What were the ideas that shaped their institutions? When and why were the rights of citizens separated from the rights of corporations? What was expected of modern cities as corporations? This book answers these questions by studying political and legal discourse—political and legal treatises, enactments, legislation, edicts, proclamations, practices (e.g., poor law administration, land settlement), commissions, inquiries, surveys—that gradually but fitfully constituted the modern city as a corporation—a subordinate body politic with delegated powers to undertake the governance of its subjects.

To put it differently, this book questions the modernity of the city as a corporation—a question of both research and politics. The modern city became a subordinate body politic, and its legal expression was a new form of corporation developed in conjunction with the dictates of the modern State. Similarly, the sphere of citizenship shifted from city to State. The overall approach of the book is to explore the political principles that the city as a corporation embodies and expresses. And in so doing, I want to call into question institutional aspects of the city that are embedded in our modern urban experience.

The focus of this book is on the origins of the modern Canadian city as a corporation, which spans the period between the 1780s and the 1850s. But the book places the Canadian city against the background of political and constitutional developments in England and America. The book traces the lineage of the city as a corporation back to the twelfth century and chronicles its transformations until the nineteenth century. The book then focuses on the transposition of the corporation idea into the New World in the seventeenth and eighteenth centuries in colonial America. Although its origins can be traced to English and American counterparts, the distinctive features of the Canadian city in this formative period were intensified in the transition to new liberal colonial politics in the 1840s, which eventually diverged from its origins. Out of these colonial conditions, by the 1850s, a city developed that was quite different from its background in either England or America. By examining the crucial ways in which the modern Canadian city diverged from English and colonial American patterns, this book provides an interpretation of the origins of the Canadian city as a corporation. But it also opens up the question of the modernity of the city as a corporation.

A few remarks about the intellectual roots of the book are perhaps in order. For some time now historians have turned toward long-term changes and transformations that enveloped shorter time spans and events—the *longue durée*. The French *Annales* school of historians, although not the first to have recognized, let alone practiced, the long duration history, were nevertheless influential in popularizing it. If we go further back in time, we should note Frederic W. Maitland (1850–1906) who focused on English law from the ninth century in order to understand nineteenth-century legal problems. His work was not a small accomplishment, and we shall have frequent occasion to refer to it. We can certainly add Otto Gierke (1841–1921), Henri Pirenne (1862–1935) and Max Weber (1864–1920), whose works never failed to take broad strokes with present concerns in mind.

But I think the French historian Fernand Braudel (1902–1985) stands apart because of his tenacious pursuit of the idea of *longue durée*. He elaborated this idea in a series of articles in the 1950s and the 1960s, which were subsequently compiled in his *On History*. What is the *longue durée*? He said: "It functions along the border between the moving and the immobile, and because of the long-standing stability of its values, it appears unchanging compared with all the histories which flow and work themselves out more swiftly, and which in the final analysis gravitate around it." Now, the significance of this idea is twofold. First, Braudel did not consider these time spans *as alternative historical frames of research but as mutually complementary*. And, second, he considered the relationship between time spans as one where the longer *embraces* the shorter. For this reason, Braudel insisted that it is an error to ignore the enveloping and conditioning limits of the long time span upon shorter time spans. Although long-term historical study is not viewed against studies that focus on short-term events, it is nevertheless privileged in providing broad perspectives within which short-term spans can be seen.

The concept of a long-term span encompassing shorter time spans is quite significant but little practiced in the case of British North American history (i.e., the history of those colonies that were opened up for settlement after the rebellion of the thirteen American colonies), although this history is often described as being an offspring of European and English histories. Actually, in histories of local government in Canada, this concept is a rhetorical device for *not* investigating the origins of city government and politics: we are often told that institutions of city government simply derive from their English counterparts. But the questions of how these English institutions emerged and evolved, how they were transposed to colonial America, why they were reproduced in British North America, under what specific political circumstances, and with what similarities and contrasts often remain neglected.

So this book differs from Braudel's focus on geography and economy as relatively stable elements of history. Instead, the *longue durée* that I study deals with legal and political institutions as relatively stable and slow-changing elements that impose real limits on how we think and act. Accordingly, I draw upon institutional and legal history that was mostly practiced in the late nineteenth and early twentieth centuries but since then has fallen out of fashion. Later in this century the concerns of the institutional and legal history were found to be too narrow and archaic by the 'new' economic and social historians. The historians who dominate the bibliography of this book, Frederic Maitland, Otto Gierke, Charles Andrews, Herbert Osgood, and their disciples, were largely abandoned except by a few followers. It is true that institutional and legal history concerned itself with technical details, and sometimes engaged in futile debates on absolute origins, but they also produced an immensely valuable body of knowledge for understanding the history of Western political and territorial institutions, such as cities, States, parliaments, counties, townships, etc.

There is an important reason why political and legal institutions must be seen in the context of the *longue durée*. Once an institution emerges, the need to articulate the reasons why such an institution and its rules and regulations exist disappears, unless an opposing vision emerges. Without such a vision these institutions become embedded in our consciousness and experience without being called into question. Moreover, the political and legal institutions of Western civilization have steadily come to form calculated components of government, and this has been concomitant with the development of the modern State. Accordingly, institutions have become objects of intense political and legal thought and action—discourse—in the modern era. Our institutions are not products of arbitrary and inevitable developments but outcomes of legal and political discourse. As this book attempts to show, the city as a political and legal institution has followed a trajectory that began in the thirteenth and fourteenth centuries and became an object of intense discourse. It is the assumptions and rationalities of this discourse that we will study in this book. To call into question our modern institutions through broad and comparative historical analyses, to cast a different light on what we are otherwise likely to take for granted is one of the tasks of historical writing. It is a task to which this book aspires.

A word about quotations and terminology. To maintain consistency I modernized the spelling and punctuation of quotations from original documents. Also, I use 'city' rather than 'town', except, of course, where they legally mean different things, and where the use of 'borough' is necessary.

1

INTRODUCTION

THE object of this book is to explore the origins of the modern Canadian city as a corporation.[1] Saint John, Montréal, Québec, Toronto, Kingston, Hamilton and Halifax were constituted as corporations by the British colonial government between the 1780s and the 1840s. Although a few changes have been made since then in their legal institutions and structure, the fundamental principles remain the same. Moreover, similar principles have been constituted in virtually all Canadian cities, and are embedded in general legislation on municipal corporations. An inquiry into the origins of the modern city as a corporation, therefore, is of more than historical interest. It is crucial for understanding the functioning of our cities as political institutions, and our role within them.

Before discussing the organization of the book, let us briefly consider how modern legal and political doctrine conceptualizes the city. Above all, the modern city is considered a legal institution created by the legislature.[2] In Canada it is often said that cities are 'creatures' of provinces. What does this mean? It means that the provincial legislature passes a statute to create a city, without which no community is entitled to exist as a city. This act of creation typically involves turning a populous community with a prescribed territory into a corporation with a name, and its governing body is guaranteed continuous succession. The modern city is thus created, with or without the consent of its inhabitants, as a subordinate government for the purposes of the local administration of provincial affairs. Yet the modern city is also said to be created to administer the 'internal' concerns of the district embraced within its corporate limits in matters peculiar to such place and not common to the province at large. It therefore has a dual legal and political purpose: one defined as 'external' (obligatory) and the other as 'internal' (permissive). That is, one class of duties and functions consists of those acts performed as a franchise of the legislature in the exercise of delegated powers, and enforcement of general laws made in pursuance of federal and provincial policies. The other consists of acts performed by the corporation for 'its' own benefit or the benefit of its inhabitants

1

alone. But modern doctrine considers the latter class of functions subordinate to the former in cases of conflict.[3]

We can then isolate two essential legal characteristics of the modern city as a corporation. First, it is created at the pleasure of the legislature, and while the province may obtain the consent of the people of the affected locality, it need not. The act of incorporation is not a contract between the legislature and the inhabitants. The province can erect, change, divide and abolish a corporation at its pleasure and as it deems appropriate. Second, the authority conferred on the modern city is not local in nature but derives from the province. The act of incorporation empowers a governing body (the city council) to exercise authority on behalf of the province. Accordingly, these characteristics are expressed in law by two principles. First, the corporation is distinct from its inhabitants. This means that with the creation of a modern city as a corporation inhabitants are not vested with any rights as citizens. It is the corporation through its governing body that is vested with rights and obligations. Most important of these include the following: (i) to exist perpetually; (ii) to hold lands; (iii) to pass regulations and bylaws; (iv) to sue and be sued; and, (v) to hold a common seal. The modern city as a corporation also has a subordinate legal status: its governing body may exercise only those powers explicitly granted to it by the legislature, or powers necessarily and clearly implied from those explicitly granted, or those which are essential to the proper functioning of the corporation.

The modern doctrine of corporations became an accepted and guiding principle of legal and political practice in British North American colonies in the 1830s, but its development spanned the period between the 1780s and the 1840s. (Throughout this book we use 'British North American colonies' to refer to Upper Canada, Lower Canada, Nova Scotia and New Brunswick, which were opened up for settlement after the rebellion of the original thirteen colonies. Those original British colonies are referred to as 'American colonies'.) As mentioned earlier, the first incorporated cities in British North America were Saint John (1785), Québec (1832), Montréal (1832), Toronto (1834), Halifax (1841), Kingston (1846) and Hamilton (1846), and these cities existed as localities or towns before they were constituted as cities.

It is generally acknowledged that the modern doctrine was being used in incorporating cities in the 1830s and the 1840s. But this fact is very rarely, if at all, seen as constituting an important element of the modernity of the city in historical literature. Why were cities incorporated? What precisely did incorporation mean? What aims were the city governments expected to accomplish? How was power exercised in these new institutions? Why did the British colonial government wait after Saint John was incorporated in 1785 until the 1830s to begin to constitute city governments? We need to emphasize now that it is neither self-evident nor was it inevitable that cities were constituted as modern corporations in the 1830s.[4] Rather, it was an outcome of a long history and specific circumstances, and these need analysis. To call into question the significance of incorporation through an historical analysis is to open up the question of the political status and legal nature of the modern city because incorporation expresses a precise political relationship between the city and the State, one whose specific features this book seeks to discuss.

The modern city did not originate in British North America, and we cannot answer the questions posed above without studying the origins and lineage of the modern city as a corporation—a long history, one that has undoubtedly shaped the practices that emerged in British North America. Without placing the emergence of the modern city in British North America within this history, it would be neither possible to understand its distinct characteristics nor to appreciate its origins. The modern city in Canada was an extension, if also a modification, of European and English legal and political traditions. To draw proper contrasts and similarities, this book sketches the broad outlines of the institutional development of the modern city in European legal and political thought and practice since the twelfth century. This was when distinct characteristics of the city as an autonomous corporation emerged. The autonomous city as a corporation was distinguished by being a sworn association whose source of authority rested with the citizenry. This book then describes two great transformations that the autonomous city as a sworn association of citizens has undergone since the twelfth century. The first happened around the fifteenth century; it saw the subjection of the autonomous city to the nascent European States. The resulting early modern city as a corporation, as it is defined in this book, was institutionally distinguished by its subordinate status and was governed by an appointed oligarchy that derived its authority directly from the State. This was when the citizenry was separated from the city. The second great transformation occurred in the early nineteenth century when the city became a municipal corporation with an elaborate and uniform constitution. The modern city as a corporation is an institutional form distinguished by its dual source of authority. On the one hand, it is authorized by the State with elaborate and prescribed powers. On the other hand, the qualified inhabitants authorize the governing body to act on its behalf within the powers prescribed. The modern city thus constituted is defined in this book as an apparatus of governance emphasizing the elaborate structures of its institutions, and its separate legal existence from its inhabitants.

After articulating the attributes that define the modernity of the city, the book then focuses on its emergence in British colonial experience. First an emphasis is placed on the British experience in the seventeenth and the eighteenth centuries in colonial America. This was when the English State attempted, without complete success, to create royal cities and boroughs as early modern corporations. This book shows that the English attributed the loss of the thirteen colonies in part to the failure to create royal cities. This experience in colonial America played a significant role when British North America was opened for settlement. The book shows how British statesmen were uncertain whether to create cities with or without corporate status. With the fear of another rebellion, until the 1830s, cities were created without corporate status and were governed by royal officials and through appointed bodies. Nonetheless, with the emergence of the city as an apparatus of governance in England and in response to problems of government in the colonies, modern cities were incorporated in the 1830s and the 1840s. The modern city was thus born as an apparatus of governance in British North America.

Accordingly, the book is organized in three parts, each of which is discussed below in a section: the first is an outline of a history of corporations in Europe with a particular focus on English political and legal traditions (Chapter Two); the second is an outline of how corporations were transposed to colonial America (Chapter Three); and, the third is a study of the specific conditions of British North America, placed within the broad outlines sketched (Chapters Four and Five).

Modernity of the City as a Corporation

"Let us imagine," said Fernand Braudel, that "we are looking at a comprehensive history of the towns of Europe covering the complete series of their forms from the Greek city-state to an eighteenth century town."[5] And he asked, "How is one to classify such a wealth of material?" His suggestion was a threefold classification of Western cities: (i) the ancient Greek or Roman city, which was open to the surrounding countryside and on terms of equality with it; (ii) the medieval city, which was a closed, self-sufficient unit; and, (iii) the subjugated city of early modern times.[6] We need also to add a fourth class, the modern city *proper*, which is not included by Braudel since his classification did not extend beyond the eighteenth century. Like any classification, this suggestion is open to criticism. But at least it highlights a problem: unless we are able to know the distinctive characteristics of each of these forms of Western cities, we will not be able to establish a workable conception of the modernity of the city. Hence we need precise comparisons and contrasts among cities with different institutional forms.

Max Weber initiated such a project in his *Die Stadt* (1921), which became a classic statement on the distinctiveness of the Western city that emerged in the late-medieval centuries.[7] He maintained that the urban autonomy characteristic of the late-medieval centuries, which included autonomies of law-making authority, autocephaly (judicial autonomy), and taxing and market rights, did not exist in either Greek or Roman cities, although these also possessed certain autonomies.[8] For Weber, the legal and political status of the city between the eleventh and fourteenth centuries, within the surrounding kingdoms and emerging States, stood out as a colossal and unique phenomenon. Braudel pointed out a distinctive element in this period. He said: "The miracle in the West was not so much that everything sprang up again from the eleventh century, after having been almost annihilated with the disaster of the fifth [the decline of the Roman Empire]. History is full of examples of secular revivals, of urban expansions, of births and rebirths."[9] And in a noteworthy insight, he added, "But these revivals always featured two runners, the state and the city. The state usually won and the city then remained subject and under a heavy yoke. The miracle of the first great urban centuries in Europe was that the city won hands down, at least in Italy, Flanders and Germany. It was able to try the experiment of leading a completely separate life for quite a long time. This was a colossal event…Soon there were no states around these privileged towns."[10] Braudel here elaborates what Weber emphasized as the uniqueness of the autonomous medieval cities.[11]

The political and legal autonomy of the medieval city was expressed in its *corporate* form. The medieval corporation was an outcome of a peculiar fusion of elements that came together in Western Europe between the sixth and twelfth centuries: Germanic folklaw, Roman law and Christian thought.[12] As Harold Berman argued in his *Revolution and Law* (1983), the fusion and split of these elements conditioned forms of legal and political tradition for centuries in the West, forms to which we still belong.[13] The historiography of corporations owes a great deal to German jurist Otto von Gierke (1841–1921).[14] It was he who opened up research in this area and who drew the attention of generations of historians, albeit with different purposes and reasons, such as Frederic W. Maitland, Brian Tierney, Walter Ullmann, Harold Berman, Joseph Canning, Gerald E. Frug and Antony Black, each of whom studied various aspects of the history of corporations. It is on the basis of this literature that it is now possible to sketch the outlines of the history of corporations from the twelfth to the nineteenth centuries, which is crucial to an understanding of the modernity of the city. We must remember that it was mainly Gierke and Maitland that Weber relied on in drawing his conclusions regarding the legal autonomy of the medieval city.[15]

Chapter Two opens with an outline of the essential elements of the autonomous city, with a focus on England. And it poses the questions: What happened to the autonomous city? How did the pendulum shift back to the side of the State which dismantled the city as an autonomous corporation? However one would attempt to answer these questions, after Gierke's research, we cannot ignore the role that legal and political discourse played in this subordination because, during the centuries in which the autonomous city triumphed, there existed no coherent or precise concept of corporation in legal and political discourse.[16] Autonomous corporations were sworn bodies of citizens who formed associations. The citizens exercised powers and liberties as corporate bodies. And in the fourteenth and fifteenth centuries they came under increasing attack from the emerging territorial States, which were marked by a growing centralization of rule. The outcome was the subjugated city of early modern Europe. Accompanying these attacks were attempts by canonical and lay jurists to formulate a concept of corporation that would fit within the emerging forms of State rule. It was then thought that when a corporation was erected, it was considered as a 'body politic' as opposed to a 'body natural', which meant a distinction between the obligations and liberties of those people who made up the corporation (citizens) and of the corporation itself (governing body). This was the moment in history when legal discourse separated citizens from cities. A parallel concept to the abstract existence of the corporation was its subordination: it could only be created by the authority of the State, and sworn associations were illegal. If the 'old' cities and corporate bodies could not be recognized as legal associations, what was their legal status? Then came the notion that corporations were subordinate bodies politic and could not possess autonomy that was not prescribed. This idea was expressed in the term 'artificial person' (*persona ficta*), an entity created by law. Therefore, the legal concepts of abstraction and subordination of corporations epitomized and legitimated the political hostility toward citizenry and multiple sovereignties within the centralizing States.

Now, during the fifteenth and the sixteenth centuries, the *legal* concept of the corporation as an artificial (created) and subordinate entity found *political* grounds of use. This was an era of the nascent modern State and the tension between the city and the State took on a different shape: autonomous corporations and their liberties were dismantled. Throughout Western Europe, in England, France, Prussia, Germany and Italy, this was an era of the subjugation of the autonomous city, notwithstanding the difference in degree of subjugation, to which Charles Tilly has drawn attention.[17] There is one clear and identifiable difference between the corporations, associations and communes of medieval Europe and those which were created, or juridically recreated by the emerging States in the fifteenth and sixteenth centuries: the former were *de facto* corporations, which possessed political and legal autonomy in the sense explained above, whereas the latter became *de jure* corporations, which were created as a result of compliance with all the constitutional or statutory requirements of the State. Maitland highlighted this difference when he stated that "during the Middle Ages, the function of the Royal Charter was not that of 'erecting a corporation' or of regulating a corporation that already existed, but that of bestowing liberties and franchises upon a body, which, within large limits, was free to give itself a constitution from time to time."[18] Since the fifteenth century, political and legal thought and State practices sustained a considerable hostility toward the 'old' autonomies practiced by intermediate entities between the State and the 'subject', and the result was incessant attacks by the nascent European States on the old corporate liberties and autonomies. This is what we will call the first great transformation: the gradual subjugation of the cities and citizens to the State, at least in terms of their juridical and political status. We can say that the constitutional identity of the city and citizenry were dramatically altered during this first great transformation.[19]

By the seventeenth and eighteenth centuries there were two processes at work: on the one hand, the dismantling of old corporate liberties and the transformation of autonomous cities into subordinate entities continued, but, in addition, new uses were found for the instrument of incorporation. The first process involved the institution of 'close corporations', which made their appearance notably in England. This type of corporation was created by the State so that the governing body of the city was now empowered to perpetuate itself and was responsible to the State and *not to the citizenry*. Thus, oligarchies were formed in cities by the State to impose legislation on citizens. Until 1688, this strategy was deployed by successive kings of England to manipulate the composition of the parliament since cities returned members to the parliament.[20] The second process actively involved the cities in the administration of relevant State legislation, primarily expressed in poor laws. The formation of incorporated workhouses and the calculated use of cities for the enforcement of poor laws were new developments. The city was not only subjugated, but was now used as an instrument of State administration. The city that embodied these two processes can best be characterized as the *early modern city* because while it had lost its old political and legal autonomy, the city was also becoming an active instrument of State administration. The former process found its clearest justification in the work of Edward Coke (1552–1634), while the latter was most forcefully advocated by Thomas Hobbes (1588–1679).

By the nineteenth century the legal and political institution we now know by the name of municipal corporation was defined and elaborated with unprecedented precision and uniformity. In England, the Municipal Corporations Act of 1835, which followed a Royal Commission on Municipal Corporations, identified the modern city as one which was a municipal corporation with a clear mandate from the State to *govern* 'its' inhabitants. How did this change come about? Since the middle of the eighteenth century, jurists, political theorists and 'social reformers' had become convinced that a great need of the times was to 'reform', if not to recast, the oppressive and negative system of law, which had been inherited from the absolutist regimes of the sixteenth and seventeenth centuries. Now, in the Age of Enlightenment, it was thought that these laws were not only barbaric in substance and often chaotic in form, they were also inefficient: they attached an exaggerated importance to the severity of punishment and ignored the importance of clarity and precision in the form of the law and certainty in its *positive* application. It was argued that government by command, by edict, by proclamation, in short, by force, was not effective; instead, government on the basis of calculated, coherent legislation was defined as the proper domain of politics. To govern, in this sense, was to direct and steer the actions or conduct of the subjects through established laws, rules and regulations, by those invested with authority.[21] This means that, in the 1830s in England, there was a shift of emphasis from *punitive* law (although this did not disappear) to *institutional* and enabling law. The modern or 'enlightened' concept of law embodied a form of government that relied on political institutions for the enforcement and implementation of State policies. Throughout this book we will use the term *governance* to mean the practice of governing in this 'enlightened' sense. In England, the cities constituted by the Municipal Corporations Act were political institutions that were seen as capable of governing inhabitants by authorizing and empowering a governing body to exercise powers that were explicitly prescribed but at the same time enabling *some* inhabitants to choose their governors. In other words, domination was no longer the modality through which the cities were governed. Rather, the corporation was used as a calculated and precise apparatus of governance. This is what we will call the second great transformation: the city was constituted as an integral part of a system of governance and was given an elaborate and articulate constitution, which enabled the governing body (the mayor and the council) to establish institutions, laws, rules and regulations to steer the conduct of its inhabitants. In this sense, the modern city can indeed be called an *apparatus of governance.* If the early modern city was simultaneously subjugated and used by the State through the oligarchies formed within them, the modern city proper became a self-governing political community. As Jeremy Bentham (1748–1832) put it, the city became an atom of the State, an indivisible and integral element of governance within the modern State.

This typology, the autonomous city, the early modern city and the modern city, is outlined in finer detail in Chapter Two. It forms the historical background that places the emergence of corporations in colonial America and British North America in the context of their constitutional history, and takes a needed articulated stance toward what constitutes the modernity of the city. Thus, Chapter Two not only provides a background history but it also gives historical precision to certain key concepts in the political and legal discourse *about* the city—a discourse that also formed part of the British colonial apparatus discussed in Chapters Three, Four and Five.

Corporations in Colonial America

When colonial America was opened up for settlement in the seventeenth century, the English State was presented with the problem of 'government at a distance', and the 'solution' (if any could be said to have been found) involved, among other things of course, the creation of incorporated cities. But, before the thought was formulated that the colonies must be made integral parts of the State and governed directly as subordinate entities, and in the absence of a solution to the problem of 'government at a distance', the New England colonies went through an interesting development as corporate colonies that exercised *de facto* powers and organized their own political culture according to their needs. In the course of this development, the much heralded 'New England town' came into being, which had affinities with the vigour of the medieval cities. Yet, as soon as the English State set out to subordinate the colonies, a new form of colonial government became predominant: the royal colonies. These colonies placed an increasing reliance on royal governors, councils, legislatures, written commissions and carefully prescribed powers.

The British colonial apparatus took on some definition and shape in the latter part of the seventeenth century, both in compliance with, and in reaction to, a colonial policy that emerged in the 1660s. Expressed chiefly in the familiar Navigation Acts of the 1650s and 1660s, this policy was based on mercantilist principles: colonies existed for the benefit of the English State and must be made to function in this capacity. But it did not take long for the Councils for Trade and Plantations and then the Lords of Trade (1675) to conclude that colonies, three thousand miles distant from the centre of the empire, would not 'naturally' promote England's economic and social well-being.[22] Hence, effective political control was necessary. And so colonial policy, epitomized at the outset in trade regulations, spilled over into government and politics, and included several innovations that targeted accustomed *de facto* political liberties of corporate colonies.

One of the innovations that targeted accustomed liberties was the formation of royal colonies—colonies with royally appointed governors, elaborate instructions (approximating a constitution) and locally elected assemblies (proprietary colonies had similar constitutions except that they were granted to an individual). The city in corporate colonies exercised *de facto* corporate powers in two senses. First, *de facto* because the colonies themselves, being of corporate status, could not create corporations. So cities took it upon themselves to constitute their own priorities, policies, rules and regulations—they exercised *de facto* corporate powers. And, second, and perhaps more important, in the absence of pressure from the English State, corporate colonies organized their towns according to their needs and the dictates of local politics and culture. By contrast, in the royal colonies, the city appeared as a *de jure* corporation with prescribed powers and early modern charters. Between the 1660s and the 1730s there was considerable effort to create *de jure* cities in the colonies to facilitate the exercise of 'government at a distance'. Many of these were close corporations resembling the early modern cities of England. Some of these attempts succeeded but some failed. By 1776 there were between twenty-four and thirty-six *de jure* corporations in colonial America. After the loss of the thirteen colonies, it became a predominant interpretation among British statesmen and colonial agents that one of the important 'causes' of the rebellion was the failure to create *de jure* corporations and to subordinate *de facto* ones. As we shall see, this diagnosis was an important backdrop against which corporations were later conceptualized and created in British North America. For example, John Graves Simcoe, the Lieutenant Governor of Upper Canada, who defended founding cities with close corporations, once stated that "it has been adopted as a principle, so to form the place for future Establishments in this Colony, as to avoid the errors which the former settlements of the United States and Canadians have fallen into…a central Capital, from whence should flow loyalty, attachment, and respect to the British Government and all those principles, qualities and manners which are of eminent use in decorating and strengthening such an attachment."[23]

The history of corporations after the formation of the United States (between the 1780s and the 1840s) is also an important backdrop against which British North American corporations can be contrasted.[24] As we mentioned, many *de jure* corporations in colonial America were close corporations with governing elites. These governing elites came to represent the last vestiges of British power in America and were considered inconsistent with the spirit of the Revolution. In turn, this legitimated and justified numerous attacks on cities by state legislatures in the new republic. In due course, this led to the doctrine of state supremacy over cities.[25]

The history of corporations in colonial America therefore has a fourfold significance for understanding the subsequent evolution of corporations in British North America. First, and this is a point that is often overlooked, the constitutional form used when British North American colonies were settled was almost identical to that of the royal colonies, and, as we mentioned, the creation of royal cities was an essential element of its constitution.[26] This aspect too was almost identical in British North America. Second, the failure of 'government at a distance' forced the British colonial apparatus to scrutinize closely existing practices and to adopt those which were considered successful (such as the constitution of the City of New York). Third, the developments in the early republic are important in terms of understanding divergencies in corporate constitutions: whereas the main concern regarding the cities in the early republic was how to subordinate local oligarchies, the main problem in British North America was how to create cities without citizens.

And, finally, the colonial experience in America taught the British statesmen and administrators that the loyalty of the subjects to the State cannot be taken for granted or viewed as an innate attribute of humans; that loyalty and attachment must be produced and constantly reproduced. Without a close supervision of settlement, colonists developed diverse allegiances and loyalties, which ultimately made impossible the exercise of royal authority. This diagnosis formed an important backdrop against which the settlement of British North America was guided.

Modern City in British North America

When British North America was opened up for settlement after the rebellion of the thirteen colonies, the colonial apparatus was hesitant as to whether and how to settle the territories. It was also extremely eager to encourage allegiance and loyalty among settlers to the English State and the nation, to prevent another potential rebellion. As a result, the early period between the 1780s and the 1830s was characterized by a tension between an antagonism toward the development of *de facto* citizenship practices and the necessity of constituting *de jure* cities for purposes of governance. The corporation as an instrument was therefore used cautiously and carefully on the grounds that unprepared and 'immature' polities could not be entrusted with such an institution. Hence, although the legal and political instrument of incorporation was used in British North America as early as 1785, widespread incorporation did not take place until the 1830s and the 1840s. The first incorporation was Saint John, New Brunswick. This city was constituted as an early modern, close corporation.[27] But the cities created in the 1830s and the 1840s had modern constitutions. The unsatisfactory record of numerous political and legal experiments (such as police towns and boards of police) that were earlier introduced to deal with the problem of governance, and the containment of the aforementioned tension, were among the reasons believed to have precipitated rebellions in both Upper and Lower Canada in 1837 and 1838. With the development of liberalism as a program of State administration in England, a new series of colonial policies emerged. And in response to rapidly changing colonial conditions, the city was being constituted in modern political and legal terms, that is, as an apparatus of governance. Therefore, the formative period can be seen as a period of transition from the early modern city to that of the modern city. The traditional interpretation of this transformation has been the "birth of local autonomy in Canada."[28] The foundations of this interpretation were laid out by liberal scholars in the early twentieth century and became, as Carl Berger put it, the 'central myth' of Canadian historiography.[29] As we shall see, such an interpretation cannot stand up to the light of the history of the specific conditions of British North America when set against the long history of corporations in England and colonial America. Thus, it is in this sense that this book is a study of the legal and political discourse through which cities were constituted as modern corporations in British North America against the outlines of the history of corporations in England and colonial America.

Notes

1. The corporation that will be under scrutiny throughout this study is not related to either business corporations (joint-stock companies, trade companies) or single-purpose corporations such as school boards. The focus of this study is on those corporations which, since the nineteenth century, were beginning to be called municipal corporations.

2. The legal authority to create cities is vested in provincial legislatures in Canada, state legislatures in the United States. We shall see later how this authority evolved.

3. See for more details Ian M. Rogers, *The Law of Canadian Municipal Corporations*, 2 vols., 2nd ed. (Toronto, 1971) and *The Encyclopedia of Words and Phrases, Legal Maxims, Canada: 1825-1985*, G. D. Sanagan, ed. (Don Mills, 1986), s.v. "municipal corporation," "city," "municipal institutions" and "municipality."

4. See Horace L. Brittain, *Local Government in Canada* (Toronto, 1951); J. H. Aitchison, "The Municipal Corporations Act of 1849," *Canadian Historical Review*, vol. xxx, 1949, pp. 107–122; J. H. Aitchison, "Development of Local Government in Upper Canada" (Ph.D. Thesis, University of Toronto, 1953); John George Bourinot, *Local Government in Canada: An Historical Study* (Baltimore, 1887); Adam Shortt, "The Beginning of Municipal Government in Ontario," *Transactions of the Canadian Institute*, 1902, vol. vii, pp. 409–524; Adam Shortt, "Municipal Government in Ontario: A Historical Sketch," Morley S. Wickett, ed., *Municipal Government in Canada* (Toronto, 1907).

5. Fernand Braudel, *Civilization and Capitalism, 15th–18th Century*, vol. i: *The Structures of Everyday Life* (New York, 1981), p. 514.

6. Braudel, *Structures of Everyday Life*, pp. 515–520.

7. Max Weber, *Die Stadt*, written c. 1911–1913, posthumously published 1921; English translation without Weber's notes by Don Martindale and Gertrud Neuwirth (Glencoe, Ill., 1958). This essay was incorporated into Weber's *Economy and Society*, 2 vols. Guenther Roth and Claus Wittich, eds. (New York, 1978) as chap. xvi.

8. Weber, *City*, pp. 181–195. Weber was aware that the specific combination and strength of these autonomies differed within different regions in Europe; he knew, for example, that in England, because of a strong bureaucratic state administration, the city did not possess the same autonomous character as in Italian city republics.

9. Braudel, *Structures of Everyday Life*, p. 511.

10. Braudel, *Structures of Everyday Life*, p. 511. Note that Braudel is using the general term "state" to designate some form of centralized political rule.

11. As two historians of the American city, E. Griffith and C. Adrian said, "a certain tension existed between the cities and their creators, at least since medieval times and probably stretching back into the ancient past." *A History of American City Government: The Formation of Traditions, 1775-1870* (Washington, 1976), p. 32.

12. See "The Evolution of Modern Western Legal Systems," *Encyclopedia Britannica*, 15th ed., vol. xxii, pp. 917–947.

13. Berman, *Revolution and Law* (Cambridge, 1983), chap 1. Berman, however, commits a fundamental error by defining the twelfth-century cities as 'modern

Western cities.' This is partly because we lack historical work on the similarities and contrasts between the medieval city and the early modern city but also between the early modern city and the modern city. For the former Braudel remarked that "everywhere in Europe, as soon as the state was firmly established it disciplined the towns with instinctive relentlessness, whether or not it used violence." Braudel, *Structures of Everyday Life*, p. 519. This remark was taken up by historians H. Trevor-Roper, *Religion, the Reformation and Social Change* (London, 1967) and Richard Mackenney, *The City-State, 1500–1700: Republican Liberty in an Age of Princely Power* (Atlantic Highlands, N.J. 1989). Of course, the emphasis on the early modern subordination of cities is important.

14. See in particular Otto Gierke, *Political Theories of the Middle Age*, trans. and intro. by Frederic W. Maitland (Cambridge, 1900).

15. We must also note that this is not readily apparent from the Martindale edition since all of Weber's original notes were replaced with those of the editor. The edition that is included in his *Economy and Society* contains numerous and illuminating references to, and discussions of, Gierke and Maitland.

16. Susan Reynolds made this point recently in her "The Idea of the Corporation in Western Christendom Before 1300," in J. A. Guy and H. G. Beale, eds., *Law and Social Change in British History* (London, 1984).

17. Charles Tilly, *Coercion, Capital and European States, AD 990–1990* (London, 1990).

18. Maitland, *Township and Borough*, p. 85.

19. As Mackenney, *City-State, 1500–1700*, chap. ii "Defeat" demonstrates in a graphic account, this subjugation was not accomplished without resistance or bloodshed.

20. Christopher Hill, *Reformation to Industrial Revolution* (Harmondsworth, 1969), pp. 142–145.

21. See an important chapter by Roberto M. Unger, "Law and Modernity," in his *Law in Modern Society* (New York, 1976).

22. Arthur B. Keith, *Constitutional History of the First British Empire* (Oxford, 1930), chaps. iii and iv.

23. Simcoe to Portland, 1794, *Simcoe Papers*, vol. iii, p. 61.

24. See Stephen L. Elkin, *City and Regime in the American Republic* (Chicago, 1987).

25. Jon C. Teaford "The City versus State: The Struggle for Legal Ascendancy," *The American Journal of Legal History*, vol. xvii, 1973, pp. 51–65.

26. Chester Martin, *Empire and Commonwealth: Studies in Governance and Self-Government in Canada* (Oxford, 1929), chap. i.

27. William Acheson, *Saint John: The Making of a Colonial Urban Community* (Toronto, 1985). We must note some differences, however. Only the mayor was appointed and councilmen were to be elected by a popular vote.

28. John H. Taylor, "Urban Autonomy in Canada: Its Evolution and Decline," in G. A. Stelter and A. F. J. Artibise, *The Canadian City: Essays in Urban and Social History* (Ottawa, 1984), pp. 478–500.

29. Carl Berger, *The Writing of Canadian Historiography: Aspects of English-Canadian Historical Writing since 1900*, 2nd. ed. (Toronto, 1986), p. 52.

2

HISTORY OF CORPORATIONS IN ENGLAND: AN OUTLINE

ITIES with autonomous political and legal status have been amongst the most vigorous forces in the history of Western institutions. The legacy of the Greek *polis* and the Roman *civitas* is still embodied in our language.[1] For example, the concept 'political' is rooted in the culture of life and thought in the ancient Greek *polis*; the concept 'civilization' is rooted in the Roman concept of man as a citizen (*civis*) living in a *civitas*. Yet the autonomous medieval cities perhaps constitute the most enduring historical legacy: about six centuries after the dissolution of the Western Roman Empire thousands of new cities and towns were founded in northern Italy, Flanders, France, Normandy, England, Germany and other parts of Europe, beginning in the late eleventh and twelfth centuries. All Roman cities had disappeared by the ninth century, and with few exceptions such as London and Rome, there was no continuity between the former Roman cities and the European cities that emerged in the late eleventh and twelfth centuries.[2] There are those who would have us forget those histories. But Lewis Mumford's *The City in History* and Murray Bookchin's *The Rise of Urbanization and the Decline of Citizenship* make it more difficult to do so.

But what is striking about the rise of cities in the late eleventh and twelfth centuries when compared with the Greek and Roman cities is not only their astounding number, but as Max Weber and Henri Pirenne demonstrated, their political autonomy came to be strongly expressed in legal autonomy. In medieval Germany, for example, *Stadtluft macht frei* (city air makes people free) became a legal maxim and spread throughout continental Europe and England; charters, which were the founding legal documents of the city, stipulated that after a year and day of breathing the town air, a serf could not be returned to bondage, for he had become a *citizen*.[3] Cities and citizens emerged as an antithesis of feudal lordships and kingships that were simultaneously emerging with cities, and stood for the supremacy of law rather than the supremacy of will—for association rather than subjugation. The medieval concept of citizenship was articulated through association with other people, a principle elaborated by the city as a mutually dependent sworn association of people. This was the birth of the city as an autonomous corporation.[4]

As Pirenne argued, the rise of the autonomous city was closely associated with the revival of industry and trade in the West after the collapse of the Western Roman Empire. The city became an economic association of merchants, craftsmen and artisans, who created the city as a means of seeking relief from surrounding feudal lordships, kingdoms and other jurisdictions of all sorts. The autonomous city and citizens were naturally in conflict with the nascent royal and territorial powers. But the autonomous city was also a potential source of revenue for the emerging monarchical bureaucracies of Western Europe: kings and lords often established new cities to encourage trade and the associated tax revenue. Monarchs also waged wars against the old cities to coerce them into their tax schemes. The charter was in fact a contract between the law-making authority and the citizens as a corporation.[5] The failure on either part to honour the contract would result in conflict or ultimately war.[6] The level of autonomy embodied in the charter was an outcome of a constellation of forces: of the city, of surrounding feudal lordships (ecclesiastical and lay) and of the monarch or prince. The result was a considerable variation in autonomy in different regions in Europe— from Italian city republics with immense powers to English boroughs with moderate liberties within a strong monarchy. But the autonomous cities of medieval Europe were eventually subjugated by the emerging European States. We must nevertheless recognize that, as Lewis Mumford said, "the historic cities of Europe today are all older than the state that legally claims these rights, and had an independent existence before their right to exist was recognized!"[7]

We must focus on the medieval city as a corporation and on its transformations if we want to understand the origins of the modern city as a corporation. This chapter is organized around the typology Braudel suggested, which was discussed in Chapter One, excluding the ancient Greek and Roman cities and, instead, including the modern city. First, we focus on the birth of the city as a sworn association: *de facto* corporations in the eleventh and twelfth centuries and the associated concept of citizenship. Second, we examine the ideas pressed into service by the State in the war against the legal and political autonomy of the city; the invention of the concept of a corporation as a human association that was both abstract (a legal entity distinct from its members) *and* artificial (created by a superior authority) was the hallmark of the early modern city as a *de jure* State institution in the fifteenth and sixteenth centuries. And, third, we discuss the modernity of the city as an apparatus of governance, which was now considered a governmental franchise of the State. Overall, the purpose of this chapter is to sketch an outline of the origins and transformations of the city as a corporation in English history since the twelfth century, as it was embodied in legal and political practice and thought. Appendix 1 surveys a literature that deals with the Anglo-Saxon origins (between the eighth and the eleventh centuries) of English cities.

Autonomous Cities: The Long 12th Century

The legal and political autonomy of the medieval city was epitomized in an institution that was named with a panoply of terms reflecting variations in autonomy in different regions of Europe. These included *commune* (French), *populi* (Italian), *communitas* (English), *universitas, urbani, burgensis populus, civitas* and *burgh* (German), which can all be translated into modern English as the corporation. The corporation was a legal and political institution that expressed the association principle of the medieval city and its autonomy.

Cities, however, were not the only corporations. Some universities, cathedral chapters, bishoprics, monasteries, manorial courts and trade and craft guilds were also corporations. But all these formations had some connections with the city, and the city protected their legal and political autonomies. Indeed, the city as a corporation was a union of these diverse associations: it was almost always founded as a sworn association of citizens to adhere to a charter that had been publicly read aloud.[8] Under the prevailing legal theory the corporation was a body of people sharing common legal functions and acting as a legal entity. Cities were by and large *de facto* corporations: their formation was an expression of its members rather than a prescription of supreme law or authority.[9] Most charters issued by kings, princes and ecclesiastical and lay lords only recognized these *de facto* corporations and their legal and political autonomies—they did not create them. A charter then was a contract between a ruler and the corporation to respect each other's powers and limits; a breach in this respect could result in violence. The twelfth and thirteenth centuries was an era of great conflict between towns and their rulers often involving bloodshed and revolving around the issues of self-determination and taxation.

As we noted earlier, however, the English borough was never as autonomous as the French communes or Italian city republics. As shown by historians, there are several reasons for this, which are discussed in Appendix 1. Here we note one significant reason: in England the rise of autonomous cities coincided with the conquest of Anglo-Saxon England by William I (1066), who declared himself the overlord of all lords in England.[10] In this way, he was able to retain effective control through the lords he installed throughout his realm. This resulted in an intimate association of feudal law with royal government and administration.[11] At any rate, cities in England found themselves in a more centrally organized and powerful kingdom with its administration and law, in contrast to their counterparts in French communes or Italian city republics. Nonetheless, English cities retained considerable liberties and autonomous rights. Let us now turn to these liberties and rights.

Typically, during the late eleventh and twelfth centuries, the recognition of a city or a borough involved the granting of mercantile and jurisdictional privileges to its citizens (burgesses) in return for a certain amount of tax (tallage). The legal form in which privileges were granted was the charter. The founding charters of towns conferred numerous and varied sets of liberties, privileges and jurisdictions, a combination of which would distinguish a city community from other communities.[12] Although a charter was not necessary for the recognition of a city (it may have had its court and particular privileges without a need for their legal expression), by the end of the twelfth century charters were widespread. When ecclesiastical and lay lords founded cities for "peaceful penetration of newly conquered districts"[13] and increased revenue (cities could produce much faster and higher rates than feudal manors), some of this 'peace' and revenues were shared with the king.[14] It was, therefore, in the interest of the king, not only to recognize old cities and even found new cities himself, but also, to encourage his lords to do so, to increase revenue. Of all new cities (172) after 1066, only 12 per cent were founded by kings, 45 per cent by lay seigneurs, 15 per cent by bishops, 18 per cent by abbots, 10 per cent unknown.[15] By contrast, of all cities (excluding new cities after 1066) 27 per cent were recognized by kings, 37 per cent by lay seigneurs, and 24 per cent by bishops and abbots, 12 per cent unknown. Maurice Beresford notes that the founding of new cities required elaborate machinery and resources (choice of proper site, inducement and recruitment of merchants and craftsmen and so on).[16] The king often relied on the expertise of his lords in founding cities in royal lands.

Although the lay and ecclesiastical lords who founded cities often sought royal confirmation, they were still required to have regard for royal authority, which became concerned about 'jurisdictions of all sorts' in England.[17] As Beresford stated "…it was not essential for the king to give permission before a seigneur made a borough on his own land, although it might be politic to seek a royal charter. Similarly, a seigneur did not have to enroll his borough charter at the Royal Chancery, although the habit of so doing grew with the passage of time."[18] By the twelfth century there was growing pressure on all the jurisdictional privileges, which had been recognized in ecclesiastical franchises, lay lords and cities.[19] On the other hand, an opposite movement from the towns was taking shape, partly in response to this increased pressure from the growing royal authority and partly following the rise of sworn corporations on the Continent. As Susan Reynolds remarked, "it seems then that by the late eleventh century towns in England had achieved a combination of corporate solidarity and administrative separation from the country which could form the basis of a campaign for independence. The campaign becomes discernible in the twelfth century and it bears a notable resemblance in nature and chronology to those waged by townsmen abroad."[20] James Tait also observed a similar pattern in that "by the middle of the eleventh century the more important boroughs had secured a legal and economic status that set them apart from the rest of the agrarian communities."[21] And he concluded that "the increasing privileges obtained by the boroughs, and the evidence of borough government anticipate the emergence of the commune that was to characterize the [twelfth century]."[22] For example, in 1130, both London and Lincoln had acquired a privilege to 'farm' their own city (*firma burgi*), which meant that the citizens could collect taxes and register it directly at the exchequer ('State finance department') as opposed to the collection of taxes by the sheriff of the county in which the borough was located.[23] Tait said that these were "the first signs that the leading English boroughs at least were no longer content to remain mere reservoirs of revenue…but had so far developed a communal spirit as to aim at collecting the borough issues themselves…They aspired, in fact, to secure emancipation of the borough from the shire in finance as well as in justice."[24] The emancipation from the shire meant the emancipation from that powerful royal official, the sheriff, who had the authority to adjust the taxation rate,[25] which was already high in comparison to other communities.[26] The liberty of a borough to tax itself was expressed as *firma burgi*.

During the twelfth century some English cities gained the status of *liber burgus* (free city), which meant the possession of autonomous law-making, taxing and trading, in short, governing powers. How was a free city governed? Government and administration were inextricably connected with legal jurisdiction: when a city gained autonomy it generally took over the royal courts.[27] The mayor was the leader of the city and he worked closely with the reeve or bailiff, who was responsible for paying royal or seigneurial dues. Some officers in cities are known to have had councils to advise or supervise them.[28] Reynolds notes that although the methods by which the mayor, officers and councils were chosen are usually obscure, it is clear that they were chosen in a congregation of the whole city.[29] Since the city was an association of craftsmen and merchants, citizenship was associated with membership in a craft or merchant guild (which also meant possession of property as a citizen); however, not all inhabitants of a city were free citizens of the city, and inheritance and admission practices varied across cities.[30]

There was constant tension between cities and the successive English kings. This revolved around the liberties of the city: on the one hand, cities were useful for revenue to support an increasing bureaucratic State administration; on the other, they constituted a major threat to royal centralization by gaining, protecting and increasing political and legal autonomies. There is a very telling medieval English proverb, which is much less known than its German counterpart on free city air (and indeed in direct contrast with it), that is said to have originated by a monk who said that the city was considered as "a rising of the people, the fear of the kingdom and the terror of clergy."[31]

Toward the end of the thirteenth century, the autonomous city and the royal power seem to enter a new relationship: the kings gradually but fitfully started to use cities against their lords and act as supreme arbitrators in these struggles. As Pirenne noted: "To accept the king as arbitrator of their quarrel was, for the parties in conflict, to recognize his sovereignty. The entry of the burghers upon the political scene had as a consequence the weakening of the contractual principle of the Feudal State to the advantage of the principle of the authority of the Monarchical State."[32] Toward the end of the thirteenth century the English State began to gain an upper hand on cities by coercing them to participate in and support the affairs of the State: the legal component of this political subordination was manifest in the invention of the idea of *representation*. The cities were slowly considered an integral part of the realm and were addressed through their representatives. Ballard saw this as the gradual 'personification' of cities by which he meant that the king could consider the city as a constituent of the realm.[33] Toward the end of the thirteenth century, the formation of the first parliament (1264) was, on the one hand, a reflection of these changing power relations and, on the other, an event which strengthened the assimilation of cities by requesting them to send *representatives* to a colloquium to discuss matters.[34] Until the turn of the fourteenth century, eleven more parliaments were convened, in each of which an average of about eighty-six cities were represented.[35] In the beginning, the writs of summons were directly sent to individual cities; but later these writs were sent to sheriffs of counties vesting them with the authority to summon cities in their county. This indicates the increasing royal administration and exercise of authority. The resistance of some cities and lords to these parliaments should not be underestimated. In 1295, for example, the sheriff of Westmorland, after listing the elected knights and burgesses, added, "but these cannot come on the day named in the writ because all men of my bailiwick between the ages of fifteen and sixty, both knights, freeholders and foot-soldiers, have been charged to appear before the lord bishop of Durham and John, Earl Warenne, and their lieutenants."[36] In another example of resistance, we learn from contemporary chronicles that, in 1316, the community of Bristol rose against the king's court when

> ...trouble arose...over customs in seaport and market, privileges and other things, in which fourteen of the greater persons of this town seem to have a special right. The community resisted, stating that the burgesses were all of one condition and therefore equal as to liberties and privileges. Over matters of this sort frequent domestic quarrels arose, until in the king's court they asked for and received judges to examine the case and bring it to just conclusion.[37]

But, when the final decision came, apparently citizens did not find it 'just' and "...started a riot and the whole people was smitten with fear and tumult. Forthwith returning with a large company they entered the hall where they proceeded to turn their right into outrage. With fists and sticks they began to assail the opposing party, and that there about twenty lives were suddenly and stupidly lost."[38] How seriously citizens took their liberties! As for the king, he wanted to punish the citizens and "they were demanded from the county, and not coming or obeying were declared to be exiles. But well fortified they remained within their town nor would obey the royal mandate unless it were carried out by force." The Bristol case demonstrates that as late as 1316 and as powerful as State administration was in England, cities could resist.

These resistances are understandable: the king summoned cities to parliaments largely by his will to obtain their consent to increase taxation as well as to retain judicial and administrative control over them.[39] It appears that the legislation passed in these parliaments and the ratification of charters put enormous burdens on cities. It must therefore be stressed that parliaments in the thirteenth and fourteenth centuries were underlined by a duality of power relations; they indicated increasing royal authority throughout the realm and a simultaneous reluctance of towns (particularly those founded by territorial and ecclesiastical lords) to participate in them. But, without participation, it would become very difficult to secure, ratify or enhance jurisdictional, mercantile and tenurial privileges from the king. By the thirteenth century, English cities were caught in a situation where they both depended on, and were becoming *incorporated* into, the emerging English State administration and law.

Invention of the City as a Corporation: 13th–14th Centuries

Maitland said that "in the history of medieval Europe we have to watch on the one hand the evolution of groups (in particular, religious groups and groups of burgesses) which in our eyes seem to display all or many of the characteristics of corporations, and on the other hand the play of thought around the idea of an *universitas* which was being slowly discovered in the Roman law books. If the facts were ready for the theory, a theory was being fashioned for the facts, those who were preparing it were Italian lawyers."[40] By "play of thought" Maitland meant those attempts of jurists to legitimate a right for the king to incorporate cities by appropriating certain elements of Roman law. We can certainly consider this play of thought as an invention of the city as a corporation, for, as we shall see, during these two centuries State jurisprudence invented an institution that radically altered the history of cities. To put it differently, medieval law and jurisprudence were pressed into royal service, which resulted in the invention of the city as a *de jure* (prescribed and created) corporation. We have seen the emergence of English cities as *de facto* corporations. Now we will focus on this play of thought on *de jure* corporations.

The work of the German jurist Otto Gierke opened up research on this invention by focusing on an immense body of juristic writing on corporations.[41] Gierke's primary concern was to trace the growth of the

Germanic law of association, based on the concept of the organized group as a corporation. As a result, his section on the medieval canonists was mainly devoted to expounding the distinction between this Germanic idea of a corporation and the opposing canonist concept of an institution. He found the origins of the corporation in medieval canon law. According to Gierke, in a *de facto* corporation the principle of unity resided in the actual members who came together to achieve an end determined by themselves. By contrast, in a *de jure* institution the principle of unity, the 'end' of association, was imposed 'from outside and above'. This external principle—in the case of the Church it would be God—was, moreover, the true 'right-subject' of the institution, its physical members being mere representatives of the transcendent authority that infused into them unity and a semblance of corporate life. Gierke thought that the doctrines of the medieval canonists were by no means lacking in traces of the 'true corporation spirit', which was especially evident in their definition of the whole Church as a corporation. But these tendencies were quickly overwhelmed by ideas on *de jure* institutions in the late thirteenth and the fourteenth centuries that the canonists applied alike to the whole Church and to individual churches.

Closely associated with Gierke's account of the distinction between the corporation and the institution was a contrast between two opposed theories of corporate personality. The 'properly medieval' doctrine recognized in the corporation a real group personality and a group will, which was distinct from the personalities and wills of individual members. The canonists, Gierke thought, progressed some way toward this conception since they did tend to personify the individual churches. However, this progress was thwarted by the acceptance of Pope Innocent IV's doctrine that the corporate personality was to be defined as a mere *persona ficta*, a fiction of the law subordinate to the whole. Gierke argued that while canon law could not find the constitutive principle of ecclesiastical human groups from within, it *did* have recourse to the idea of creation.

Gierke maintained that the canonist idea of the corporation as *persona ficta*, without recognition of the *real* personality of the group, left the way open for the absolutist State doctrines of the fourteenth and fifteenth centuries in secular law. Before the fifteenth century, in political and legal discourse, even the partisans of the idea of monarchy were wont to concede to cities an active right of participation in the life of the State because, cities being what they were, some such concession was almost unavoidable. In the medieval power configuration coexistence of multiple sovereignties was a reality, and the kings and their jurists had to concede. The principle of representation of cities, however, had already made it possible to think that the powers ascribed to the cities were not the private rights of a sum of individuals, but the public right of a constitutionally compounded association. Gierke argued that it was at this time, around the fifteenth century, that the formulation of a distinction between positive law and natural law in legal and political thought made it possible to think of cities as subordinate entities within the State. According to this doctrine, before the State existed, natural law already prevailed as an obligatory statute. The rules of right to which the State owed even the possibility of its own rightful origin, and the highest power on earth was subject to the rules of natural law. The positive law, on the other hand, expressed the will of the ruler. It was made and enacted by the ruler for the people. In this doctrine, then, the State was below the rules of natural law and above the rules of positive law. The autonomous city found no place in this doctrine because natural law now asserted that the State was founded on a social contract between sovereign individuals and the sovereign State. Gierke said that we see "…a drift [in the fifteenth century] which makes for a theoretical concentration of right and power in the highest and widest group on the one hand and the individual man on the other, at the cost of all intermediate groups. The Sovereignty of the State and the Sovereignty of the Individual were steadily on their way toward becoming the two central axioms from which all theories of social structure would proceed, and whose relationship to each other would be the focus of all theoretical controversy."[42] As we shall see below, Gierke isolated an important aspect of the beginnings of modern political theory that became hostile to any autonomy expressed other than the individual and the State. Or, put in other words and following Benjamin Barber, according to Gierke modern political theory was being founded on the deathbed of free cities and citizens: the coexistence of multiple sovereignties became unthinkable in the modern configuration of power.[43]

Gierke isolated a significant difference between medieval and early modern political theory with regard to corporations. Gierke wrote as a historian of ideas, but he was aware that the idea of the corporation, of whose history he was writing, was as powerful a weapon as the medieval knight's sword in battle. He said:

> It is true that speculation was also affected by action, and that every development of the world of thought in this period was an echo and reverberation of historical events. But the relation of the natural law theory of the state to the actual process of history was never fully passive. On the contrary, it served as a pioneer in preparing the transformation

of human life; it forged the intellectual arms for the struggle of new social forces; it disseminated ideas which, long before they even approached realization, found admittance into the thought of influential circles, and became, in that way, the objects of practical effort.[44]

Gierke's insight here is important: the role that was played by political and legal discourse cannot be overlooked in articulating the concept of the city as an outpost of modernity.

Walter Ullmann, a medievalist, elaborated on some of the ideas of jurists on corporations. He argued that during the fourteenth and the fifteenth centuries jurists and lawyers were beginning to make a distinction between legal and illegal associations.[45] But jurists soon found that Roman law was not clear on whether individuals were at liberty to organize and associate themselves in corporate bodies or whether the legality of an organization depended upon an act of a superior authority. Neither of these problems was sufficiently clarified in the Roman texts.[46] The canon law, on the other hand, had important ideas as to the status of human groups within the context of a broader rule. There was, for example, the distinction between permitted or permissible associations and those associations instituted by law for a definite purpose. The concept of a 'just cause' hence received an ever widening interpretation and the legality of a human association was judged by its purpose. The conception, for example, that every organization that was founded by a just cause was legal, was already the core of Pope Innocent IV's teaching, who, as previously noted, is often credited with formulating the ideas of fictitious personality.

Following these principles, medieval jurists and lawyers introduced a scheme of classification of human associations to ascertain their 'illegality' and 'legality'. According to them the legal associations were (i) tax farming partnerships, trade guilds, charities, universities; and, (ii) cities, boroughs, city councils, townships. But their legality derived from their purpose that was given to them by royal will. They asserted that (i) monopolies, criminal societies, seditious associations; and, (ii) leagues and confederations between city-states, federations of cities for the purpose of ousting other cities in politics or economics were illegal associations. Note here that having articulated the legality of a corporation, medieval jurisprudence proceeded to declare federations and leagues of cities as illegal. Here legal and illegal came to mean, of course, whether or not an association was prescribed by the royal authorities. Hence, Ullmann concluded that "the writings of the jurists provide ample testimony of the alarming growth of sectional organizations, and of the people's desire to found associations with more or less justifiable ends."[47] To put it in other words, if a *de facto* corporation was deemed unjust by royal authorities it would be declared illegal.

Walter Ullmann also maintained that since corporations began to be considered as subordinate it was not possible to solve the problem of the territorial sovereignty of the State, since the State was also considered in juristic thought as a corporation.[48] This constituted an obstacle as well as an inducement for jurists to reflect on the State, which resulted in a unique formulation of corporation theory. In canon law the corporation was considered as minor, underage and incapable of expressing 'its' will. "The consequence of this point of view was that, since the corporation could not act on its own accord, just as a minor could not, it had to have a tutor who was also called a procurator or an administrator, whose function differed in no way from that tutor who acted on behalf of individual minor."[49] In secular law, which developed against the background of canon law *and* Roman law, the same relation was sustained. In order to have legal status any corporation had to have approbation from the superior. For ecclesiastical bodies, this demand followed logically since, as the whole Church was instituted by divinity, individual bodies could not be created without its authorization. The formulation of the concept of corporation by canonists and legists (secular jurists) assisted the process of equating the corporation with a natural person in the shape of a minor. It was now thought that corporations should have, as did their natural counterparts, heads and organs. In ecclesiastical bodies, bishops were heads and the elected monks and priests were the organs. The bishop governed the ecclesiastical body. In charters to cities a similar formula was used. The mayor represented the body of citizens who represented the inhabitants of the city. The ideas of representation and corporations therefore presupposed each other. Of course these ideas were formulated in practice over time and only gradually acquired uniformity and coherence. Thus a corporation was called *persona ficta*, a person created by a superior authority 'who' in the public sphere had neither an autonomous standing nor enjoyed rights which were not, at least by construction, conferred upon 'him'.[50] Baldus (1327–1400), an Italian jurist, expressed it thus: "We commonly hold that corporations enjoy the rights of a minor and can benefit from restitution...And there is a reason for this, because they are always under the protection and government of administrators, and thus they are equivalent to churches and minors."[51] From the emergence of these ideas in practice until their formulation in juridical political thought, corporations were considered as subordinate entities in canon and secular laws, which prompted

Ullmann to say that he has "not found one jurist who expressed a different standpoint [in the later medieval centuries]."[52]

A principal element of this new concept was that the corporation was an *abstract* entity separate from its citizens; in other words, the corporation was at one and the same time a body of citizens *and* an abstract entity perceptible only by the intellect.[53] As Baldus stated, "...separate individuals do not make up the people, and thus properly speaking the people is not men, but a collection of men into a body which is mystical and taken as abstract, and the significance of which has been discovered by the intellect."[54] Accordingly, the corporation had rights and duties other than the rights and duties of all or any of its citizens. This abstract entity "...acts and wills, in that members act and will as a unity, that is either in assembly...or through elected representative councils or magistrates. In short, the members are the physical expression of the corporation, which acts through its members who express not the wills of separate individuals but that of the corporation as a whole."[55] There is a clear distinction made between the corporation as an entity and its members.[56] Thus the superior authority who created a corporation, a king, a bishop or a lord was also the authority which gave direction and purpose to the body. Citizens of the corporation had to accept this purpose and direction.

Incorporation of the City: 15th–18th Centuries

Now let us turn from the realm of legal theories to the realm of practices in which these theories found grounds for use. As mentioned earlier, in England, during the fourteenth century, parliaments became more regular and the knights and citizens became regular elements of them. With few exceptions, every city that was summoned to parliament made a return.[57] Also, there appears to be much less variation among the wordings of writs of summons sent to sheriffs, indicating an increasing uniformity and standardization of parliamentary procedures. Accompanying this increasing uniformity and regularity was an increasing control on the part of the English State over the knights and citizens who participated in parliaments. From 1350 to 1355 the sheriffs were reminded to see that "the knights, citizens, and burgesses chosen be not pleaders, nor maintainers of quarrels nor such as live by pursuits of this kind, but responsible men of good faith, devoted to the *general welfare*."[58] The phrase 'general welfare' should not be underestimated here as it manifests a broadening in the conception of interests from cities and scattered territories to a larger territorial domain and its influence on its *constituent* parts. Now the English State could legitimate the cities and citizens as subordinate to the larger interests than that which concerned them. Cities became permitted or permissible constituencies insofar as their interests also furthered the general welfare.

With the formulation of corporation as an abstract and subordinate legal *creation*, certain attributes were articulated designating such an entity. In 1345, Coventry received the earliest charter of *de jure* incorporation, which contained one of the five attributes of a modern corporation which we discussed in Chapter One. This was the perpetual succession: "that the said men, their heirs and successors, shall in future have a community among themselves, with power to choose a mayor and fit bailiffs of themselves yearly."[59] And, in an interesting clause, the charter ordained that "there shall be a prison in the said town...for punishing malefactors."[60] Similarly, in 1348, Hedon received a charter of incorporation ordaining that "the burgesses and their successors shall have a community among themselves and may choose a mayor and bailiffs...who after taking the usual oaths shall do and keep all that pertain to their offices in the said town."[61] This time Hedon was asked that "the mayor and bailiffs...shall have return of all the king's writs and executions thereof and of summonses of the exchequer."[62] While this clause ensured that the incorporated city was obliged to appear in parliament, to summon the city still remained within the king's discretion. The citizens in Hedon were also conferred with the liberty of suing as a whole "provided always that the burgesses render to the king the said farm."[63] With similar clauses of charter, Bristol (1373) and Basingtoke (1393) were incorporated.[64] Yet these early uses of the new invention of corporation were rudimentary and, as Weinbaum noted, lacked the legal precision of later incorporations that we shall shortly discuss.[65]

Toward the end of the fourteenth century, in 1395, the first general statute of the State concerning cities in English history was issued.[66] This statute ordained that all cities in the realm should have a perpetual community status, that is, even though the mayor and the citizens of the city died, the city could still continue to exist. Or, in royal words, the king wanted to deal with cities under more stable conditions: the citizens may die but the city must remain a city for the king, for the king never dies. Moreover, this statue enabled the king to extend the principles of incorporation throughout the realm without having to issue separate charters for each.

Early Modern Cities in England

If we were to choose a specific date for the birth of the early modern city in England we could certainly choose the year 1440. That was when Kingston-Upon-Hull was incorporated as a city.[67] The charter issued by the king recognized the city of Kingston-Upon-Hull as a body politic. And, to the burgesses, that is, the citizens of the city, being recognized as a body politic meant being endowed with particular rights as well as being required to fulfill certain duties for the State. All these were explicitly specified in the charter. Let us take a look at the charter itself to see what these rights and duties were.

The charter opened by specifying the liberties that were granted:[68] (i) "the said town of the mayor and burgesses shall be corporate and the mayor and burgesses shall be perpetually corporate." This meant that the mayor and burgesses would assume the role of leadership in the community and this role would exist perpetually independent of the citizens who occupy these positions; (ii) "the mayor and burgesses by that name shall be persons able to pursue and defend all pleas, suits, plaits and demands, and real, personal and mixed actions in any court"; (iii) "the said mayor and burgesses shall be persons able and capable in law acquiring lands, tenements, rents, services and possessions within the said town and its liberty, to be held by them and their successors, notwithstanding the statute of mortmain or any other ordinance or statute to the contrary, saving always to the king the services due"; (iv) "commonalty of the town so incorporated under the name of the mayor and burgesses" with a seal; and, (v) "the burgesses shall have all fines, forfeited issues and amercements pertaining to the office of justice of peace within the said town and liberty, with power to levy the same by their own ministers in aid of the payment of their farm and of the daily charges of the town." To rephrase, the liberties then were as follows: perpetual succession, that is, even when the particular burgesses that made up the corporation died, the corporation would not cease to exist as a legal person; the power of suing and being sued, that is, burgesses were liable as one person independent from their own persons; the power to hold lands as a corporation; the power to hold a common seal and name; and, the power to issue rules and regulations (or bylaws). These liberties came to be identified as the essential attributes of a corporation after this date. But, as was discussed, these liberties were practiced before the fifteenth century; what is novel here is that they are codified and prescribed by the authorities of the nascent State rather than being an outcome of negotiation on *de facto* rights.

If these were the liberties or the rights, then what were the duties? The duties of the corporation included an annual lump sum tax to the king and the sending of burgesses to the parliament when summoned. In other words, being recognized as a corporate body with specific liberties also required participation in the affairs of the State both politically and financially. The 1440 charter inaugurates a series of incorporations in the early modern era.[69] This was the time when the nascent modern State subsumed the creation and incorporation of cities as entirely under its own jurisdiction. The legal incorporation of the city then meant the institution of a franchise relationship between the city and the State: the State delegates certain governing powers to the city to be exercised on citizens. Thus the charter of 1440 described a set of privileges and duties that were already in existence but "the relevant clauses are characterized by a remarkably careful handling of language, which is a sure sign of experience, and the service of draftsmen behind the scenes."[70] What this remarkably precise language also indicates is an increased ability to conceptualize this relationship of franchise and to reflect it in legal practice with political effects. As we have seen, since the fourteenth century jurists were elaborating on the nature, sphere and purposes of corporations within the State as the State was itself becoming a predominant form of political existence. By the fifteenth century it was possible to claim that a corporation was a subordinate jurisdiction within the State and that the State was the only authority that could create a corporation with a specific purpose. Such corporations were called *persona ficta*, that is, *artificial* or juristic persons. Such a juristic person could be created by the State and could be dissolved by the State. Its purposes, nature and sphere of jurisdiction were beyond and above those of its members, that is, it had an *abstract* but legal existence. The incorporation of Kingston-Upon-Hull thus was the beginning of the subordination and political integration of autonomous cities within the nascent modern State.

The incorporation of Kingston-Upon-Hull was followed, with similar clauses containing all attributes of incorporation, by Southampton (1445), Ipswich (1446), Rochester (1446), Nottingham (1448), and Tenderden (1449), to list the most important ones. Throughout the fifteenth century, city charters took the form of either full incorporations or mere ratification of earlier privileges. In 1503, a general act of parliament ordained that corporations of the realm could not make or enforce ordinances without the approbation of the justices of peace who were State officials in county courts.[71] This act was followed by another one in 1558, which ordained that the State could enforce ordinances and rules directly on corporations who were responsible for carrying out these rules and regulations.[72] These two acts demonstrate unmistakably that the concept of State supremacy over cities had become an articulable legal and political principle: this is what constitutes the early modernity of the city. Although not yet modern, it already contains important elements of the modern city: its subordinate and abstract status with respect to State law had explicit and prescribed corporate attributes. Technically, cities and citizens could no longer boast their *de facto* rights and liberties based on extant charters; if they were not explicitly stated in law, issued in either a formal incorporation or a general law, they could not possess these liberties—of course, technically; it was yet another matter politically. As we shall see, that was not settled so easily until the 1830s. To give an example of resistance let us hear an anonymous "Discourse of Corporations" written c. 1587–1589. It was argued in that discourse that "it is the site and place where every town or city built which is the chief cause of the flourishing of the same, or else some special trade, and not the incorporation thereof."[73]

To conclude, as the English State apparatus was more stabilized and the parliament became an instrument through which the English State was governed during the fifteenth century, the incorporation of cities assumed a more consistent and calculated pattern.[74] To put it in other words, the *political* subjugation of cities within a wider system of power gradually found expression in the invention of *legal* incorporation, which was being slowly formulated in legal thought. There is no doubt that the political subjugation of cities within the State coincided with the elaboration of the corporation as an institution, a subjugated body politic. Although the interplay of ideas and practice is never simple, the idea of corporations as subjugated bodies politic, as elaborated mostly by Italian jurists, was influential in the emergence of the modern State and in the dismantling of intermediate jurisdictions. The appearance of the 'five attributes' of *de jure* corporations (perpetual succession, the capacity to sue and be sued, land possession, common seal and name, power to issue rules and regulations) must be seen in the context of the idea of early modern corporations as subjugated bodies politic (*persona ficta*). We must note again that what we described above was the *beginning* of the subjugation of cities within the nascent modern State. It was by no means total or even extensive. As we shall see, as late as the nineteenth century, by the time of the famous Royal Commission on 'municipal corporations' in 1835, there were cities which could claim autonomy on the basis of extant charters. The point here is that while before the fifteenth century the subjugation of cities was politically impossible and legally unthinkable, after the fifteenth century it became not only legally articulable but also politically enforceable.

Close Corporations and Oligarchies

Between the fifteenth and the late seventeenth centuries the general strategy of the English State administration was to force corporations to surrender their old charters and liberties and accept new charters of incorporation.[75] These new charters were often aimed at forming a governing body that was either directly in contact with the State or appointed by it.[76] The result was what came to be known as 'close corporations', which meant that the governing body (city council) of the corporation was empowered to co-opt members to perpetuate itself rather than through popular elections. Throughout the early modern period the State administration went as far as appointing many city officials. In 1661, this strategy became a legitimate legal principle in a hallmark general act on the early modern city as a State institution.[77] The statute ordained that the State would appoint commissioners in all cities of the realm and all officials would take the oaths of allegiance and supremacy: "I declare and believe that it is not lawful upon any pretense whatsoever to take Arms against the King and that I do abhor that traitorous position of taking by his authority against his person or against those that are commissioned by him." As much as this act indicates the rising subjugation of what we have called *de facto* corporate bodies within the State, it also indicates that the subjugation did not happen without resistance. At any rate, toward the end of the seventeenth century, cities became subordinate to the State and were separated from the body of citizens who had originally made up the governing bodies of cities. Instead, the 'new' *de jure* corporations became closed, oligarchic bodies of a governing elite who performed their duties as officials of the State. By 1688, in England there were 128 such incorporated cities.

The jurists and lawyers who gradually elaborated the idea of cities as *de jure* corporations were also representing significant political struggles of their own times; struggles which lay beneath their practices. They were not passive observers of broader battles but active participants in power relations between the cities and the nascent modern State. Their writings, therefore, did not only consist of only 'theoretical' treatises but also included numerous 'practical' treatises that addressed the issues of power, governance and cities. Sir Edward Coke (1552–1634), for example, was an influential jurist and statesman whose practice, as a lawyer, a crown legal officer and a royal court judge, spanned the most important period of the transition we are here discussing; the transition, that is, from *de facto* to *de jure* corporate institutional arrangements in the cities.[78] In several judgments he ruled consistently against old corporate liberties of cities on the grounds that they were a breach of "the liberty of the subject" and contrary to the "sovereignty of the State."[79] He came to express the hostility of the early modern political thought toward city liberty succinctly and effectively. The axis formed by the two polar entities of the State and the subject was, in fact, to constitute a pillar of modern political thought. Briefly, I would like to draw attention to his work.

Coke's major treatise on law defined the borough as "an ancient town, held by the king or any other lord, which sent burgesses to the parliament and it is called a borough because it sent members to the parliament."[80] Here the definition may sound like a circular one but it expresses an important seventeenth century conception of the city. The city was recognized only if it sent burgesses to the parliament. But there were important boroughs before the parliament became a regular part of State administration in the fourteenth century. Coke's definition recognizes only the *de jure* corporations of the fourteenth and fifteenth centuries and ignores the *de facto* corporations of the eleventh, twelfth and the thirteenth centuries. In other words, he renders the history of corporate bodies from the point of view of the State and acknowledges them only in the form in which they were recognized in the seventeenth century.

For example, Coke says: "If a town be decayed so as no houses remain, yet it is a town in law. And so borough be decayed, yet it shall send burgesses to the parliament it still is a borough in law."[81] This definition presupposes the perpetual existence of the city, that is, independent of the citizens, the city has a legal life of its own. Coke elaborates on this by stressing that "every city is a borough, but every borough is not a city...for a city is a borough incorporate" which implies that unless a borough is incorporated it cannot be a city.[82] Now, here corporation presupposes representation "for the towns that now be cities or counties, in old time were boroughs, and called boroughs; for of such old towns called boroughs, come the burgesses of the parliament to the parliament, when the king summoned his parliament."[83] In order to become a city, the borough must be both represented in the parliament *and* also be a corporate unit, a creation of royal law. The definition of the city by Coke then is predicated on its relationship with the State: a city is that multiplicity which is governed by a body politic and corporate through delegated powers of the State.

Coke then moves on to consider the importance of cities within the State: "Cities are instituted for three purposes: For conservation of laws, whereby every man enjoyed his own in peace; for tuition and defence of the king's subjects; and for keeping the king's peace in time of sudden uproars; and lastly, for defence of the realm against outward or inward hostility."[84] The city as an institution thus enforces legislation, takes care of both the king's subjects and his peace, and can be used for defence purposes. What Coke is expressing here is the early modern concept of the city, instituted by the State as a subordinate body politic for the purposes of State administration.

He defines the parliament as "the highest and most honorable and absolute court of justice in *England*, consisting of the king, the lords of parliament, and the commons."[85] This highest court of justice comprises representatives or royal officers of territorial institutions, which contain subordinate courts: "sheriffs from shires or counties, citizens out of cities, and burgesses out of boroughs."[86] As was discussed, this conception of boroughs as juridical persons represented in the parliament gradually appeared in charters issued to boroughs in the later thirteenth and throughout the fourteenth centuries.[87] But here it is interesting to note that while Coke describes the emergence of the early modern city with remarkable skill and precision, he is equally obscure about the *de facto* corporations. Is this a simple problem of historical research or something altogether different? Upon reflection about the conditions under which corporations were conceptualized in the seventeenth century, we will realize that the latter is the case. By obscuring the *de facto* corporations and focusing on created corporations, Coke was legitimating the early modern attack on corporate liberties and 'ancient privileges'. Let us take, for example, the hallmark "act for the well governing and regulating of corporations" which was mentioned earlier. This act stated that:

> Whereas questions are likely to arise concerning the validity of elections of magistrates and other officers and members in corporations, as well in respect of removing some as placing others during the late troubles contrary to the true intent and meaning of their charters and liberties; and to the end that the succession in such corporations may be most probably perpetuated in the hands of persons affected to his majesty and the established government...: be it enacted...that no charter of any corporation, cities, towns, boroughs, ports and their members, and other port towns in England or Wales...shall at any time hereafter be avoided for or by reason of any act or thing done or omitted to be done before the first day of this present parliament.[88]

The act sent a clear and strong message to those who attempted to interpret the "true intent and meaning of their charters and liberties" that such interpretation can only be authenticated by the State. In 1682, this message was dearly received by the citizens and mayor of London when the State opened *quo warranto* proceedings before the court of the king's bench against them.[89] In conclusion of these proceedings, the king's right was upheld and the corporation was condemned to forfeit all its old customary liberties. The king restored these liberties thereafter on the condition that the incorporation should henceforth install no officials without his confirmation in writing.[90] In these proceedings Robert Sawyer, the attorney general, argued that corporations which 'abuse' their power could be seized into the king's hands. If, he said, it were impossible to proceed thus against corporations, and to punish them for their misdeeds, "it were to set up independent commonwealths within the kingdom and this...would certainly tend to the utter overthrow of the common law, and the crown too, in which all sovereign power to do right both to itself and the subjects, is only lodged by the common law of this realm."[91] Indeed, "the law would be deficient if such inferior jurisdictions, or corporations, were not subject to the common law upon the like conditions, as other liberties, franchises and inferior jurisdictions are."[92] As Holdsworth observed, the principle "that in the interests of public order, the modern State should never allow large numbers of men an unlimited and unregulated power of grouping themselves for a common object" and "the need for the sanction of the State for the creation of a corporation was steadily adhered to in this period [the seventeenth century], and it has never been abandoned."[93] By the seventeenth century, the sovereignty of the State was established in law as an inviolable principle, and the autonomous corporations were considered a violation of this principle.

Although the Glorious Revolution of 1688 reversed the London case, attacks continued on corporate liberties.[94] More interestingly during this period, the history of corporation came to be rewritten, as we have seen in Edward Coke, who was interpreting the entire history of cities from the perspective of the English State. These efforts of rewriting the history of cities as corporations resulted in two very significant historical treatises. The first was in 1704 by Robert Brady, *An Historical Treatise of Cities & Burghs or Boroughs.*[95] Brady's purpose was to show that whatever immunities and liberties cities and corporations may have had, they were derived from the king and thus could be annulled by the king. The belief on the part of many lawyers that these liberties were held independently of the king and did not originate in him is the one which Brady sets out to dispel by opposing "matter of fact, through the whole discourse, to these fond imaginations, and easy notions, and for the clearer demonstration of what I intended to evince."[96] The treatise uses historical truth on the side of royal power: "whoever will seriously peruse this treatise, shall find the dates of their originals, and gradual augmentations, and must confess [cities] have nothing of the greatness and authority they boast of, but from the bounty of our ancient kings, and their successors."[97] Like Coke, Brady focuses on 'parliamentary boroughs', that is, boroughs from the fourteenth century onwards and leaves the earlier history in obscurity without isolating the sharp difference between earlier *de facto* and *de jure* corporations.

The second treatise was by Thomas Madox, *Firma Burgi, Or an Historical Essay Concerning the Cities, Towns & Boroughs of England.*[98] Madox considered a number of cases where a borough failed or refused to render the lump sum owed to the king. The conclusion is as might be expected: "The grace and indulgence of the kings of England to their cities and towns and boroughs should be a powerful motive to engage them from time to time to a loyal and dutiful behaviour toward the King, their patron and benefactor."[99]

These treatises laid the foundations of modern historical conceptions of corporations. And this perhaps explains why there has been little interest in cities as corporations and why we take their existence for granted. If you recall we began this section by considering the importance of 1440 in the history of corporate cities. One view was that 1440 did not constitute any significant break or threshold, while another view took it for granted that that was the year when corporations came into being.[100] In either case, we can see that the interpretation is made from the perspective of the State, that is, *de facto* corporations are considered either as the same as *de jure* corporations or as archaic and 'immature' forms of cities. Both interpretations were advanced in the earliest historical treatises on cities, which were written to attack the legitimacy of the rights and liberties of corporate bodies that were not explicitly derived from the State. In other words, we belong to an era when the liberties of corporate bodies and communities cannot be assumed unless they are conferred by the State. But cities and citizens did not originate that way.[101]

Early Modern Cities and Poor Laws

The era that we focus on in this section is also known in historical literature as the era of the great absolutist States in Europe.[102] The kingdoms and territorial States of medieval Europe were transformed into powerful

States with elaborate administrative, financial, legal and war machines. Because of a general demographic upswing, the governing of populations became a major concern for kings and their State apparatuses. With this in mind there were numerous political treatises addressed to the art of government: how to govern the State and its population, how to avoid rebellions, how to inculcate habits of obedience, etc. French historian Michel Foucault has specifically drawn attention to issues of government in the early modern States. He said:

> the theory of the art of government was linked, from the sixteenth century, to the whole development of the administrative apparatus of the territorial monarchies, the emergence of governmental apparatuses; it was also connected with a set of analyses and forms of knowledge which began to develop in the late sixteenth century and grew in importance during the seventeenth, and which were essentially to do with knowledge of the state, in all its different elements, dimensions and factors of power, questions which were termed precisely 'statistics', meaning the science of the state; finally, as a third vector of connection, I do not think one can fail to relate this search for an art of government to mercantilism and the science of police.[103]

The concerns with obedience, discipline, rebellion and the duties and rights of the State were also the concerns expressed in general legislation that were passed in the sixteenth and seventeenth centuries in England. A series of general legislation known as poor law is relevant in understanding the subsequent development of cities as corporations. If we distinguish poor relief from poor law it becomes apparent that poor law was closely associated with the issue of governing masses. Poor relief existed in England since the Middle Ages and was administered through the church parishes for destitute people.[104] The poor law, however, operated through an elaborate and general legislation of State administration: the idea that the strength of a State was an industrious, numerous, obedient population, provided the English State with the complex of reasons to wage a battle against 'idleness', 'vagrancy', 'impotence', a battle which took the form of proclamations, statutes, orders and regulations. What emerges from the poor law legislation and administration is that the sovereign State constituted its population as an object of practical concern for the wealth and strength of the State. The early modern poor law legislation thus worked with general principles and culminated in a distinction between the deserved and the able-bodied poor, which reflected an abstract work ethic. The early modern poor law, then, was less aimed at relief than governing of *subjects*.

The importance of this series of laws for cities as corporations is twofold. First, although poor law begins with brutally suppressive measures, it gradually shifts, toward the eighteenth century, to more complex institutions of discipline and government. This constitutes the beginnings of the liberal approach toward governance. And, second, a shift in the administration of poor law, which now worked with general principles and aimed at the governance of subjects, used the cities as corporations. In poor law administration, cities began to play an important role as instruments of governance. The State legislation would often specify in general terms how each jurisdiction (counties) or corporation (boroughs, cities and towns) should administer the determined 'policy'; the rest was done in these bodies politic. The central legislation was accomplished through statutes and proclamations. The statutes were directed often to the justices of peace (counties) and mayors (corporate boroughs, cities and towns). Therefore, a new relationship of franchise between the State and the city was being worked out in the practice of poor law by delegating certain powers and duties to cities. Let us now turn to the poor law legislation of the sixteenth and the seventeenth centuries in England.

In a statute of 1531 about vagrancy, a distinction was made between those who were impotent and those who were capable of work; impotent persons were allowed to beg with authorization. If any impotent person without such an authorization was caught, "the constables shall cause every such beggar to be taken to the Justice of Peace; and thereupon the said Justice of Peace shall command that they shall strip him naked from the middle upward, and cause him to be whipped."[105] Those who were capable of work were less tolerated: "If any person being whole and mighty in body and able to labour be vagrant and can give none reckoning how he does lawfully get his living, that then the Justice of Peace shall cause him to be tied to the end of a cart, naked, and be beaten with whips throughout the same Market Town or other place till his body be bloody by reason of such whipping."[106] It was also ordained that "Scholars of the Universities of Oxford and Cambridge that go about begging, not being authorized under the seal of the said universities...shall be punished and ordered in manner as is above rehearsed of strong beggars."[107] The interpretation of these penances in local courts and by officials was varied; the justices of peace and justices in cities were limited only by their imagination. On December 15, 1547, a city of London justice ordered that:

Thomas Yonge, a sturdy vagabond shall tomorrow, and two market days more, in example of other offenders, be set upon the pillory with a paper upon his head declaring his said offenses. And that he shall stand there three hours every of the said days in the market time. And that the last of those three days, one of his ears shall be nailed to the pillory. And that he, after this his penance done, shall avoid the city forever.[108]

The king occasionally issued proclamations to the inhabitants of a city. On April 28, 1551, in such a proclamation to the people of London, it was declared that "...there is at this present a great number of idle persons and masterless men, which seek rather by Idleness, or mischief, to live by other men's labours and industries, than to travail by any pains taking, to live like good and obedient members of the common wealth: His Majesty immediately charged and commanded by his prerogative royal, to depart all such out of the City of London, and the Suburbs of the same within four days after the making of this proclamation, home to the place either where they were born, or where they have dwelt last three years within the realm, going at least eight miles a day."[109]

These measures of explicit suppression were gradually displaced by more subtle measures of governance toward the end of the sixteenth century; this also resulted in the more precise definition of the duties of agents and agencies of local administrations. In the statutes and proclamations that were produced in this earlier period, justices of peace in counties appeared as the most significant agents of local administration, although corporations gained gradual predominance.[110] The distinction between these jurisdictions was increasingly clarified. On January 12, 1562, a statute ordained that

> ...in every city, borough, and town corporate, the mayor and other head officers for the time being, and in every other parish the parson and churchwardens, shall have written in a book the names of the householders within their town or parish as well as the names of all such impotent aged and needy persons which are not able to live by their own labour.[111]

This statute reveals an important new principle: corporate cities, boroughs and towns are explicitly viewed as agencies of State administration, and as such they are expected to fulfill obligations that are prescribed for them. In a further statute, in 1572, it was enacted that

> ...all Justices of Peace, Mayors, Sheriffs and other officers, shall make diligent search of all aged, poor, impotent and decayed persons, and shall make a Register Book containing the names of all such poor people. And when the number be truly known, then the said justices and other officers shall [find]...convenient places to settle the same poor people for their habitation...And they shall set down what the weekly

charge will amount to within their Divisions; and that done, they shall tax and assess all and every inhabitant in every city, borough, town village, hamlet, and place, to such weekly charge as they and every one of them shall weekly contribute to the relief of the poor people.[112]

In a statute of 1575, such "convenient places" were called the houses of correction and the officers of the city administration were asked to appoint "governors of the poor" to manage such places.[113] The same statute ordained "to the intent that youths may be brought up in labour and work and to the intent also that such as be already grown up in idleness...[that] within every county of this Realm, one, two, or more [such] Places, convenient in some Market Town, shall be provided."

When we examine these statutes, proclamations and court cases, we can see the reason of State at work: how the battle against idleness was waged; how industriousness and obedience were first brutally enforced and then were inculcated through houses of correction; and, how cities were integrated and used as agencies of State administration. The sixteenth century can be considered then as a threshold in the history of corporations: the question shifted from the nature of cities as corporations to the problem of their integration within the State administration.

As Webb and Webb observe, in the first half of the seventeenth century, there was an attempt, gradually developing out of orders and legislation, and which continued for half a century, to establish a comprehensive administrative hierarchy, by which the legislation relating to the condition of the population (but of particularly the poor) could be systematically put into operation throughout the realm.[114] The most important development from our point of view was the establishment of Corporations of the Poor, or Incorporated Boards of Guardians. Here I would like to draw attention to one pamphlet on the subject, which John Locke said was "the best discourse I have ever read on that subject," and which was to result in immediate legislation.[115] The pamphlet was published in 1695 by John Cary, *An Essay on the State of England in Relation to its Trade, its Poor & its Taxes.* Cary had gained experience in Bristol by inducing the mayor and aldermen of the city and other principal inhabitants to apply to parliament for a local act. The reasons for the application, as stated in the preamble, were that

...it is found by experience that the poor in the City of Bristol do daily multiply, and idleness and debauchery amongst the meaner sort greatly increase, for want of workhouses to set them to work, and a sufficient authority to compel them thereto, as well as to the charge of the inhabitants and grief of the charitable and honest citizens of the said city, as the great stress of the poor themselves for which sufficient redress had not yet been provided.[116]

Cary put forward a set of proposals, which, according to Webb and Webb, "were destined to be copied up and down the kingdom for a whole century."[117] Cary proposed that "a spacious workhouse be erected at a general charge, large enough for the poor to be employed therein; and also for room for such as, being unable to work, are to be relieved by charity"; "that the rules of the house may force all persons to work that are able, and encourage manufacturers to furnish them with materials to work upon"; "that persons not able to maintain their children may put them into this workhouse or hospital at what ages they will, so that these children may be bred up to labour, principles of virtue implanted in them at an early age, and laziness be discouraged"; "that the governor be empowered to force all poor people to work who do not betake themselves to some lawful employment elsewhere, but spend their time lazily and idly"; "that the governor have power to settle out the young people at such ages as may be thought fit..."; "that this will prevent children from being starved by the poverty of their parents and the neglect of parish officers, which is now a great loss to the nation, inasmuch as every person would by his labour add to the wealth of the public."[118] On January 18, 1696, the parliament passed the bill to incorporate the Board of Guardians in the city of Bristol. The spread of incorporated workhouses was significant in the history of the city as a corporation. Did the incorporated workhouses constitute the beginnings of the corporation as an apparatus of governance?

This new deployment of corporations toward the second half of the seventeenth century illustrates the shift in the conception of the role of corporations within the modern State. Between 1440 and 1688, the English State was often concerned with limiting the liberties of corporations and increasing their obligations as they were assimilated into the State apparatus. The period is therefore marked with encroachments by the State on corporations. This contrasts with the earlier period, between the twelfth and the fourteenth centuries, when the autonomous city triumphed. This period also contrasts with the later period when corporations were used for the purposes of State administration. There was also a parallel shift in juridical and political thought as well. As we have seen, Edward Coke was more concerned with limiting the liberties of corporations. Whereas Thomas Hobbes (1588–1679), writing at the moment of this shift, was more concerned with the use of corporations, which anticipates, but also participates in a transformation toward the modern city. As Gierke pointed out, Hobbes "was the first to introduce into the theory of Natural Law a conception of Group-persons, which was not simply borrowed from the civilian or Roman-law theory of corporations, but was genuinely deduced from the actual principles of Natural Law; and he was the first to make such a conception the pivot of both public law and the law of corporations."[119]

When Thomas Hobbes stated that "there are two kinds of Cities, the one natural the other institutive, which may be also called political," he was making a crucial and clear distinction between *de facto* and *de jure* corporations.[120] By this distinction he was also expressing the rudiments of the modernity of the city in political and legal thought: the city was not only an entity for subjugation but could be instituted for purposes of government. Although, and expectedly, he was coterminous with the rudiments that were already appearing in new poor law, his conceptualization possessed a remarkable clarity. Hobbes contended that the accomplishment of the objectives of the art of government requires creating subordinate cities "to divide the burdens, and charge of the [State] proportionally."[121] According to Hobbes, the State would expect that certain functions *and* consequences of administration, exercise of authority, and governance of subjects, must reside in cities to govern an *increasing* population. In fact, only by consenting to the formation of a multitude of people into cities does it become possible to govern with more and more general principles. This was a significant leap toward the modernity of the city.

To conclude, the sixteenth and seventeenth centuries, the age of absolutism, were an era of both systematic, theoretical and practical exercises in the "art of government"—ordering and maintaining the multiplicity of subjects. And both exercises paid considerable attention to the city as a corporation. First, the subjugation of the corporations drew attention and then, toward the end of the seventeenth century, the focus shifted to their use in government. The early modern city, as we call it in this book, embodied both of these aspects of the art of government. At the same time, it increasingly became the handmaiden of the king in parliament since the governing bodies of corporations (the mayor, council and the officials) became close, self-perpetuating bodies politic and separated themselves from citizens who initially *were* the city. Citizens were now considered as subjects of government.

But toward the end of the eighteenth century, for reasons which are debated among historians, the English State in particular and European States in general became too complicated to be governed through edicts, proclamations, enforcement and governing elites. Toward the end of the eighteenth century in England, there was already concern about 'rotten boroughs' as close corporations. The dawn of modernity—modern concepts of law, politics, society and the city—was already in the making.

City as a Government Franchise: 19th Century

After the middle of the eighteenth century, jurists and political econo-mists became convinced that a great need of the times was the 'reform' if not the total recasting of the oppressive and negative system of law that had been inherited from the absolutist regimes. The 'enlightened' view stated that these laws were not only barbaric in substance and often chaotic in form; they were also *inefficient* because they attached a quite illusory importance to the severity of punishment and ignored the im-portance of clarity and precision in the form of the law and certainty in its application. The belief that the main principle of State administration could be legislation guided by a conception of punishment as a means of preventing misconduct, and by a scientific understanding of human nature, formed an important part of the European enlightenment of which Jeremy Bentham (1748–1832) was the principal English voice. The enlightened view argued that government by command, by edict, by proclamation, in short, by force, was not effective; instead, go-vernment on the basis of calculated, coherent legislation was defined as the proper domain of politics. To govern, in this sense, was to direct and steer the actions or conduct of the subjects through established laws, rules and regulations, by those invested with authority.[122] This marked the emergence of the modern concept of law and government.

As was described earlier, however, in political and legal practice, the beginnings of a change from suppressive control to an "art of go-vernment" can be observed as early as the 1680s (particularly in poor law). But toward the end of the eighteenth century, these ideas begin to form the essentials of political and legal discourse. From our point of view the significance of this shift is that the city as a corporation soon came under the gaze of this new thinking. It went through an important transformation: the political and legal aspects of the modern city as a corporation were founded in this period, between the 1780s and the 1830s. It is important for us now to see what was new in the enlightened view of the city as a corporation. Let us begin by outlining some ideas and proposals Bentham formulated, which not only reflected their times but also helped induce changes in England and elsewhere.[123] Bentham is important not only because he was the principal English voice of enlightened governance, but also because the principal figures who launched a new liberal colonial politics in Canada in the 1830s and 1840s—Edward Gibbon Wakefield, Robert Baldwin, John Arthur Roebuck and Lord Durham—often aligned their ideas with Bentham.[124]

Jeremy Bentham and the Modern City

Here we cannot get more than a glimpse of the most important aspects of the new concepts of law and government embodied in Bentham.[125] First, we will outline his concept of 'enlightened' or liberal governance. Then we will focus on how the city as a corporation was viewed within enlightened governance.

Bentham coined the term 'pannomion' to describe a comprehensive and precise legal system. He said that "by a Pannomion, understand on this occasion an all-comprehensive collection of law, that is to say, of *rules* expressive of the will or wills of some person or persons belonging to the community, or say society in question, with whose will in so far as known, or guessed at, all other members of that same community in question, are regarded to act in compliance."[126] We notice here a distinction between those who *will* and those who *obey* in the State where pannomion prevails. And law is a set of rules of conduct that expresses the will of legislators. There was no doubt that "law supposes government: to establish a law, is to exercise an act of government. A law is a declaration of will—of a will conceived and manifested by an individual, or individuals, to whom the other individuals in the society to which such will has respect are generally disposed to obey. Now government supposes the disposition to obedience: the faculty of governing on the one part has for its sole efficient cause, and for its sole measure, the disposition to obey on the other part."[127] If you recall, Hobbes also presupposed the obedience of subjects for the existence of the State; but there is a significant difference between Bentham and Hobbes: the latter thought that the obedience to leaders was found in nature (natural law) whereas for Bentham it was a product of discipline. Bentham clearly expressed this when he said that the disposition to obey is "the result of a system of conduct of which the commencement is lost in the abyss of time."[128] The disposition of obedience then is a learned habit and it forms the foundation of the State. For this reason there are branches of pannomion: an effective branch that deals with giving direction to the conduct of the subjects of the State, and a constitutive branch that is occupied with determining who the subjects of the State are, and by whom the powers belonging to the effective branch shall be exercised.[129] But how can the direction of the conduct of subjects be manipulated?

Here we embark upon, once again, corporations as apparatuses of governance.

Let us note that what Bentham's pannomion embodies are the main principles of the liberal concept of law (generality and precision) and its emphasis on institutions as the means of governance for steering the conduct of subjects. If we contrast these principles with the series of State legislation in the seventeenth and eighteenth centuries we will see that what Bentham epitomizes as the genuinely modern political and legal exercise of power is no longer predicated on proclamation, edict and force, but on positive law *and* carefully calculated institutions for steering the conduct of subjects.[130] Bentham called the latter "indirect legislation": calculated institutions, which both presupposed and precipitated a precise body of knowledge about subjects in question.[131] Also, presupposed and precipitated by these new calculated institutions was an apparatus of governance. Bentham's enthusiasm about institutions to govern the conduct of subjects and a comprehensive legal system (pannomion) epitomize genuinely modern principles of State administration and power.[132]

But there was one more principle that Bentham formulated, which is of significance for us: the principle of self-government as obligation. By this Bentham understood means of instruction through which the citizens of the State were taught to govern themselves. Bentham thought that such instruction could best be accomplished in what he called "fields of action" in which citizens participated.[133] Each field of action was centred on a territorial institution: districts, subdistricts and trisubdistricts.[134] Since Bentham wrote the "Constitutional Code" for the use of any State, the names of territorial institutions were his. But he said that the names could be adjusted to any existing territorial system of the State in question. In England the equivalent of his territorial institutions, he said, would be counties, townships and towns.[135] The city, Bentham said, was the atom of the State, which could not be further subdivided.[136] Here what we see is the distinctively modern concept of the city, which is conceptualized as an integral component of a hierarchical apparatus of administration and governance—the city as the atom of the State.[137]

If we summarize the modern concept of law and governance as epitomized in Bentham, its main features were an emphasis on positive legislation setting out boundaries for permitted and permissible conduct *and* a concern with institutions to enable subjects to govern their own conduct. But this transformation in the concept of law was also embodied in new legislation in the 1830s. As Maitland diagnosed, in modernity "the parliament begins to *legislate* with remarkable vigour...but about the same time it gives up the attempt to *govern* the country, to say what commons shall be enclosed, what roads shall be widened, what boroughs shall have paid constables and so forth."[138] Instead, Maitland observed, the parliament "begins to lay down general rules about these matters and entrust their working partly to officials, to secretaries of State, to boards of commissioners, who for this purpose are endowed with new statutory powers, partly to the law courts."[139] With such a transformation in the concept of law and governance, the modern city was beginning to be considered within the framework of representative institutions within the State. Let us now look at how these concepts were embodied in legislation for cities as corporations.

Corporations and State Legislation

The beginning point of exploring how the city figured in the liberal State administration is the well-known act on parliamentary representation in 1832, which presupposed and affirmed a legislative supremacy over cities.[140] This legislation overhauled the centuries-long established patterns of parliamentary representation of cities and disfranchised more than fifty cities that returned members to the parliament. Another set of thirty-one cities was reduced to sending only one member. But at the same time, forty-two new cities were constituted with the *elective franchise* to send one or two members to the parliament. We do not need to deal with the details of occupation, residence and property qualifications for the new relationship of franchise that was established between the city and the State. But it should be pointed out that this act brought about a significant change in terms of the corporate status of the early modern city. Until then, the city was a political community that sent a member to the parliament. As we have seen in our discussion of Coke, the early modern city was associated with its parliamentary franchise.[141] But now, sending a member to the parliament or, in other words, to participate in the affairs of the State was no longer an exclusive property of a city.[142] There was now a distinction between municipal franchise and parliamentary franchise. Another novel aspect of this legislation from our perspective was the constitution of a number of counties as corporate bodies for the purposes of elective franchise. As we shall see, incorporation of counties with distinct corporate capacities was an important aspect of the emergence of municipal corporations in British North America.

Of course, the 1832 act made it necessary to rethink all the corporate cities throughout England: How many corporations existed?

What authorities constituted them? What were their corporate status, capacities and powers? What were their responsibilities and duties? How were they governed? In 1834, a commission of inquiry was appointed and assistant commissioners were sent out to examine how corporations were governed.[143] The commissioners were surprised that "they were unable to find any correct list of such corporations in any of the departments of the state."[144] But from local records it was ascertained that in 1835 there were 246 cities in England (cities were now beginning to be called municipal corporations). Of these, the greater number of the incorporations were granted between 1440 and 1688 and "the general characteristic of these documents," the report stated, was "that they were calculated to take away power from the community, and to render the governing class independent of the main body of the burgesses...for the purpose of influencing the choice, or nomination, of Members of Parliament."[145] Here the report quite accurately detected the era and the nature of the early modern city discussed earlier: the subjugated and close corporation. The conclusion of the report was that "the most common and most striking defect of the Municipal Corporations of England and Wales is, that the corporate bodies exist independently of the communities in which they are found. The Corporations look upon themselves, and are considered by the inhabitants, as separate and exclusive bodies; they have powers and privileges within the towns and cities from which they are named, but in most places all identity of interest between the Corporation and the inhabitants disappeared."[146] In other words, the report found the English cities without their citizens: instead, each city was governed by a close oligarchy of elite families since the fifteenth and sixteenth centuries. As a result, some corporations were so decayed as to be virtually nonexistent; many did nothing of value for the local inhabitants; some were corrupt. Most of them lacked police or watch functions; municipal institutions such as prisons, workhouses, and correction houses were unregulated by the corporations. The commissioners concluded "that the existing Municipal Corporations neither possess nor deserve the confidence or respect of the subjects, and that a thorough reform must be effected, before they can become useful and efficient instruments of government."[147] This conclusion, the importance of which we should not underestimate, epitomizes the modernity of the city: a useful and efficient instrument of government. Although the report revealed and recognized the cities without citizens, it was not about to entertain the possibility of autonomous cities governed by its citizens. Instead, a new, distinctively modern, notion of the city as a corporation was forged. Let us now see this modern notion.

The Municipal Corporations Act, 1835, gave the cities a new and uniform constitution that embodied rudiments of their modernity.[148] The act stated that it was passed because "diverse bodies corporate at sundry times have been constituted within the cities, towns and boroughs of England and Wales, to the Intent that the same might for ever be and remain well and quietly governed." The act applied to 178 towns, cities and boroughs. This means that the act considered only these entities as municipal corporations and no other. The act is therefore exclusively about the modern city constituted as a municipal corporation.[149] The act included a schedule listing the cities and towns to which the act was addressed and specified the number of wards, the number of councilmen and the explicit name of each corporation. The city council was empowered to "make such bylaws as to them shall seem meet for the good rule and government of the borough, and for prevention and suppression of all such nuisances as are not already punishable in a summary manner by virtue of any Act in force throughout such borough, and to appoint by such bylaws such fines as they shall deem necessary."[150] But, it required that the council send a copy of any such bylaw to one of the principal secretaries of the State who had the power to disallow the bylaw. In other words, cities were to be governed within limits set by the State. Other important aspects of the act were as follows: the administration of justice was separated from local administration and the borough justices were separated from the borough council. For this purpose some cities were constituted as counties. The exclusive rights and customs of all cities, guilds and trading companies within cities were abolished. And, most importantly, the qualifications for mayor, councillors, aldermen and voters were specified, following the guidelines of the 1832 act.

Let us make no mistake about it: the modern city as a corporation retained the principle of separation of the city from its citizens. The city was governed by an elite. While in the autonomous city, citizens among themselves decided who belonged to the city and who was to govern; in the early modern city, it was the State administration who appointed a governing elite that exercised power over citizens. Both the early modern and modern cities were cities without citizens; if citizens were 'subjects' in the former they became 'voters' in the latter. The modernity of the city as a corporation consists in rules specified by the State within which a governing body authorized by the voters (whose qualifications are determined as citizens of the State) exercises its franchised rights and fulfills its governmental obligations.

As to the governmental obligations of the city as a corporation, it was the maintenance of law and order: separate clauses were provided to detail the duties of the city council. It was ordained that the city council appoint a watch committee to observe and enforce order. "Watch Committee shall, within three weeks after their first formation, and so from time to time thereafter as occasion shall require, appoint a sufficient number of fit men, who shall be sworn in before some Justice of the Peace having Jurisdiction within the borough to act as constables for preserving the Peace by day and by night."[151] The watch committee was empowered to make regulations concerning the police force in the city, subject to approval of the city council. The justices of the peace were empowered to nominate and appoint some inhabitants of the city to act as special constables who could be called for duty as required. The watch committee was required to submit a quarterly report to one of the principal secretaries of the State. This aspect of the municipal constitution is not surprising: one of the reasons that precipitated the act was widespread riots and rebellions in Bristol and other cities.[152]

We must note that the Municipal Corporations Act was passed at a time when a great series of laws was being enacted in the parliament to establish cities for the purposes of governance. The act contains frequent references to other legislation thereby coordinating tasks of the city council with that of other authorities which were established in cities. We need to discuss briefly three areas of such legislation that were closely associated with the Municipal Corporations Act: poor law, public health, and elementary schooling. These three fields eventually became responsibilities of modern city government (social services, planning, and education).

Modern Poor Law

We discussed earlier how from 1688 onwards the State legislation on poor law shifted its emphasis from brutal suppression to calculated discipline of the poor, which culminated in incorporated workhouses. Here, as in earlier discussion of poor laws, our aim is not to enter into this complex subject but to point out how the liberal poor law related to municipal corporations. When a Poor Law Commission was appointed to report on the working of the existing arrangements, the commission sent out investigators to examine conditions in about three hundred parishes.[153] Among the recommendations of the committee was a well-regulated workhouse system. If this system was put into operation, the pauper class would be made into a labouring class with improved moral and social conditions and with frugal habits: the paupers will be divided into classes (male, female, old, children) and each class will be located in a separate building or area.

The well-known Poor Law Amendment Act, 1834, based on the commission's recommendations, provided a new and uniform administration for poor relief. A central body in London, the Poor Law Commission, was to supervise the whole system—the start of the State control over the details of local administration. The central body incorporated parishes into convenient areas for poor law purposes and in so doing ignored other territorial institutions. The reason for this was that when the poor law report was written, the royal commission on municipal corporations was in progress and the municipal corporations were not yet reformed. The poor law administration could not rely on existing 'municipal' corporations because, as we have seen, even the exact number of them was unknown. Thus many corporate parishes overlapped county boundaries. The Poor Law Commission laid down strict rules covering the distribution of relief. The unions were to build workhouses, and the distribution of relief other than to workhouse inmates was banned. The regime in the workhouse was to be severe in order to deter applications for admission. Local boards of guardians were elected by the taxpayers to run the workhouses, subject to State control and approval.

Public Health

In the 1840s the concern of the State administration was concentrated on "public health."[154] This concern was largely stimulated by Edwin Chadwick, secretary of the Poor Law Commission, who was convinced that disease was the main cause of poverty, and that the best way to help the poor was to remove the causes of sickness.[155] A further belief, of importance for towns, was that the character, morals and health of the working classes was conditioned by their living spaces. Much of the concern of public health then turned toward urban spaces in which the working classes lived and the planning of these spaces so as to make them conducive to better morals and health. In 1840, the Report of the Select Committee on the Health of Towns "...laid down as a general position, that persons of the same class, and engaged in the same sort of occupations in different populous towns, are subject, more or less, to the same evils...that their health and comfort are affected by the same causes, and that the remedies suggested...would be applicable to improve the condition of all or most of them."[156] This meant that a high level of legislative generality was reached and that the modern urban space also became a field of intervention. The focus of the report was predominantly on working-class housing: it was argued that the irregular and crowded dwelling conditions and particularly "...the position of rows of small houses in closed courts, built up at the sides and end, and having only one entrance, frequently under a narrow archway, [are] injurious to the health of inhabitants."[157] The recommendation was that "...the opening of a fresh thoroughfare, giving light and air, would not only remove or abate the evil, but would give additional value to the property through which it passes."[158] This report established a principle that made possible the application of general considerations to urban spaces throughout the realm. In 1842, a committee was formed to produce the first general building and design regulations in England.[159] Modern city planning *practice*, as yet not codified as such, arose out of a will to induce in the working classes habits and customs that were conducive to industry and health through a minute and unprecedented attention to the design of their living spaces.

The two major reports on the *Sanitary Condition of the Labouring Population* (1842)[160] and the two reports of the committee on the *State of Large Towns* (1844, 1845) applied this principle to numerous towns.[161] Commissioners were sent out to towns to conduct inquiries and inquisitions; numerous building designs were compiled and tested; numerous model working-class district plans were debated; and, numerous working-class district design principles were reached. The minute detail of these principles is breathtaking: there were more than thirty specific recommendations in the second report that dealt with the enforcement of cleanliness, width of courts and streets, interior and exterior of buildings, public walks and appointment of medical officers, to mention only a select few. The Public Health Act, 1848, authorized the establishment of local boards of health to put these recommendations into practice. The work of local boards was to be supervised by a Central Board of Health. Earlier, in 1846, the poor law guardians had been given limited powers to deal with the sanitary conditions of their jurisdiction.[162]

Schooling

Throughout this period, the concern of the modern State administration was the education of working classes. From an early date it was recognized that the education of the "lower classes" was of utmost importance. Education, of course, was never meant to be what we would understand; it was the pure and simple domestication of pauper children for useful labour. Joseph Lancaster was important in the diffusion of "...an institution of attaining primary education amongst the industrious classes of the community...wherein 300 children are educated, and trained to habits conducive to the welfare of society."[163] Lancaster considered that the most important principle of the school was its partitioning: "The school is divided into classes, to each of these a lad is appointed as monitor: he is responsible for the morals, improvement, good order, and cleanliness of the whole class. It is his duty to make a daily, weekly, and monthly report of progress."[164] And he defended this system on the grounds that it "...effectively commands quietness, by commanding attention; and as certainly prevents idleness, by actively employing every boy in the class at the same instant of time."[165] This system, in fact, rapidly spread throughout England. In 1818, once again, a royal commission, was formed to inquire into the education of "lower orders."[166] The committee concluded that "the means of educating the poor are steadily increasing in all considerable towns as well as in the metropolis."[167] The committee observed from the returns made to the commission "...that a very great deficiency exists in the means of educating the poor, wherever the population is thin and scattered over country districts." The recommendation that followed from this observation was that in certain areas perhaps it was desirable to concentrate the population through incorporation.

To conclude, from this brief review of modernity of the city as a corporation, the governability of the State was associated in modernity with the capacity of its legal and political institutions to direct and guide the conduct of its subjects. To govern in a modern State was to structure the possible field of action of subjects with precise and calculated limits. Here, recall what Maitland said about modern legislation: it gives up governing but focuses on setting limits. Accordingly, in modernity only subjects with liberty can be governed, and only insofar as when they are free. How could the conduct of humans be steered, let alone influenced by willing compliance if they were chained? Since the nineteenth century a new, modern body of knowledge developed that had constitutional *and* administrative law as its main components and the State *and* the subject as its main referent. This body of knowledge constituted a sophisticated kind of thought about power, characterized by an urge toward both generality and precision, systematization and completion. The modern concept of law combined then, on the one hand, general principles and, on the other hand, calculated *apparatuses of governance*, both of which were represented in the works of Bentham as discussed earlier. The modern city as a corporation was beginning to emerge as such an apparatus of governance by the 1830s.

Modern City within a Municipal System in England

It will be useful here to outline some of the developments in the latter part of the nineteenth century with respect to municipal authorities in England. By the 1830s the city was only *beginning* to emerge as one of the most important apparatuses of governance, within a municipal system of governance. Yet, until the 1880s the system of municipal governance was by no means complete, let alone established. Although by 1870 there were 65 counties, 224 municipal corporations, 667 incorporated boards of guardians, 637 local boards of health, and 15,414 townships and parishes, there was little integration or coordination among and between these authorities to warrant designation as a system.[168] At least this was the conclusion reached in the decades between the 1850s and the 1880s among legislators, reformers, statesmen, administrators and political economists. There was an agreement to coordinate this immensely proliferated number of local authorities in an efficient and coherent *system*.[169] A reformer, Toulmin Smith, for example, argued that such a system was compatible with national interests since the "true patriotism finds in Local Self-Government its constant nurse and that Local Self-Government affords the only true Education...the school of the active exercise of all the faculties in the earnest work of real life."[170] This was a theme that was repeated time and again in these debates.

But it was John Stuart Mill who articulated more cogently the importance of what he called "local representative bodies" for purposes of governance and "want of a system" in his *Considerations on Representative Government* (1861). At the outset, according to Mill, there were two purposes for which local bodies were established. First, central authorities must diffuse the burden of governance and let local bodies govern their 'local' affairs.[171] For there is little reason for central authorities to govern localities in their minute and local concerns. But at the same time, since their local concerns are the concerns of the State in general, a central supervision must be established to inspect the workings of the powers that are vested in them. Or, as he put it, "The authority which is most conversant with principles should be supreme over principles, while that which is most competent in details should have the details left to it."[172] And he added, "Power may be localized, but knowledge, to be most useful, must be centralized."[173] What Mill envisaged was that the coordination of local authorities must be accomplished by the central authorities according to demands and wants of national interests. Second, local bodies are the means to cultivate useful political habits in citizens of the State. But he cautioned that "government and administration do not exist for...the education of the citizens...alone, great as its importance is."[174] Thus the second purpose must always be subordinate to the first in establishing a system of local authorities.

A step toward such a system was first taken in 1882 when the Municipal Corporations Act was passed to constitute the cities that were excluded in the act of 1835.[175] Still, it was not until 1888 and 1894 that counties, townships and parishes were constituted as part of a system of municipal governance. The Local Government Act, 1888, constituted counties as bodies politic with chairmen, aldermen and councillors.[176] The powers of the county were styled after the municipal councils of boroughs, but the act clearly separated the jurisdiction of county councils from municipal councils already established with county boroughs and more than fifty thousand inhabitants. The Local Government Act, 1894, constituted district and parish councils as bodies politic and corporate.[177] The act constituted urban sanitary authorities as urban district councils and their districts as urban districts unless they were constituted as boroughs.[178]

To conclude, although by 1835 the rudiments of the modern city as an apparatus of governance had emerged in England, it was not until the 1880s and the 1890s that it was integrated within a municipal system of governance. In fact, as Keith-Lucas argued, it was not until the Local Government Act of 1972 that the city was fully integrated within a municipal system in England![179] As we shall see, such an integration and a system of municipal governance was accomplished in British North America in the 1840s.

Modern City: An Apparatus of Governance?

The main thrust of this chapter is that the modernity of the city can be properly understood only within the context of, and in contrast to, the rise of the autonomous city in the eleventh and twelfth centuries. We emphasized that the birth of communal liberty was expressed within a unique institution: the corporation. After that period, we discerned two great transformations that we designate with dates from English history. The first spanned the period between 1440 and 1688 in which the city was subjugated to the nascent modern State. And the second spanned the period between 1688 and 1835 in which the city gradually became an integral component of governance and administration within the modern State. The shared characteristic of both of these transformations was that the city as a corporation was considered to be a creature of the State.

Our point is that regardless of how one accounts for these transformations, after the research of Gierke it is impossible to underestimate the active role political and legal discourse played in these transformations—hence our focus. Both transformations embodied considerable thought as to the status and nature of the city as a corporation: jurists, administrators, statesmen, political theorists and philosophers not only expressed the tension between local autonomy and central authority but were participants in it. We have seen how the articulation of an abstract conception of the corporation and its fictitious nature during the fourteenth and fifteenth centuries became a weapon of State authority, which interpreted local autonomy as a creation of the State; and how the representation of cities in the parliament marked the beginning of a franchise relationship between cities and the State. The five attributes of the corporation codified by jurists signified that corporations were recognized by *de jure* franchises granted to cities by the State, as opposed to their *de facto* emergence. The subjugation of communal liberties by State authorities between 1440 and 1688 was justified and rationalized by this principle. This was the first great transformation of the autonomous city into the early modern city—the city that was subjugated to the State, a concept that came to be succinctly expressed in the thought *and* practice of Edward Coke.

From 1688 onwards we detected a shift in legal and political thought and practice toward the calculated use of cities and corporations for the enforcement of State legislation, including poor laws. Thomas Hobbes had already reached such a formulation in the 1650s, indicating the emergence of the modernity of the city, but the second great transformation of the autonomous city was not complete until the 1830s when liberalism became the main credo of State administration. The liberal credo set itself apart from the extremely centralist policies of State administration, which distinguished the early modern era. Liberalism did not question governance; it questioned government by command, by decree and by proclamation, which was predominant in the early modern era: the essence of the liberal attack was on the grounds that government by command was inefficient and ineffective. Instead, governance through institutions was the pillar of a new concept of power: to govern meant that those invested with authority established laws, rules and regulations to direct and steer the actions or conduct of citizens of the State. And within this credo, a general and precise legal discourse emerged as an instrument of governance.

The modern city was one of the first institutions that came under the gaze of this new discourse. From this we can draw the conclusion that the modern city as a corporation became an apparatus of governance. And, connected with the municipal corporations, for the first time in the history of the modern State, the urban space itself became a precise field of governance (from which modern city planning emerged). A new political and legal discourse was born to deal with all the intricate details of the corporation as an apparatus of governance, the modern city. But, parallel to these developments, and by no means less important, a new franchise relationship was being articulated between the city and the State: the city was now being considered a legal and political institution with explicit delegated powers and liabilities to undertake the governance of citizens of the State.

Notes

1. Lewis Mumford, *The Culture of Cities* (New York, 1938) and *The City in History* (New York, 1961); Murray Bookchin, *The Rise of Urbanization and the Decline of Citizenship* (San Francisco, 1987), rev. ed. *Urbanization Without Cities: The Rise and Decline of Citizenship* (Montreal, 1992).

2. Berman, *Revolution and Law*, p. 358; Werveke, "The Rise of the Towns," pp. 5–8.

3. Max Weber, *Die Stadt*, written c. 1911–1913, posthumously published 1921; English translation by Don Martindale and Gertrud Neuwirth (Glencoe, 1958); Henri Pirenne, *Medieval Cities* (Princeton, 1922).

4. Weber in his *General Economic History* stated this very clearly: "In the middle ages, the distinguishing characteristic of [a city] was the possession of its own law and court and an autonomous administration of whatever extent. The citizen of the middle ages was a citizen because and insofar as he came under this law and participated in the choice of administrative officials." Quoted in Derek Heater, *Citizenship* (London, 1990), p. 21.

5. A charter is a document recording and providing proof of a juridical act, such as a deed, contract, constitution, privilege, or mandate. The name comes from the Latin *c(h)arta* or *c(h)artula*, originally meaning a sheet of papyrus, with something written on the papyrus, parchment, or paper (a document, letter or booklet). The charter is associated with the emergence of legal systems in Western Europe in the late eleventh and twelfth centuries. Most charters (those issued by authorities such as popes, emperors, kings and rulers) were produced in the author's chancery, the responsible agency for composing and copying the written text. A charter had two main parts: protocol and text. The first included at the beginning the names and titles of the author (whose legal disposition was being recorded) and the recipient (in whose favour the charter was issued), a greeting, and possibly an invocation, and at the end it might include subscriptions of the author, witnesses, chancery officials, and scribes, along with the dating, a prayer, a seal, and other signs of validation. The text usually had a notification and exposition, and possibly a preamble preceding the disposition which might itself be followed by various concluding clauses. For more details see Joseph R. Strayer, ed., *Dictionary of Middle Ages*, 13 vols. (New York, 1982–1989).

6. Mumford, *City in History*, p. 302.

7. Mumford, *City in History*, p. 305.

8. Berman, *Revolution and Law*, p. 393.

9. Yet despite these numerous corporate institutions, both canon law and lay juristic thought did not have an articulate concept of the corporation until the late fourteenth century. Susan Reynolds made this point recently in her "The Idea of the Corporation in Western Christendom Before 1300," in J. A. Guy and H. G. Beale, eds., *Law and Social Change in British History* (London, 1984).

10. Here we are not concerned with the problem of whether feudal law existed in Anglo-Saxon England and whether Norman feudal law constitutes continuity with Anglo-Saxon institutions; we can be content with the minimalist position: that feudal relations were different after the Conquest. See Helen Cam, *Law-Finders and Law-Makers in Medieval England* (London, 1962), pp. 44–58.

11. Cam, *Law-Finders and Law-Makers*, p. 58. She added: "Looked at as a whole, the most characteristic quality of English feudalism seems to be its intimate association with royal government. Knight service, baronial courts and feudal revenues in the Anglo-Norman period; feudal land law the basis of the national common law as it developed from Henry II to Edward I; the traditions of counsel and consent handed down from the great councils of the Normans and Angevins to the parliaments of the later Middle Ages; the integration of the franchise holder into the national system of government by the rule of responsibility."

12. Frederick Pollock and Frederic W. Maitland, *The History of English Law before the Time of Edward I*, 2 vols. 2nd ed. (Cambridge, 1898). This work was envisaged as a joint venture and bears the name of both Pollock and Maitland. It is, however, substantially the work of Maitland, with the exception of chap. i in vol. i. That is why it is often cited as Maitland, *History of English Law*; Frederic W. Maitland, *Domesday Book and Beyond: Three Essays in the Early History of England* (Cambridge, 1897). See also G. R. Elton, *F. W. Maitland* (London, 1985). Maitland, *History of English Law*, seems to have adopted the best strategy to approaching the problem of the definition of the borough by not defining it; instead he focused on all these privileges and their nature: (i) jurisdictional; (ii) tenurial; (iii) mercantile; (iv) firma burgi; (v) property holding; (vi) election of officers; (vii) bylaws and self-government; (viii) self-taxing powers; (ix) guild-merchant.

13. Tait, *Medieval English Borough*, p. 350.

14. "Yet kings of England were more than grand seigniors; they were sovereigns; and with sovereignty came revenues from towns that were not planted on royal demesnes. For example, it came to be accepted that new markets and fairs, wherever held, needed a royal charter: and his subjects paid the sovereign for his grant. Seigniors who were creating organic boroughs or planting towns could enfranchise their villains by private charter, but it became increasingly common for seigniorial boroughs to be backed by a royal charter confirming the liberties: for this charter, payment was made to the king, and after the accession of a new sovereign it was often thought prudent to ask (and to pay) for a renewal of the charter." Beresford, *New Towns*, p. 85.

15. Beresford, *New Towns*, p. 100.

16. Beresford, *New Towns*, chaps. iii–vii.

17. Tait, *Medieval English Borough*, p. 212.

18. Beresford, *New Towns*, p. 60.

19. Tait, *Medieval English Borough*, p. 212.

20. Susan Reynolds, *An Introduction to the History of English Medieval Towns* (Oxford, 1977), p. 98.

21. Lyon, *Constitutional and Legal History*, p. 73.

22. Lyon, *Constitutional and Legal History*, p. 73.

23. Tait, *Medieval English Borough*, p. 140.

24. Tait, *Medieval English Borough*, p. 158.

25. Tait, *Medieval English Borough*, p. 150.

26. James F. Willard, "Taxation Boroughs and Parliamentary Boroughs, 1294–1336," in *Historical Essays in Honour of James Tait* (Manchester, 1933), pp. 417–435.

27. Reynolds, *English Medieval Towns*, p. 119.

28. Reynolds, *English Medieval Towns*, p. 121.
29. Reynolds, *English Medieval Towns*, p. 122.
30. Gierke, *Community in Historical Perspective*, p 40.
31. Richard of Devizes, *Chronicle* quoted by Reynolds, *Kingdoms and Communities* (Oxford, 1984), p. 62.
32. Pirenne, *Medieval Cities*, p. 180.
33. See charters collated and listed in Adolphus Ballard, *British Borough Charters, 1042–1216* (Cambridge, 1913); cf. p. c.
34. May McKisack, *The Parliamentary Representation of the English Boroughs* (Oxford, 1932).
35. McKisack, *Parliamentary Representation*, p. 11.
36. Quoted by McKisack, *Parliamentary Representation*, p. 13.
37. Mundy and Riesenberg, *Medieval Town*, document no. 13, pp. 119–120.
38. Mundy and Riesenberg, *Medieval Town*, document no. 13, p. 120.
39. McKisack, *Parliamentary Representation*, p. 126.
40. Maitland, *History of English Law*, ii, p. 486.
41. Otto Gierke, *Das Deutsche Genossenschaftsrecht*, 4 vols. (Berlin, 1868–1913). This work had an unfortunate history of translation: parts of vol. iii which focused on the law of associations in classical antiquity were translated in *Associations and Law* (Toronto, 1977); *Political Theories of the Middle Age* (Cambridge, 1900); *Natural Law and the Theory of Society, 1500–1800* (Cambridge, 1934); and, more recently, *Community in Historical Perspective: A Translation of Selections From* Das Deutsche Genossenschaftsrecht *(The German Law Of Fellowship)* Deutsche Genossenschaftsrecht. *English Selections* (New York, 1990).
42. Gierke, *Political Theories*, p. 87.
43. Benjamin Barber, *Death of Communal Liberty* (Princeton, N.J., 1974); Chapter One contains a brief but useful discussion of the attitude of modern political theory towards communal liberty and autonomy.
44. Gierke, *Natural Law*, p. 35.
45. Walter Ullmann, "The Medieval Theory of Legal and Illegal Organizations," in his *Law and Jurisdiction in the Middle Ages* (London, 1988).
46. Ullmann, "The Medieval Theory of Legal and Illegal Organizations," p. 285.
47. Ullmann, "The Medieval Theory of Legal and Illegal Organizations," p. 291.
48. Walter Ullmann, "Juristic Obstacles to the Emergence of the Concept of the State in the Middle Ages," *Annali di Storia diritto*, vols. xii–xiii (1968–1969), pp. 43–64.
49. Ullmann, "Juristic Obstacles," p. 54.
50. Ullmann, "Juristic Obstacles," p. 58.
51. Quoted in Joseph P. Canning, *The Political Thought of Baldus de Ubaldis* (Cambridge, 1987), p. 196.
52. Ullmann, "Juristic Obstacles," p. 54.
53. Joseph P. Canning, "Law, Sovereignty and Corporation Theory, 1300–1450," J. H. Burns, ed., *The Cambridge History of Medieval Political Thought, 350–1450* (Cambridge, 1988), pp. 454–476.
54. Quoted in Canning, *Baldus de Ubaldis*, p. 187.
55. Canning, "The Corporation in the Thought of Thirteenth and Fourteenth Century Jurists," *History of Political Thought*, vol. i, p. 14.
56. Ernst H. Kantorowicz, *The King's Two Bodies* (Princeton, N.J., 1957).

57. McKisack, *Parliamentary Representation*, p. 29.
58. Quoted in McKisack, *Parliamentary Representation*, p. 25 (emphasis added).
59. Text is translated in Weinbaum, *Incorporation of Boroughs*, p. 48.
60. Weinbaum, *Incorporation of Boroughs*, p. 48.
61. Text is translated in Weinbaum, *Incorporation of Boroughs*, p. 51.
62. Weinbaum, *Incorporation of Boroughs*, p. 53.
63. Weinbaum, *Incorporation of Boroughs*, p. 53. Farm here means a lump sum paid in lieu of detailed accounting.
64. Weinbaum, *Incorporation of Boroughs*, pp. 56–58.
65. Weinbaum, *Incorporation of Boroughs*, p. 5.
66. 15 Richard II (1395), Weinbaum, *Incorporation of Boroughs*, p. 60.
67. See Weinbaum, *Incorporation of Boroughs*, which contains the full text of the charter (with slight omissions), pp. 93–96.
68. The charter is translated in Weinbaum, *Incorporation of Boroughs*.
69. See Charles Gross, *The Gild Merchant* (Oxford, 1890). He argued that it is misleading to designate 1440 as the first date of formal incorporation, which was first used in H. A. Merewether and A. J. Stephens, *The History of Boroughs and Municipal Corporations of the United Kingdom* (London, 1835). However, as Gross himself conceded, the designation of 1440 marks a moment of clarification and self-consciousness on the part of the lawyers, which makes it a significant turning point. This debate was largely predicated on a confusion between *de facto* and *de jure* corporations of the medieval and early modern Europe.
70. Weinbaum, *Incorporation of Boroughs*, p. 66.
71. "An Act Against Unlawful Statutes Made by Corporations," 14 Henry VII, c. 7, 1503, *The Statutes of the Realm*, vol. ii, pp. 652–653.
72. "An Act whereby the Queen's Highness May Make Ordinances and Rules in Corporations," 1 Elizabeth, c. 22, 1558, *The Statutes of the Realm*, vol. iv, part 1, pp. 397ff.
73. Quoted in Peter Clark and Paul Slack, *English Towns in Transition, 1500–1700* (Oxford, 1976), p. 7. The full document is reprinted in R. H. Tawney and E. Power, *Tudor Economic Documents*, vol. iii, pp. 273–274.
74. Weinbaum, *Incorporation of Boroughs*, Chapter Two discusses these particular charters in detail.
75. Peter Clark and Paul Slack, *Crisis and Order in English Towns, 1500–1700* (Toronto, 1972), p. 27. Also see their *English Towns in Transition, 1500–1700*.
76. *First Report of the Commissioners Appointed to Inquire into Municipal Corporations in England and Wales*, 30 March 1835, *Parliamentary Papers*, xxiii, pp. 5–51.
77. "An Act for the Well Governing and Regulating of Corporations," 13 Charles, c. 2, *The Statutes of the Realm*, vol. v, pp. 321ff.
78. See Stephen D. White, *Sir Edward Coke and "The Grievances of the Commonwealth," 1621–1628* (Chapel Hill, 1979).
79. Black, *Guilds and Civil Society*, p. 159.
80. Coke, *Institutes*, vol. i, chap. x, section 162. This is also quoted in Maitland, *History of English Law*, vol. i, p. 642.
81. Coke, *Institutes*, vol. i, chap. x, section 171, p. 116a.
82. Coke, *Institutes*, vol. i, chap. x, section 164. In describing the historical practice of constituting cities, Coke here is not quite accurate; for though in general the description is accurate, there were cases which did not fit this description. This

is, however, understandable, if not more revealing, for the role assumed by a jurist in this text is to bring coherence to existing practice; the interest is, therefore, in lieu of the nature of the text, less of historical accuracy than practical efficacy.

83. Coke, *Institutes*, vol. i, chap. x, section 164, p. 109b.
84. Coke, *Institutes*, vol. i, chap. x, section 164, p. 109b.
85. Coke, *Institutes*, vol. i, chap. x, section 164, p. 110a.
86. Coke, *Institutes*, vol. i, chap. x, section 164, p. 110a.
87. A useful list of these charters is compiled in the following sources: Ballard, ed., *British Borough Charters, 1042–1216*; Ballard and Tait, eds., *British Borough Charters, 1216–1307*; Weinbaum, ed., *British Borough Charters, 1307–1660*. A discussion of charters beyond 1660 is contained in Weinbaum, *Incorporation of Boroughs*.
88. Carl Stephenson and F. G. Marcham, *Sources of English Constitutional History: A Selection of Documents* (New York, 1937), document 114J, pp. 542–543.
89. Quo warranto is an English legal practice, which originated in the thirteenth century, a writ of right for the king against those who claimed or usurped any office, franchise or liberty, to inquire by what authority he supported his claim, in order to determine the right.
90. Stephenson and Marcham, *Sources of English Constitutional History*, document 117C, pp. 581–582.
91. Quoted by Holdsworth, *A History of English Law*, vol. ix, p. 46.
92. Holdsworth, *A History of English Law*, vol. ix, p. 46.
93. Holdsworth, *A History of English Law*, vol. iii, p. 479; vol. ix, p. 47.
94. Frug, "The City as a Legal Concept," p. 1094.
95. Robert Brady, *An Historical Treatise of Cities and Burghs or Boroughs; showing their original whence, and from Whom they Received their Liberties, Privileges, and Immunities; What they were, and What Made and Constituted a Free Burgh, & Free Burgesses* (London, 1704).
96. Brady, *Historical Treatise*, p. ii.
97. Brady, *Historical Treatise*, p. i.
98. Thomas Madox, *Firma Burgi, Or an Historical Essay Concerning the Cities, Towns & Boroughs of England* (London, 1726).
99. Madox, *Firma Burgi*, p. 249.
100. As late as 1981, Susan Reynolds could still say, in a casual remark, that "in England it looks as though the first so-called charters of incorporation—that is, charters giving explicit right to perpetual succession, etc.—were a response to legislation on mortmain." Susan Reynolds, "The Idea of Corporation in Western Christendom before 1300," in J. A. Guy and H. G. Beale, eds., *Law and Social Change in British History*, papers presented to the Bristol Legal History Conference, July 1981 (London, 1984). An opposite view was Weinbaum, *Incorporation of Boroughs* and Charles Gross, *Gild Merchant*. Gross argued, however, that the incorporation of Coventry in 1345 should be considered as the first incorporation.
101. See, however, his essays on corporations in Frederic W. Maitland, *Selected Essays*, H. D. Hazeltine, G. Lapsley and P. H. Winfield, eds. (New York, 1936).
102. Perry Anderson, *Lineages of the Absolutist State* (London, 1974) and Charles Tilly, *Coercion, Capital, and European States, 990–1990* (London, 1990). See Bibliography under "On the State and Corporations."

103. Michel Foucault, "Governmentality," in *Studies in Governmentality*, G. Burchell, C. Gordon and P. Miller, eds. (London, 1991).
104. Brian Tierney, *Medieval Poor Law: A Sketch of Canonical Theory and Its Application in England* (Berkeley, 1959).
105. 22 Henry VIII, c. 12, quoted by R. Liddesdale Palmer, *English Social History in the Making: The Tudor Revolution* (London, 1934), p. 74.
106. Palmer, *English Social History*, pp. 74–75.
107. This clause is quoted by George Nicholls, *A History of English Poor Law: The Legislation and Other Circumstances Affecting the Condition of the People*, 2 vols. (London, 1854), p. 118.
108. The case is quoted by Palmer, *English Social History*, p. 78.
109. Palmer, *English Social History*, p. 80.
110. Sidney Webb and Beatrice Webb, *English Local Government*, vol. vii: *English Poor Law History: The Old Poor Law* (London, 1927, hereafter Webbs, Old Poor Law), chap. i; Nicholls, *Poor Law*).
111. 5 Elizabeth, c. 3, quoted by Palmer, *English Social History*, p. 84.
112. 14 Elizabeth c. 5, quoted by Palmer, *English Social History*, pp. 87–88.
113. 18 Elizabeth c. 3, quoted by Palmer, *English Social History*, pp. 88–89.
114. See Webbs, *Poor Law*, chap. ii.
115. John Locke is quoted by Webbs, *Poor Law*, p. 108.
116. Quoted by Webbs, *Poor Law*, p. 117.
117. Webbs, *Poor Law*, p. 117.
118. These proposals are listed in Webbs, *Poor Law*, pp. 117–118.
119. Gierke, *Natural Law*, p. 84.
120. Thomas Hobbes, *De Cive* (1642) trans. *Philosophical Rudiments Concerning Government and Society* (New York, 1949), section 22.
121. Hobbes, *Elements of Law*, p. 144.
122. See an important chapter by Roberto M. Unger, "Law and Modernity," in his *Law in Modern Society* (New York, 1976).
123. See John Dinwiddy, *Bentham* (Oxford, 1989) for a discussion of the influence of Bentham. See also Norman Chester, *The English Administrative System, 1780–1870* (Oxford, 1981) for the influence of Bentham on English state administration.
124. *The Life and Letters of John Arthur Roebuck* (London, 1897), p. 217.
125. On Bentham we draw on Dinwiddy, *Bentham* and H. L. A. Hart, "Introduction," *Jeremy Bentham, An Introduction to the Principles of Morals and Legislation*, J. H. Burns and H. L. A. Hart, eds. (London, 1982).
126. Jeremy Bentham, "Pannomial Fragments," in *Works*, John Bowring, ed., vol. iii (London, 1838–1843), p. 211.
127. Bentham, "Pannomial Fragments," p. 219.
128. Bentham, "Pannomial Fragments," p. 219.
129. Bentham, "Pannomial Fragments," p. 216.
130. Dinwiddy, *Bentham*, pp. 61–65.
131. Dinwiddy, *Bentham*, p. 30.
132. See Dinwiddy, *Bentham* for a detailed discussion, pp. 73–89.
133. Jeremy Bentham, "Constitutional Code," in *Works*, John Bowring, ed., vol. ix (London, 1838–1843).
134. Bentham, "Constitutional Code," pp. 147–148.
135. Bentham, "Constitutional Code," p. 149.

136. Bentham, "Constitutional Code," p. 150.

137. The modern state was very attentive to space and territory. In fact, the calculated and strategic manipulation of territory was considered an essential element of governance: the partitioning of space could be done in ways that would govern the conduct of subjects in question. Robert Sack expands on this theme in his *Human Territoriality: Its Theory and History* (Cambridge, 1986).

138. Frederic Maitland, *The Constitutional History of England* (Cambridge, 1908), p. 384.

139. Maitland, *Constitutional History*, p. 384.

140. "An Act to amend the Representation of the People in England and Wales," 2 William, c. 45, 1832.

141. See a discussion in Maitland, *Constitutional History*, pp. 495–496.

142. 2 William, c. 45, clause lxxix.

143. "First Report of the Commissioners Appointed to inquire into the Municipal Corporations in England and Wales," *Parliamentary Papers*, vol. xxiii, March 30, 1835; see Bryan Keith-Lucas, *The Unreformed Local Government System* (London, 1980); Derek Fraser, ed., *Municipal Reform and the Industrial City* (London, 1982).

144. First Report, Municipal Corporations, p. 3.

145. First Report, Municipal Corporations, p. 17.

146. First Report, Municipal Corporations, p. 32.

147. First Report, Municipal Corporations, p. 49.

148. "An Act to provide for the Regulation of Municipal Corporations in England and Wales," *Statutes of the Realm*, September 9, 1835, 5 & 6 William IV, c. 76.

149. This point is important because, as we will see, in British North America the municipal corporations act also constituted townships, villages and counties as municipal corporations, although with distinct and limited corporate capacities.

150. 5 & 6 William IV, c. 76, clause xc.

151. 5 & 6 William IV, c. 76, clause lxxvi.

152. Keith-Lucas, "Municipal Corporations," p. 74.

153. Peter G. Richards, *The Reformed Local Government System*, 4th ed. (London, 1980), p. 15. It should be pointed out for reference that the commission established a principle which marked a clear break from earlier poor law policies with regard to criteria of relief: "that his [the pauper] situation on the whole shall not be made really or apparently so eligible as the situation of the independent laborer of the lowest class." *Report from His Majesty's Commissioners for inquiring into the Administration and Practical Operation of the Poor Laws* (London, 1834), p. 228.

154. George Rosen, *A History of Public Health* (New York, 1958); also see his collected essays in *From Medical Police to Social Medicine* (New York, 1974).

155. Richards, *Reformed Local Government System*, p. 17.

156. Select Committee on the Health of Towns, *Parliamentary Papers*, vol. vi, 1840, p. v.

157. Select Committee on the Health of Towns, p. viii.

158. Select Committee on the Health of Towns, p. xxi.

159. Report from the Committee on Buildings Regulation and Improvement of Boroughs, *Parliamentary Papers*, vol. x, 1842, pp. 161ff. The report contains numerous model designs for buildings and districts for laboring classes. Also there are detailed discussions of each by medical and other experts in the field.

160. Edwin Chadwick, *Local Reports on the Sanitary Condition of Laboring Population* (London, 1842).

161. First Report on the State of Large Towns and Populous Districts from the Royal Commission, *Parliamentary Papers*, vol. xvii, 1844; Second Report, *Parliamentary Papers*, vol. xviii, 1845.

162. The Central Board of Health never achieved the dominance of the Poor Law Commission. The Central Board was reorganized in 1854 and dissolved in 1858. The original Poor Law Commission had been displaced in 1847 by a Minister, the President of Poor Law Board, who was directly answerable to the Parliament.

163. Joseph Lancaster, *Improvement in Education, as it Respects the Industrious Classes of the Community* (London, 1803); extracts printed in *English Historical Documents*, vol. xi, p. 711.

164. Lancaster, *Improvement in Education*, p. 711.

165. Lancaster, *Improvement in Education*, p. 712.

166. Report from the Select Committee on the Education of the Lower Orders, June 3, 1818; printed in *English Historical Documents*, vol. xi, pp. 715–718.

167. Report on Education, 1818, p. 716.

168. Norman Chester, *The English Administrative System, 1780–1870* (Oxford, 1981), p. 347.

169. H. J. Hanham, ed., *The Nineteenth-Century Constitution, 1815–1914: Document and Commentary* (Cambridge, 1969), pp. 372–400.

170. Toulmin Smith, *Local Self-Government and Centralization* (London, 1851), quoted in Hanham, *Nineteenth-Century Constitution*, p.378.

171. John Stuart Mill, *Consideration on Representative Government* (London, 1861; Oxford 1975).

172. Mill, *Representative Government*, p. 377.

173. Mill, *Representative Government*, p. 377.

174. Mill, *Representative Government*, p. 379.

175. "Municipal Corporations Act, 1882," *Statutes of the Realm*, 45 and 46 Victoria, c. 50. See also Maitland, *Constitutional History*, pp. 413–414.

176. "The Local Government Act, 1888," *Statutes of the Realm*, 51 & 52, Victoria, c. 41.

177. "Local Government Act, 1894," *Statutes of the Realm*, 56 & 57, Victoria, c. 73.

178. 56 & 57, Victoria, c. 73, clause xxi.

179. Keith-Lucas, "Municipal Corporations," p. 81.

3

HISTORY OF CORPORATIONS IN COLONIAL AMERICA: AN OUTLINE

T HE history of corporations in colonial America (the thirteen colonies, which became the United States of America in 1783) affords not only an opening to the history of the modern city in British North America, but also clarifies the outlines sketched in Chapter Two. The history of the thirteen colonies spanned a period from the seventeenth century to the late eighteenth. This was, as we have seen, a time of the ascendancy of and transition from the early modern city to the modern city in England. The following is one of the most fascinating, and from our perspective, the most important aspects of colonial history: how to govern "those distant possessions" became a vexing question for the English State in the seventeenth century, and its inability to resolve the question created favourable conditions in which *de facto* corporations that were dismantled at home could flourish in the colonies. The governing of distant territories was new and the legal and political problem of integrating these territories within the English State was to constitute the core of the colonial question—'government at a distance' as Jeremy Bentham later insightfully put it—a question of how to bend the colonies to the will of the English State.

There were between twenty-four and thirty-six *formally* incorporated cities by 1783 in colonial America.[1] But beneath these numbers lurks an important political issue: the numbers refer to *de jure* corporations that were created by colonial legislatures or proprietors in accordance with State prerogatives, and mostly in the late seventeenth and eighteenth centuries. Another series of corporations not included in that number exercised *de facto* liberties and powers. These *de facto* corporations came into being in the New England colonies at a time when the English State had not yet built up an apparatus to govern the colonies (before the 1660s). How the English State gradually built up a colonial apparatus and how this apparatus approached the city (both as part of and solution to the colonial question) in colonial America is the subject of this chapter. Therefore, our attention is focused more on the colonial apparatus rather than on how the colonists conceptualized cities, since our ultimate aim is to shed some light on how the colonial apparatus constituted cities in British North America in the aftermath of the American Revolution. What follows are the outlines of a history of corporations in colonial America from the perspective of 'government at a distance'.[2]

When the British colonial apparatus was expanding, the early modern city as an instrument of State administration figured as an essential element of that apparatus. But, by the time the colonial apparatus appeared, the towns in the corporate colonies had already developed communal attributes, which can be likened to *de facto* corporations of medieval Europe. Furthermore, the colonial apparatus consistently failed to constitute cities as *de jure* corporations in the new colonies (proprietary and royal): as mentioned earlier, by 1783 there were only between twenty-four and thirty-six *formally* incorporated cities in colonial America. As a result, the colonial apparatus associated the failure to keep the colonies obedient with its inability to constitute *de jure* corporations. This assessment formed a backdrop against which corporations were conceptualized in British North America.

Colonial Question: 'Government at a Distance'

From the late sixteenth century onwards, English statesmen, administrators, merchants, planters and jurists were gradually engaged in a debate as to whether, and if so how, to colonize North American territories. In the early period (roughly from the 1580s to the 1660s) the perceived advantages of colonization varied from 'the spreading of the gospel' to the exile of 'criminals', 'idles' and other 'undesirables' such as the poor. The extraction of raw materials, particularly of gold and silver, figured quite significantly as economists argued. We can also add the aim, which seemed possible at the time, of domesticating or 'christianizing' native populations. Perhaps more than any other text published in this period, Richard Hakluyt's *Discourse Concerning Western Planting* (1584), expresses succinctly these reflections and arguments. His was a veritable discourse on the colonial question.[3] His main argument was that the territories could be colonized for extraction of wealth (gold and silver) or the transfer of idle population.[4] It is important to note that his conception of 'plantations' as penal colonies and as sources of 'extracted' wealth did not create a problem for the 'administration of the colonies'. The colonies were simply seen as possessions, which could be used for different purposes and were kept in part "for fear of the danger of being prevented by other nations which have the like intention."[5] At this early stage, and under these circumstances, the building of an apparatus of colonial government did not present itself as a particular focus of English State administration; instead, incorporated trade companies were entrusted with maintaining and settling the colonies.

But in the late seventeenth century, the problem of colonial administration was defined anew. The target, and hence the object of administration, shifted from that of the territory with its material wealth and the possibilities of absorbing undesirables, to that of the population that inhabited the territory, which had to be governed if it was to be made useful. As we have seen in Chapter Two, this was the era in which the whole problematic art of government emerged in European States. Mercantilism was now taking hold of the State administration, and the colonies were gradually appearing as an integral part of the realm. It was now thought "that a small country and few people may be equivalent in wealth and strength to a far greater people and territory"[6] and that "a small country well peopled will be able to effect things of more advantage and grandeur, than a great dominion ill stocked."[7] And also that "from reason and experience it is certain that the power and riches of a nation depend not upon its having mines of gold and silver, but upon its having a numerous and industrious people."[8] The British colonial apparatus was about to explore new forms of government in the colonies as population, territory and wealth came to define the field of colonial government. Charles Davenant, an expert on 'political arithmetic', put this very clearly in 1698:

> As many empires have been ruined by too much enlarging their dominions, and by grasping at too great an extent of territory, so our interest in America may decay, by aiming at more provinces, and a greater tract of land, than we either cultivate or defend...it may perhaps be sometime or other worth the consideration of the State, whether a way may not be proposed of collecting within a narrower compass, the scattered inhabitants of the continent, by inviting some to cultivate...where their labour is certainly most profitable to this Kingdom, and by drawing the rest, if possible, to four or five of the provinces best situated and most productive of commodities, not to be had in Europe.[9]

With the shifting view of colonies new questions arose: What were the relations between the corporate colonies and the realm? When colonies were founded, did the English constitution spontaneously extend to them? Did all the laws which secured the rights of the State, and also those which were intended to secure the liberties of the subjects, extend to the colonies? Did the colonies become subject to the authority of the

State, and if so, under what capacity and status? and, Would these corporations be represented in the parliament like boroughs of the realm?[10]

From our perspective the rise of the colonial question had two important consequences. First was the gradual build-up of an apparatus of State administration that dealt with the colonies. An examination of this apparatus and its development is important, not only for understanding how the city as a corporation was used, but for understanding how this apparatus was extended to the settling of British North America after the American Revolution. And second, an interest on the part of jurists and political theorists helped to integrate the colonies within the administration of the State. The colonial apparatus was not built without intense debates, and ideas embodied in these debates are important for understanding how the colonial apparatus emerged and changed. The establishment of the Board of Trade and Plantations in 1696 and its instructions,[11] the formation of royal colonies, and the termination of earlier charters, proclamations, edicts, series of laws, all aimed toward regulating the colonies "in a more effectual and uniform manner"—a series of events that colonial historians explored.[12] Toward the end of the seventeenth century jurists, administrators and statesmen worked out, after experiments with corporate and proprietary colonies, a royal form of government in the colonies. The creation of *de jure* corporations in proprietary and royal colonies was an important part of State administration. "As such, an administration of government may put [the colonies] into a better state of security and make them duly subservient and useful."[13] Now let us discuss these different colonies and how the political and legal status of cities changed with them.

Colonial American Cities as Corporations

In 1768, a British jurist, William Blackstone, espoused his classification of British colonies in America.[14] "With respect to their internal polity," he said, "our colonies are properly of three sorts": chartered colonies, proprietary colonies and royal colonies as "provincial establishments."[15] What follows is an outline of the essential constitutional elements of each form of colony that Blackstone identified and how corporations figured in each.[16]

Cities in Corporate Colonies

Before the seventeenth century all grants made by the English State in colonial America were for purposes of discovery not of settlement.[17] This changed with the Virginia charter of 1606 to the London Company; the first attempt was made to regulate somewhat in detail the settlement and government of a colony. This first charter transferred limited powers to the company with petitioners given the right to trade and to establish settlements. The charter provided a royal council resident in London. This council in turn was to appoint a council resident in Virginia. The London Company established Jamestown in Virginia in 1607. The second charter to the company was granted in 1609, which this time incorporated the company and gave it direct ownership of the land. The control of the company and of the colony was handed over to the officers of the corporation, although these officials were appointed by the English State. The third charter, granted in 1612, was a 'regular' trade incorporation.[18] The governor and council were elected by a majority of the 'stockholders' and charged with the practice of governing the corporation. But for "the handling, ordering, and disposing of matters and affairs of greater weight and importance," the stockholders were to meet in four general courts each year. These general courts had the power to make 'laws' and 'ordinances' for the government of the corporation and the colony, subject only to the limitation that the laws for the colony "shall not be contrary to the laws and statues of our realm of England." With this charter the English State temporarily relinquished its attempt at direct control of the colony in Virginia. The charters granted thereafter followed the pattern of the third Virginia charter, the most important being that granted to the Massachusetts Bay Company.[19]

The Massachusetts charter was modelled after the third Virginia charter of 1612, and included a provision for a general court which was to meet four times a year during the law terms, and the Easter session, which was called the court of election.[20] A provision was also made for a governor and a board of eighteen, all of whom were to be chosen by the general court. The power to increase its own membership was also vested with the corporation. "The word freemen also made appearance in the Massachusetts charter as the designation of the members, whereas in the earlier patents for colonization the terms associates and adventurers had been commonly used."[21] This company, like Virginia, was located in London and was essentially a trading company.

In 1630, however, the Massachusetts Bay Company was moved from London to the colony. As colonial historians duly noted, the consequences of this change were quite important in terms of the purposes of the corporation. First, the corporation was now faced with the problem of territorial administration and settlement; trade became a concern insofar as it was related to territorial legislation and administration.[22]

Second, which follows from the first, the land was now considered as part of the problem of administration as opposed to only a source of revenue or profit as in the case of land companies.[23] This resulted in a township or town system of government that will be discussed shortly. The important point here is that the transfer of the company from London to New England brought consequences that were neither intended nor insignificant in the formation of new polities and practices in colonial America. One such important consequence was best represented in the concept of 'freemen'. When the members of the corporation were located in London, the freemen were considered adventurers, a body of persons who were incorporated and conferred with the power of engaging in trade and exploration. But with the transition from a company to an incorporated colony, freemen now were the settlers or citizens of the corporation, like burgesses of medieval cities. This meant that, as mentioned, the corporation encountered the problem of government of a multitude of men and women: the principle of representation was instituted to enable the general court to govern. As Governor Winthrop stated retrospectively in 1634: "When the patent was granted, the number of freemen was supposed to be (as in like corporations) so few, as they might well join in making laws; but now they were grown to so great a body, as it was not possible for them to make or execute laws, but they must choose others for that purpose."[24]

To summarize, the corporate colonies came to possess rights and privileges as communities of citizens. Other corporate colonies (Connecticut and Rhode Island) were based upon similar legal forms as outlined above. The colonies of New Plymouth and New Haven, although they never legally gained the status of corporations, also shared the similar legal status of corporate colonies.

How did the city as a corporation figure in corporate colonies? It was an essential polity: the general court consisted of an assembly of elected representatives from the cities, the council elected by the assembly, and the governor appointed by the State administration in Westminster. Cities were legally granted by acts of the general court.[25] But because the New England colonies of Massachusetts, Connecticut and Rhode Island were corporate colonies, they could not create corporations: in early modern English law, as we have seen, a *de jure* corporation could not exercise other powers than those which were explicitly granted, and a corporation was never empowered to create another corporation; only the English State had the authority to create a corporation. Since the corporate colonies could not create cities as corporations, the principle of representation was instituted through granting townships to proprietors who undertook to settle the township and organize elections for representation.[26] Thus, cities themselves were not corporate entities in legal terms but, in practice, cities acted as *de facto* corporations.[27] We need to see some of the details of this practice.

In the corporate colonies, the terms township and town in legal discourse were used interchangeably. This is indeed an important clue to the legal concept of the town: the term 'town' referred to both the territorial domain of the township and to the body of people who inhabited this domain.[28] In other words, there was no separation between the town and its inhabitants or the city and its citizens. The town was not, of course, the only territorial institution within the colonies; parish, precinct, village, plantation and county were also terms and units used.[29] But, the town (township) differed from these others in three significant respects.[30] First, it was the fiscal area from which rates and taxes were assessed, collected and accounted for by its own officers. Second, it was the unit of militia organization as each town was required to maintain a "train-band." Finally, it was the area of representation in the general court and thus acted as a *de facto* corporation. Thus, the town was both a community of incorporated people and an explicit territorial domain. Or, rather, the town was a *de facto* corporation.[31]

The general courts of corporate colonies, as a practice, did not sell or grant land to individuals but only granted land to towns.[32] Towns acted as agencies of land distribution, which were empowered to dispose of land themselves within the rules and regulations of the general courts, which through time became increasingly clear and general.[33] The first general act on towns in colonial America was passed in the General Court of the "Colony of the Massachusetts Bay in New England" at a session "held at New Town" on March 3, 1635.[34] The act ordained that

> whereas particular towns have many things which concern only themselves, and the ordering of their own affairs, and disposing of businesses in their own town, it is therefore ordered that the freemen of every town or the major part of them shall only have power to dispose of their lands and woods, with all the privileges and appurtenances of the said towns, to grant lots, and make such orders as may concern the well ordering of their own towns, not repugnant to the laws and orders here established by the General Court.

Four years later the General Court of Connecticut passed its first general act on towns. The act was passed October 10, 1639, and it provided that the towns within Connecticut should "each of them have power...to choose their own officers and make such orders as may be for the well-ordering of their own Towns, being not repugnant to any law herein established, as also to impose penalties for the breach of the same."[35] In both of these general acts, the clause "well-ordering of towns" should be interpreted as towns being territorial institutions; that is, what was ordered was not simply the shape and appearance of houses and streets, the building and repair of roads and bridges, but also the admission of settlers to the town on the basis of their morals and religion; the disposal of lands; the assessment of rates; the care and disciplining of the poor and the idle; and the maintenance and enforcement of peace, the registry of deeds, and of births, deaths, and marriages. In other words, *de facto* corporations were the means through which power was exercised in its most minute detail in the colonies.

Let us take, as an example of how power was exercised in towns, the rules and orders passed concerning the school of Dorchester, a Massachusetts town, on January 14, 1645.[36] These rules and orders required that three men in the town be chosen as wardens or overseers of the school who should choose a schoolmaster. The schoolmaster was vested with the power of "training the Children of the Town in religion, learning and Civility." Likewise, the schoolmaster was also authorized "to minister Correction to all or any of his students without respect of persons according as the nature and qualities of the offence shall require whereto, all his students must be duly subject and no parent or other of the Inhabitants shall hinder or go about to hinder the master therein." A second example are the instructions issued in a Boston town meeting in 1662 to the 'watchmen' "to see to the regulating of other men's actions and manners..." which demonstrate the wider affects that towns had on the disciplining of the populace.[37] These instructions ordered that the watchmen "silently but vigilantly walk their several turns in the several quarters and parts of the Town, two by two, a youth always joined with an elder and more sober person, and two be always about the market place." In the course of the watch "if they find any young men, maids, women or other persons, not of known fidelities, and upon lawful occasion walking after 10 of the clock at night, that they modestly demand the cause of their being abroad...and in case they obstinately refuse to give a rational account of their business then to secure them until the morning." In another Boston town meeting "it [was] ordered that no inhabitant shall entertain man or woman from any other town or country as a sojourner or inmate with an intent to reside here, but shall give notice thereof to the selectmen of the town for their approbation within 8 days after coming to the town upon penalty of twenty shillings." Insofar as the governors, the general courts and the assemblies of corporate colonies were concerned, the towns were, when created, expected to fulfill these and numerous other minute exercises of power, surveillance and discipline, and were regulated accordingly through general acts. The general court and the governor of corporate colonies therefore acted not only by creating towns, but by continuously regulating matters that were of concern to the government of the populace. In Massachusetts, for example, the general court determined the boundaries of all the towns, settled disputes and, by an act of 1647, required that all towns perambulate their bounds once every three years; all of which suggests that the general court kept some control over towns and their practices.[38]

In corporate colonies, with the exception of the earliest towns in Massachusetts Bay, all towns were erected, organized and regulated under definite legal grants from the general courts and operated as *de facto* corporations. This is important here, for the incorporation of towns in the strict juridical sense—that is, as legal entities, capable of maintaining a continuous existence despite changes in membership, capable of holding property separate from the property of its members, of suing and being sued and otherwise acting as a unit distinct from their members, and empowered to make regulations—did not take place in the corporate colonies. Therefore, the towns were not under prescribed authority of the English State and hence they were not *de jure* corporations. As *de facto* corporations they exercised the powers of associations within the limits and meaning attached to them under colonial conditions.

We must note here that legal terms such as 'incorporate', 'corporation', 'body politic' and 'charter' were not used with legal precision and uniformity in the colonies. In 1694, for example, the General Court of Massachusetts passed an act "to enable Towns, Villages and proprietors in Common and Undivided lands, etc., to sue and be sued"—an action which, insofar as the towns were concerned, would seem to have been unnecessary if the towns were created as formal corporations.[39] Governor Bernard, writing to the Lords of Trade in 1762, said that until that time only two corporations had been established by the general court—a statement which could not have included towns if the towns were *formal* corporations.[40] And it seems no corporate powers were conferred on towns in Massachusetts until 1785. In conclusion, in Massachusetts, as the trustees of Yale College said in a petition in reference to towns to the assembly in 1717, "...towns are not bodies corporate yet as the common law allows are *as it were* incorporate to do some things without which they could not well manage."[41] This was also the case with other corporate colonies. The point here is that towns, whether they had attained full corporate status or not, were important political instruments in corporate colonies. Hence, the New England town possessed some of the political vitality of medieval corporations which colonial historians have never failed to notice and praise.

Now, the importance of New England towns from our vantage point is twofold. First, as soon as the British colonial apparatus was formed and had concluded that the colonies existed for the benefit of the mother country, it then identified the exercise of *de facto* autonomy as being detrimental to the government of colonies. Hence it began to search for other constitutional arrangements that would resolve the tension between local autonomy and central authority. And let us recall that also at this time English legal and political thought had not yet reached a creative solution to this tension other than through acts of suppression. Second, New England towns are important in the extent of local autonomy exercised by them as *de facto* corporations; as we shall see, such exercise of local autonomy was considered one of the reasons for the rebellion of the thirteen colonies, which in turn coloured early policies of settlement in British North America. To conclude, if we consider that for a series of complex reasons the English State failed to integrate the corporate colonies and that this vacuum of power made possible the possession of some liberties and autonomy, the existence of *de facto* corporations in New England colonies makes sense. What also makes sense under these conditions is the consistent attacks on those corporate liberties by the English State as we mentioned above; attacks that resulted in experimenting with centrally organized colonies, such as the proprietary colonies where proprietors were empowered to create *de jure* corporations.

Cities in Proprietary Colonies

Proprietary colonies were created with grants of large tracts of land to proprietors.[42] In legal terms, the grantee of the land was a person, as opposed to a governing body, as in the case in corporate colonies. The transmission of powers, however, included more than the use of land. It included the powers to govern the territory within boundaries specified in the charter and within the established frame of law and rights in England. The proprietor was authorized to legislate through an assembly of 'freemen' all matters concerning public interest, to bestow titles of honour, and to erect *de jure* corporations.[43] The proprietor was also empowered to frame the government in his territory, and he was vested with the power to levy taxes upon the people. The important point we must observe here is that the proprietor was granted land as a property as well as governing powers. The proprietor was thus interested in disposing land as well as securing revenue from it. This required the formation of an elaborate and centralized frame of government in which *de jure* corporations were prominent.[44]

Since the corporate colonies themselves were chartered by the English State and lacked explicit powers to incorporate other entities, the boroughs, cities and towns remained as *de facto* corporations. In the proprietary colonies the legal status of boroughs, cities and towns was prescribed, that is, *de jure*: the powers to incorporate cities and towns were conferred by the State to the proprietors although there was considerable variation in terms of legal practice. In Pennsylvania, for example, the corporate powers of boroughs and towns were more definite than those of Virginia under proprietary government.[45] Let us look at some incorporations in the proprietary colonies.

In Maine, in 1632, Ferdinando Gorges was given "power to erect, raise, and build, from time to time, in the province, territory, and coasts aforesaid so many forts, fortresses, platforms, castles, cities, towns, and villages; and to the said cities, boroughs, and towns, to grant Letters and Charters of incorporation, with all the liberties and things belonging to the same."[46] The same provision appears in Carolina grants of 1663 and 1665 with some more precision: "...and to the said cities, boroughs, towns, villages, or any other place or places within the said province, to grant, 'letters of charters of incorporation', with all liberties, franchises, and privileges requisite and useful."[47] In Maine, in 1641, based on these clauses, Gorges incorporated "the Planters and Inhabitants of Acomenticus into one body politic and corporate." This was the first full incorporation in colonial America, with some legal precision.[48] The second incorporation was New York on June 12, 1665, when a proclamation was issued by Governor Nicols which declared that "the inhabitants of New York...are and shall be for ever accounted, nominated and established as one body politic and corporate."[49] Until 1686, however, New York did not receive a charter until what is known as the Dongan Charter was issued, which contained precise corporate powers.[50] The third *de jure* incorporation in colonial America was in Maryland, where Lord Baltimore incorporated St. Mary's City in 1667.[51]

Two more incorporations were created in proprietary colonies in the seventeenth century, both of which were in Pennsylvania. The proprietor William Penn granted a borough charter to the settlers of Germantown, dated in London, 1689, which went into force in legal terms in 1691.[52] The second charter was to Philadelphia in 1691 but lost its force when, in 1692, Penn was temporarily ousted from the colony. In

1701, however, he issued a new one, similar to that of 1691, which remained in force until 1776.[53] In 1718, the provincial council of Pennsylvania received a petition from the 'inhabitants' of Bristol "requesting that for regulating their streets and preserving the better order among the inhabitants, the said town might be erected into a borough by Charter of Incorporation."[54] On November 14, 1720, the governor issued the formal patent and Bristol was incorporated. We must note that these incorporations reflect only a fragment of what James Lemon called "a town-making fever" in early Pennsylvania.[55] For although Penn was determined "on the need for towns to foster the expansion of the economy, to maintain order and to sustain social values," many planned or laid out towns did not materialize.[56] By 1776 there were five incorporated cities in Pennsylvania and at least four county towns that exercised *de facto* corporate powers.[57]

In New Jersey three incorporations were created by the proprietors. In 1682 it was enacted "that the town of Burlington has liberty, and hereby empowered to choose amongst themselves some persons who have power to regulate the affairs of the town...in all such things, as usually fall within the compass of ourselves in corporations in England."[58] In 1693, the corporate powers were articulated with more precision and detail, which included a description of the election of a burgess for the purpose of making laws. Salem and Perth Amboy were incorporated in 1678 and 1680 respectively. By 1776 there were six incorporated cities in New Jersey three of which were by royal charter (see Appendix 2: American Colonies and Cities).

All this suggests that the creation of corporations was a deliberate and legal act in proprietary colonies. As Ernest Griffith demonstrated, many of these incorporations were early modern, that is, they were created as close corporations.[59] A close corporation, as we have seen, was a model constitution in which the governing body (the mayor and the council) was co-opted as opposed to elected. The charter often named the members of the governing body and the body perpetuated itself. This system was used in England between 1440 and 1688, as the royal commission's report on municipal corporations observed, to influence the composition of the parliament and to create a governing class in cities. It seems then that the proprietors were authorized to create close corporations, which became an established component of their administration before the English State began to transform these colonies into royal colonies.

Cities in Royal Colonies

The formation of royal colonies coincided with the changing objectives of the British colonial apparatus: after the 1660s a gradual increase can clearly be seen in colonial administrative offices and practices. State offices and organs such as secretaries of State, the privy council, law officers and various committees and commissioners were created or reformed to focus their attention on the 'colonial question'. The most important of the subordinate organs to the secretaries of the State were the Commissioners of Trade and Plantations, which evolved into the Board of Trade and Plantations—the most important office of administration in the later history of the colonies.

The report of the Board of Trade on proprietary governments on March 26, 1701, which we mentioned earlier, is one of the most succinct accounts of 'reformed' policies toward these forms of colonies. This report urged strongly that the 'irregularities' observed in proprietary governments convinced the board that "those colonies in general have [in] no ways answered the chief design for which such large tracts of land and such privileges and immunities were granted by the Crown."[60] The report argued "that [the proprietors] have assumed themselves a power to make laws contrary and repugnant to the laws of England..."; "that they do not in general take any due care for their own defence and security..."; "that many of them have not regular militia and [some of them are] in a state of confusion..."; and, "that these chiefly arise from the ill use they make of the powers entrusted to them by their charters." The report thus stated that "introducing such an administration of government and fit regulation of trade as may put them into a better state of security and make them duly subservient and useful to England, does everyday become more and more necessary..." which led to the conclusion that "it may be expedient that the charters of the several proprietors and others entitling them to absolute government be reassumed to the Crown and these colonies put into the same state and dependency as those of other plantations." This report was the foundation for a bill introduced in parliament voiding those clauses in proprietary and corporation charters by which the State granted the authority and power of government.[61]

The Lords of Trade emphasized three objectives during their term of office between 1675 and 1782.[62] The first was to strengthen the control exercised upon royal colonies, which required increasing the powers of royal governors. The second was to prevent the creation of more corporate or proprietary colonies and to convert those already in existence into royal colonies. Upon the recommendation of the Board of Trade, for example, the New Hampshire towns were separated from Massachusetts Bay in 1679 and made into a royal colony.[63] Although the Lords of Trade were unable to block the grant of Pennsylvania to William Penn in 1681, they did secure the insertion in the charter of a series of limitations that subjected the proprietor to much stricter controls than earlier proprietary charters.[64] Third, and most ambitiously, the Lords of Trade attempted to consolidate the colonies under broader regional governments. The formation of the Dominion of New England, for example, intended to include all of the colonies from Maine south to Pennsylvania. Thus a new form of colony in legal and political discourse was worked out: royal colonies.[65] By 1776, as a result of these policies, Virginia, Georgia, North Carolina, South Carolina, New York, New Jersey, New Hampshire and Massachusetts were all royal colonies.[66] Only two corporate colonies, Connecticut and Rhode Island, and only three proprietary colonies, Pennsylvania, Maryland and Delaware, remained outside direct royal control.[67] For our purposes, whether or not these attempts at centralization of government bore fruits as envisaged by statesmen is not an issue. We need to look more closely at how the royal government was constituted and how the incorporated cities figured in this constitution.

The royal government was operated by officials who received their appointment and instructions not from any proprietors or body of colonists, but directly from the English State.[68] The royal colony had a tripartite system of government: a royal governor, an appointed governing council and an elected assembly. Throughout the eighteenth century an increasing conflict arose between the royal prerogative and the colonial assemblies in the exercise of power.[69] The governor and the council were vested with authority to exercise royal power but the assemblies were constituted through elected representatives from townships and counties. Thus the assemblies represented the popular rights, privileges and liberties of colonists as English settler communities, while the governor and the council were entrusted with the enforcement of general State policies.

The commissions issued to the royal governors replaced the charter, which was the characteristic form of the transmission of powers and rights to the colonies. The commission, as the expression of the State prerogative, contained strict legal and formal language detailing the duties and tasks of the governor and of the council thus constituted.[70] It established that, without the commission, there could be no legal political authority in the colony. An immense class of documents followed the commission as important instruments of government. These included detailed instructions to governors, which accompanied the commission; proclamations that addressed issues of concern to all or some colonies; and the correspondence of officials and departments, the most notable being the Board of Trade and the secretaries of State.[71] Of all the instruments used to enforce royal prerogative in colonial America, the commission of the governor and the instructions were most influential in the shaping of the colonial constitution.[72] The specific instructions, prepared for governors by the Board of Trade and Plantations in close connection with the Privy Council over which the king presided, attest to this. Although drawn up in the king's name, these instructions were normally prepared by the Board of Trade, often after extensive consultation with other officials, with merchants engaged in colonial trade, and with leading colonial agents. These instructions were submitted in draft form to the Privy Council and reviewed by its committee before receiving formal sanction and authentication by the king. The instructions elaborated and explained the general powers laid down in the governor's commission and touched upon nearly every matter with which the British colonial apparatus had to deal. The Board of Trade and its proceedings, correspondence and relations with the British colonial agents attest to colonial political discourse in this period, until the American Revolution.

Among these instructions, and what is important for us, permanent, regulated and systematic land settlement through townships was considered essential for government and administration of the colonies. Townships were constituted as both units of representation in the house of assembly and of taxation. By the middle of the eighteenth century, there was already an accumulated experience of township planting. Through numerous similar instructions, toward the middle of the eighteenth century, certain general principles of township planting were gradually established in royal colonies. First was contiguity, that is, "townships should be settled on the frontiers [of settlement]."[73] Second was uniformity, "that [is] each township may consist of about twenty thousand acres of land, but not to exceed six miles square."[74] Third was centrality of the towns, that is, "in each such township a proper [often designated as central] place shall be laid out for the site of the town itself."[75] Fourth was density, that is "no town be set out or any such lands or lots granted until there be fifty or more families ready to begin the settlement."[76] And, finally, there was threshold: "that so soon as any such township has got one hundred or more families settled therein, it shall have and enjoy all immunities and privileges as do of right belong to any other parish or township in the said province."[77] The township then emerged as a unit of both representation and taxation in royal colonies. The instruction that the governor of Nova Scotia received in 1749, for example, stated that "for the better security, regulation, and government of our said settlement, it will be necessary that such persons as we shall judge proper to send to our said province should be settled in townships."[78]

The instructions sent to governors from the Board of Trade and Plantations during the eighteenth century indicate the emphasis that emerged on systematic land settlement as a means of good government. Needless to recall that the latter was, in turn, considered a prerequisite of national wealth throughout the eighteenth century. But township and town building cannot be said to have originated in the eighteenth century. On the contrary, throughout the seventeenth century, town building practices were present in Virginia, Maryland and in the New England colonies.[79] However, what was novel in the eighteenth century is that the British colonial apparatus was determined to coordinate and centralize settlement, incorporate towns and establish territorial institutions such as townships as part of the instruments of government.[80]

There is enough evidence that shows the creation of cities as *de jure* corporations became one of the major concerns of royal colonies. Perhaps more than any other colony, Virginia experienced an unprecedented concern for establishing cities. But before we proceed to discuss the attempts at creating cities, it should be pointed out that in royal colonies the county emerged as the most significant unit of local administration.[81] Therefore, the creation of cities was often considered within the context of the county government, which contrasts with the experience in New England colonies where the county was not significant.

"Virginia's Cure:" Cities

Between 1662 and 1711 numerous acts were passed to create towns (some of which also involved Maryland), and pamphlets were published on the city. There are a number of reasons why particularly in Virginia the city became a prevalent concern. The first is the manner in which the land was administered when the London Company first settled the colony: in contrast to Massachusetts and other New England colonies, the land in Virginia was granted to individual settlers in large counties, which facilitated the dispersion of settlers. The towns thus did not become agents of land administration.[82] Second, the cultivation of tobacco, the continuous search for new land and the geography of the region all contributed to the scattering of settlements.[83] Hence the colonists in Virginia remained rather reluctant to build towns.[84] What follows is a somewhat detailed discussion of a series of laws passed in the colonial legislature, instructions and some correspondence. Our particular emphasis will be on two pamphlets, which provide graphic details of the reasons for the creation of towns.[85]

In 1662, instructions were sent to Sir William Berkeley, governor of Virginia, to induce the people to erect a town on every important river.[86] Following the suggestions of the governor, the general assembly passed an act to erect towns in December 1662. Although the immediate practical results of this act were unimpressive, within the next two decades some growth in population was accomplished. The reasons this act was passed reflected the influence of certain pamphlets addressed to the creation of cities. One such pamphlet, *Virginia's Cure,* was presented to the Lord Bishop of London and carried the initials R. G.[87] The paper argued that the cure to the 'problems' Virginia experienced was simply to create towns. We will focus on this extremely interesting pamphlet.

The paper considers "the manner of our peoples scattered habitations…the sad consequences of such scattered living, the cause of scattering their habitations…and the remedy and means of procuring it."[88] R. G. informs that the colony is divided into large counties, each containing parishes for representation in the assembly. The fact that the counties are large, he argues, causes colonists to scatter to distant and remote places in the colony. The most important consequence of this manner of settlement is "that the most faithful and vigilant pastors, assisted by the most careful Church-wardens, cannot possibly take notice of the vices that reign in their families, of the spiritual defects in their conversations…," for "…if they should spend time in visiting their remote and far distant habitations, they would have little or none left for their necessary studies, and to provide necessary spiritual food for the rest of their flocks."[89] Furthermore, "their almost general want of Schools, for the education of their children, is another consequent of their scattered planting."[90] Their "scattered planting being the cause of such consequence, the consequences will remain, so long as that continues, as at this day does and therefore from the premises, it is easy to conclude, that the only way of remedy for Virginia's disease…must be procuring towns to be built, and inhabited in their several counties."[91] If the building of towns is procured

> the Planters will…enjoy the benefits of Christian Offices, of frequent civil commerce and society, which begets mutual confidence, trust, and friendship, the best groundwork for raising companies of the best qualified and most able persons to combine in designs, most advantageous to

their own and the public welfare…and by good discipline and careful tending, in well ordered societies, under faithful teachers and magistrates, both parents and children grow into habits of Christian living.[92]

The religious purpose of promoting towns here should not deter us from seeing that this is considered as the best groundwork for civil and commercial societies, which cannot be created without discipline and order. Therefore "that [these] benefits will accrue to [planters], needs no proof; the experiences of all united well ordered Christian societies, sufficiently confirms it."[93]

At one point R. G. deals with an important objection that could be raised against his argument that perhaps no other

ecclesiastic writers have told us, that Christians for this end ought to be united in societies in towns, that is the glory of the graces and virtues of many Christians shining, not in scattered corners, but in visible united societies, which is so persuasive and powerfully prevailing with the heathen to embrace the Christian faith; nor do they use any arguments to persuade Christians to *live together in towns and to incorporate into societies for this end*.[94]

R. G. answers this objection with an argument which claims that "if neither ancient, nor modern writers have told us, that Christians (if they have liberty) ought to live together in visible united societies, in cities, towns or villages, for the fore-mentioned ends; it was, because they knew no present need of writing anything of it, nor could charitably conjecture there would be any for the Future."[95]

Another objection that could be raised against the creation of towns was that the earlier attempts to build towns in Virginia failed. Here R. G. recounts an earlier act that was passed on March 27, 1656, and which was repealed, for it failed to bring about the intended results. "These things considered, men may wonder why the attempts made by the aforementioned Honorable Governors to reduce Virginia's planters into towns did never succeed."[96] R. G. claims that the unwillingness of the Virginia assembly to create towns must lie with the burgesses themselves who "by reason of their poor and mean education they are unskillful in judging of a good estate either of Church or commonwealth, or of the means of procuring it."[97] And he concludes that "if the best proposals, which have been made to such persons, for reducing them into towns, offending in the least against their present private worldly interest (though never so promising for the future) have been from time to time bandied against by such major parts of their burgesses, and the fewer wise heads over-voted by them."[98] For these reasons, R. G. outlines a program that contains seven measures to make the creation of towns effective in practice but acceptable to, and hence in the interests of, the burgesses.

On June 9, 1680, upon his appointment as governor of Virginia, Lords Thomas Culpeper addressed the general assembly and made a particular point of emphasizing towns.[99] He had been instructed by the Lord of Trade that he "shall endeavour all [he] can to dispose the planters to build towns upon every river, and especially one at least on every great river, as tending very much to their security and profit. And in order thereunto, [he is] to take care that after sufficient notice to provide warehouses and conveniences, no ships whatsoever be permitted to load or unload but at the said places where the towns are settled."[100] In the aforementioned speech the governor stressed that "without towns no other nation ever began a plantation, or any yet thrived (as it ought)."[101] The assembly passed An Act of Cohabitation and Encouragement of Trade and Manufacture shortly after this address.[102] Under the terms of this act, it was provided that within two months after the publication of the act, fifty acres should be purchased by each of the counties to be set aside as a town for storehouses, dwelling houses and so on.[103] And every product of the colony was to be brought to these towns, there to be sold and then to be carried on board for exportation. As Riley put it, "This act was as farseeing as any law passed by the assembly on this subject. Everything that could possibly entice people into towns was included."[104] And yet the immense scale and immediacy of its requirements made it very difficult in terms of the practical results that were envisaged with the act. In the first decade or two after the act was passed some development occurred within about eight towns out of the twenty specified in the act.[105] In a memorandum of December 1681, the commissioners of customs presented their ideas regarding the act to the Lords of Trade.[106] In the first place, they argued that insufficient time was allowed for putting the act into operation. They also thought that the idea of appointing places for ports and landings was the wrong approach to the problem, since it forced towns to be built and merchant vessels to call there. It was wiser, they thought, to build towns wherever trade carried itself. Following this advice, the Lords of Trade and Plantations recommended to the king that the act be suspended. On December 12, 1681, Charles II suspended the act and referred the matter to Governor Culpeper, his council, and the assembly of Virginia.[107] On May 4, 1683, the council of Virginia wrote to the Lords of Trade and Plantations requesting the consideration of the king on the act for towns so that they would "know better how to proceed."[108] After a number of attempts to repeal and modify the Cohabitation Act, in 1691 the general assembly passed an Act of Ports under the new Governor, Francis Nicholson.[109] This act contained some of the articles of the Cohabitation Act of 1680 but its requirements were less grandiose in scale and immediacy. One difference that stood out was the justification for the erection of towns. In the earlier act it was to relieve the distress in Virginia, whereas this time it was for the better collection of customs and duties. On April 1, 1693, however, the act of 1691 was suspended by the general assembly.[110]

In 1705, Francis Makemie, a tradesmen, minister and lawyer published *A Plain & Friendly Persuasive for Promoting Towns & Cohabitation,* which was dedicated and presented to the new governor, Edward Nott.[111] Although there is no explicit reference to *Virginia's Cure* of 1662, Makemie adopts similar narrative devices on similar issues. An important difference is that *Persuasive* was addressed to inhabitants and legislators about the town question, whereas *Virginia's Cure* had proposed a program of action considering various bodies and agencies on the town question. The focus of *Persuasive* is thus more attuned to the benefits that will accrue to the people when towns are established rather than the benefits of towns for administration. Makemie urges his readers that their colonies possess natural characteristics for posterity and trade, but without promotion of towns and cohabitation an improvement in wealth would be impossible. Makemie thus asks his readers to "peruse, consider and weigh this plain Persuasive [about] advantages and universal benefits...of towns and cohabitation."[112] The purpose of the work is then simple: it is not designed to "impose upon, or dictate to our legislators, or set any limits to the counsels of government, but humbly to address, and lay before you, the advantages others do enjoy, and we have not yet tasted of, by towns and cohabitation." But, Makemie adds, "a Persuasive of this nature would appear to most people a superfluous undertaking, if from many years experience in America, and particularly in Virginia and Maryland, I had not been an eye and ear witness to...narrow and inconsiderate policy and some unthinking inhabitants...exposing their small stock of reason, in multiplying Arguments against their own felicity, upon this present theme."[113]

Makemie then considers a number of advantages of towns and cohabitation connected to wealth: that towns and cohabitation "would soon add a worth and value upon our...land, woods and timber"; "towns, and nothing but cohabitation, would soon fill our Country with people of all sorts, and so add to our strength..."; "towns and cohabitation would render trade universally more easy, and less expensive...";

"towns and cohabitation would effectively prevent, and soon regulate a great many frauds, irregularities, abuses, and imposition on trade..."; "towns and cohabitation would highly advance religion, which flourishes most in cohabitation: for in remote and scattered settlements we can never enjoy so fully, frequently, and certainly, those privileges and opportunities...in towns and cities"; and, "cohabitation would highly advance learning and school education: for this flourishes only in such places, for the smallest and meanest of schools cannot be maintained without a competent number of scholars."

Makemie then considers some objections that can be raised against towns and cohabitation. First he considers the objection "if towns are promoted in Virginia and Maryland, they will grow too rich and great, and soon cast off their dependence on England, for supplies of goods, and so the trade and tradesmen of England shall suffer by it."[114] He answers this objection by claiming that the wealthier the colonies are the better relations they shall have with England, "purchasing more superfluities for maintaining extravagance, as we see evident in all other growing plantations as Jamaica, Barbados, Carolina, Pennsylvania, New York and New England." A second objection he considers is "if they fall upon towns they will in a great measure fall off from planting tobacco, and this will be injurious to the queen's revenue and interest."[115] This idea is superfluous, Makemie contends, because without towns and ports tobacco planting cannot improve at all. As a third possible objection, Makemie deals with the thought that "in process of time [colonies] will cast off their allegiance to England, and set up a government of their own." But Makemie immediately raises the question: "Why should such a thought be improved only against us, and not against Carolina, Pennsylvania, New York and New England, who began with towns as their original settlements?"[116] The fourth objection is perhaps that "the inhabitants themselves are against towns, and judge it a hardship and invincible charge to bring their commodities to towns." The answer for this is simple for Makemie: "We are not the only people in the world that are enemies to ourselves, and see not our own interest and happiness [and] I am sensible, they are the most irrational and unthinking part of the inhabitants." He adds: "I presume and hope, after a serious consideration of this *Persuasive*, in all its parts, there are none of our legislators, from the highest to the lowest, for whom it was designed, that shall ever open their mouth against towns and cohabitation. And if any should, he should have a mark fixed on him, as an enemy to his country."

Upon reading the *Persuasive*, Edward Nott urged the assembly to pass an act setting out lands for building the towns and warehouses as he had also received an instruction from the queen to deal with the town question and "...to lay this whole affair and the several acts in this behalf before our council there and to recommend to the general assembly of Virginia...to pass an act for that purpose... and to give us and our Commissioners of Trade and Plantations a constant account of your proceedings herein."[117] In October 1705, the General Assembly of Virginia passed an Act for Establishing Ports and Towns.[118] This act provided for the establishment of fifteen towns in the colony and outlined their government in detail. The sites of the proposed towns were practically the same as the places named in the Act of Ports of 1691.[119] The most significant difference, however, between the act of 1705 and all the earlier ones lies in the special privileges and rights offered to inhabitants of towns to encourage their settlement. The more important of these privileges gave town inhabitants exemption from three-fourths of any duties that would be laid after the passage of the act and from the tobacco poll, for fifteen years, as well as the privilege of not being mustered outside their own towns unless the colony should be at war. Elaborate plans were embodied in the act for the government of the proposed towns. Each town was to pass through various stages of control according to the growth of population. At each advance, the town was to be given more corporate powers. In 1709, however, a document appeared entitled *Reasons for Repealing the Acts passed in Virginia & Maryland relating to Ports & Towns*, which argued that "the whole Act is designed to encourage by great privileges the settling in townships, and such settlements will encourage their going on with the woolen and other manufactures there, And should this Act be confirmed, the establishing of towns and incorporating of the planters as intended thereby, will put them upon further improvements of the said manufactures, And take them off from the planting of tobacco."[120] This was one of the objections Makemie had foreseen (or perhaps heard) against towns and cohabitation that was put forward by tobacco merchants and proved to be influential. The governor of Virginia repealed the act by proclamation on July 6, 1710.[121] Another act was proposed and defeated in 1711 to establish towns. This proposed act was the last attempt of the legislature of colonial Virginia to undertake the establishment of towns through legislation and wholesale implementation. Through the acts passed between 1662 and 1711, however, important steps were taken toward the incorporation of towns and cities in Virginia, which continued after 1711. The seat of the general assembly was, for example, moved from

Jamestown to Williamsburg, which received a royal charter of incorporation in 1722. In 1736 the town of Norfolk received a borough charter from Governor Gooch. Norfolk had been first settled under the influence of the act for cohabitation in 1680. In spite of the suspension of the act, the town continued to grow, and in 1736 the inhabitants petitioned for a charter of incorporation, which when granted remained in force until the middle of the nineteenth century.[122]

Our emphasis on Virginia is to demonstrate that in royal government there was considerable eagerness toward establishing cities. The reasons given for these attempts ranged from disciplining and inculcating useful habits in settlers to promoting trade. It should be emphasized that this discourse on the city originated with the desire to establish effective government in the colonies. If, in the aftermath of the rebellion of the thirteen colonies, the British colonial apparatus found the local autonomy exercised by the New England town to be one of the reasons for dissension, it was also thought that the failure to establish cities without autonomy was among the reasons for failed government.[123] The essence of the tension was how to build cities without citizens, for it was thought that without building cities it was impossible to establish a civilization, whereas at the same time it was recognized that cities must be subordinated to the centralized authority. It can certainly be suggested that the tension between the city and the State took on an intense dimension in the New World where creating cities without autonomy was a more formidable task, given the resources of the State (administrative apparatus, legal and political techniques, and so on) compared to subjugating those which existed in England.

Other Royal Colonies

Virginia was not the only royal colony in which the cities were created with intense legislation. Most of the towns that were originally incorporated under proprietors, after their respective colonies were under royal government, received royal charters that possessed more uniform corporate powers, privileges and duties. In these royal colonies there were also new incorporations. In New Jersey, in 1713, An Act for Confirming a Patent by his Excellency Robert Hunter for the Incorporation of the Town of Bergen was passed in the legislature.[124] The same governor in New Jersey granted another incorporation a month later to the inhabitants of Newark.

In North Carolina, towns were first established either by order of the governor and council or by legislative act; these towns were represented in the assemblies. By about 1754, however, most of the acts establishing both towns and counties were repealed by order of the State administration, and the governor was instructed "to confirm by Charters of Incorporation, all the rights and privileges derived to certain towns and counties" by the acts repealed. In 1755 this instruction was revoked, "at the humble request of the Assembly." In 1760, Governor Dobbs reported to the Board of Trade that nearly all had applied for charters of incorporation, which he had granted. The response from the Board of Trade stated that "as to granting Charters of Incorporation to those towns, the acts for establishing of which had been repealed, it was meant only as a more regular mode of reestablishing in them those powers and offices of corporations which had been taken away by the repeal of the laws."[125]

The general importance of the royal colonies from our vantage point is twofold. First, it was this constitutional form that was used when early British North America was settled. One significant difference was that those colonies that were converted into royal colonies had originated as settler communities under diverse political and legal conditions. Hence, throughout their histories there were incessant political conflicts between lower assemblies, which were composed of elected representatives of the settler communities, and the royal appointee, the governor.[126] As we shall see, similar conflicts also existed between assemblies and the governor and his council in the 1820s and the 1830s in British North America. And, second, the tension between creating cities for purposes of government and circumventing autonomy existed in colonial America, and this tension was heightened following the political and legal failure to retain the thirteen colonies.

With the gradual build up of a colonial apparatus, the creation of early modern cities became an established component of government in colonial America. Both in proprietary and royal colonies, governors were anxious to create cities for government. Griffith asked, "Why was 'government' in the majority of the colonies anxious to have cities?"[127] His answer was that cities were associated with civilization; they promoted trade and commerce; they regulated trade and hence provided revenue and, in some instances, they helped in defence.[128] But he did not draw the conclusion that these reasons must have included government itself. Whatever the reasons for the creation of cities, the shift from corporate to royal colonies seemed to be precipitated by the desire of the colonial apparatus to make the colonies useful to the English State. And it was known that unless a successful system of government was in place, the colonies would not bend their will to the State. As early as 1620, when Sir Edwin Sandys (1561–1629) stated at the Virginia court in

England that "…the particular government by way of incorporation for every city and borough [which was] to be for all of one and the same model uniformity, being not only a supporter of amity, but also a great ease to the general government…," he was clearly expressing how the corporations were considered as a solution to the problem of government.[129]

It was also known that as much as corporations were engaged in trade regulations (which is itself an act of government), they were also engaged in policing the conduct of city inhabitants and the regulating of numerous aspects of city life.[130] We have seen some of the arguments in favour of creating and incorporating cities for inculcating useful habits. The early modern doctrine that it was the prerogative of the State to create cities guided the legal practice of creating incorporations in proprietary and royal colonies. The creation of cities in colonial America was for the most part initiated by the proprietors, the English State, the royal governors and the colonial legislatures.[131] And, again, as Griffith said, "In point of time it represented a later stage for the inhabitants of a given community themselves to seek incorporation."[132] When they did, in the eighteenth century, the reasons given for a demand for incorporation were overwhelmingly related to government and good order.

But all of this does not create successful colonial government, for the desire to command the colonies, to bend them to become useful for the English State, came relatively late. Once liberties and rights of *de facto* corporations were in place, it was difficult to encroach upon them. Boston, for example, resisted becoming a *de jure* corporation until 1822. When there was an attempt to make the city a *de jure* corporation in 1714, the citizens came together and drew up a lengthy petition with at least ten reasons, which included the burden of administration, fear of turning into a close corporation and objection to giving up the practice of town meetings.[133] Hence, the tension between the city and the State (as expressed in the tension between *de facto* and *de jure* corporations) also prevailed in colonial America. The fact that corporate colonies seized liberties and rights as settlers and forged for themselves powers of self-determination was to have profound consequences. When the thirteen colonies rebelled against the State, the British colonial apparatus largely blamed its inability to institute *de jure* corporations, particularly in the New England colonies—a diagnosis that formed a significant backdrop against which corporations were conceptualized in the settlement of British North America in the aftermath of the rebellion. We could suggest that the inability of the colonial apparatus to transform citizens into subjects was ultimately the decisive factor in the loss of the thirteen colonies, and the colonial apparatus correctly diagnosed its failure.

Cities in the Early American Republic

It will be useful here to outline briefly the legal status of cities in America after the Revolution. This will help to compare and contrast the legal status of cities in British North America in the same period. It is interesting, or perhaps ironic, that the cities that contributed to the spirit of independence and rebellion against central rule were subordinated to state legislatures after the rebellion. This, it seems, is what happened.[134] Between the years immediately after the rebellion and the middle of the nineteenth century, urban politics in America was dominated by a conflict between the cities and the legislatures of the states in which they were situated. But the members of the legislatures, having been locally elected, were "viewed as compatible with the spirit of the Revolution."[135] The cities as close corporations were considered inconsistent with republican doctrine and, ironically, formed the basis for attacks on cities by state legislatures: close corporations represented the last vestiges of British power in America.[136] Hence, the power that had rested in the State-appointed governor and the council before the Revolution shifted to the legislatures, with a powerful legitimation to create and regulate cities and municipal corporations. This principle came to be enhanced by the judge John F. Dillon whose treatise, *The Law of Municipal Corporations* (1878), laid the basis of many court cases in the United States and was influential abroad.[137] What came to be known as "Dillon's Rule" was put forward as follows:

> It is general and undisputed proposition of the law that a municipal corporation possesses and can exercise the following powers, and no others: First, those granted in express words; second, those necessarily or fairly implied in, or incident to, the powers expressly granted; third, those essential to the accomplishment of the declared objects and purposes of the corporation—not simply convenient, but indispensable. Any fair, reasonable, substantial doubt concerning the existence of a power is resolved by the courts against the corporation, and the power is denied.[138]

Dillon's Rule became the core of the modern doctrine of the corporation and was embodied later in state constitutions. But there was also resistance to the doctrine of state supremacy over cities. The legacy of cities with citizens persisted in the early republic. This legacy came to be expressed in two legal principles: right to local self-government and municipal home rule. The first was expressed by judge Thomas M. Cooley but did not become an accepted rule.[139] The other was more influential and stipulated that the creation of a city could not be complete without the consent of the inhabitants.[140] As a reflection of this legacy, and like some European cities, some American cities still uphold their historical rights and liberties.

Another noteworthy aspect of the legal status of cities after the Revolution was the predominance of special-act charters. Since the legislatures established the doctrine of state supremacy over cities, many cities were created by charters that were drafted for the specific city in question. This created considerable variation in terms of the particular powers that were granted to cities, and depended on numerous political forces related to the city, the legislature and the inhabitants of the city. In addition, villages, counties and townships were gradually being given some corporate powers with special-charter incorporations. Although there was a growing tendency toward general acts, it was not until the 1850s and 1860s that the first prohibitive clauses appeared in state constitutions about special charters, and it was not until the 1870s that some state constitutions included clauses that were somewhat comparable to general act provisions such as the 1835 English Municipal Corporations Act.[141]

Notes

1. G. Frug, "The City as a Legal Concept," *Harvard Law Review*, vol. xciii, April 1980, no. 6, pp. 1096.
2. I would like to note here that the history of corporations in colonial America has not been approached from the perspective of "government at a distance" and that it remains curiously neglected. A recent and massive article by G. Frug, "City as a Legal Concept," for example, contains some four pages on colonial American corporations, which is only a synopsis of an earlier literature on corporations. Ernest S. Griffith's *History of American City Government: The Colonial Period* (1938), which was followed by Jon C. Teaford, *The Municipal Revolution in America: Origins of Modern Urban Government, 1650–1825* (1975) remain the only book-length studies on the subject that I was able to draw upon. Yet both neglect to place the subject within the context of "government at a distance" since they do not focus on the connections between the building up of an apparatus of government in the colonies and the creation of corporations. There are also a series of papers written by legal historians around the turn of the twentieth century amid the increased concern about municipal politics and reform (see Bibliography). We need to make a special mention of J. S. Davis, *Essays in the Earlier History of American Corporations* (Cambridge, 1917), which contains important facts and suggestions about corporations in colonial America.
3. Richard Hakluyt, *Discourse Concerning Western Planting* (1584), in C. Deane, ed., *Documentary History of the State of Maine* (Cambridge, 1877).
4. Hakluyt, *Discourse*, pp. 36f.
5. Hakluyt, *Discourse*, p. 95.
6. Sir William Petty, *Political Arithmetic* (1690), in *Economic Writings*, C. H. Hull, ed. (Cambridge, 1899), vol. i, p. 249.
7. Slingsby Bethel, *An Account of the French Usurpation upon the Trade of England* (London, 1679), p. 15.
8. David Bindon, *A Letter from a Merchant Who Has Left Off Trade* (London, 1738), p. 4.
9. Charles Davenant, *Discourses on the Public Revenues and the Trade of England* (London, 1698), 2 vols. vol. i, p. 232.
10. Jack P. Greene, *Peripheries and Center: Constitutional Development in the Extended Polities of the British Empire and the United States, 1607–1788* (London, 1986).
11. These instructions are collected and edited in a monumental work by L. W. Labaree, *Royal Instructions to British Colonial Governors, 1670–1776*, 2 vols. (New York, 1935).
12. Charles M. Andrews, *The Colonial Period of American History*, 4 vols. (New Haven, 1934–1937), particularly vol. iv: *England's Commercial and Colonial Policy*, and H. L. Osgood, *The American Colonies in the Seventeenth Century*, vol. iii: *Imperial Control: Beginnings of the System of Royal Provinces* (London, 1926).
13. *Report of the Board of Trade* (March 26, 1701), Proprietary Governments, *English Historical Documents*, ix, document 32b, pp. 251–252.
14. William Blackstone, *Commentaries on the Law of England* (London, 1768), Introduction, section 4.
15. Although in 1896 Osgood questioned the accuracy of differentiating between chartered and proprietary colonies (for proprietary colonies were chartered), this

classification remains useful in considering the juridical status of colonies in British America. Herbert L. Osgood, "The Corporation as a Form of Colonial Government I," *Political Science Quarterly* (1896), vol. xi, no. 2, pp. 259–277. What Osgood found as problematic in wording was the use of "chartered colonies." He argued that this term missed the fact that indeed the charter was a legal document used for the transmission of powers and was characteristic of proprietary colonies as well.

16. A word of caution should be noted here. As Appendix 2 shows, the transition from earlier corporate colonies to royal colonies was neither without resistance nor chronologically consistent. Therefore, the organization of this section is more thematic than chronological.

17. Osgood, "The Corporation as a Form of Colonial Government I," p. 264.

18. "The third charter of the Virginia Company" (March 12, 1612) in Merrill Jensen, *American Colonial Documents to 1776* (London, 1955), pp. 65–72.

19. Jensen, *Colonial Documents*, pp. 72–84.

20. Herbert L. Osgood, "The Corporation as a Form of Colonial Government II," *Political Science Quarterly*, vol. xi, no. 3, pp. 502–533.

21. Osgood, "The Corporation as a Form of Colonial Government II," p. 504.

22. Osgood, "The Corporation as a Form of Colonial Government II," p. 509.

23. Osgood, "The Corporation as a Form of Colonial Government II," p. 510; Egleston, *The Land System of New England*, p. 24.

24. John Winthrop, *The History of New England*, vol. i, p. 153.

25. J. R. Pole, *Political Representation in England and the Origins of the American Republic* (New York, 1966), pp. 38–54. Although Pole uses the term incorporated, in New England towns incorporation came much later for reasons we will see below.

26. Roy Akagi, *The Town Proprietors of the New England Colonies, 1620–1770* (Philadelphia, 1924).

27. Herbert L. Osgood, "The Land System in the Corporate Colonies of New England," in his *The American Colonies in the Seventeenth Century*, vol. i: *The Chartered Colonies* (New York, 1904), p. 424.

28. Edward Channing, "Town and County Government in the English Colonies of North America," Herbert B. Adams, ed., *Johns Hopkins University Studies in Historical and Political Science* (Baltimore, 1884).

29. Channing, "Town and County Government," p. 35.

30. George E. Howard, *An Introduction to the Local Constitutional History of the United States*, vol. i: Development of the Township, Hundred, and Shire (Baltimore, 1889), p. 60.

31. Osgood, *The American Colonies in the Seventeenth Century*, vol. i, uses the term "land community," which implies a voluntary aggregation of persons as opposed to legal inducement, a point which Osgood himself does not overlook.

32. See Akagi, *Town Proprietors of the New England Colonies*.

33. Osgood, *American Colonies*, stated that indeed in corporate colonies "there was no land system apart from the towns," vol. i, p. 436.

34. *Records of Massachusetts*, vol. i, p. 172. See also H. W. Rogers, "Municipal Corporations," in *Two Centuries' Growth of American Law, 1701–1901*, by Members of the Faculty of the Yale Law School (New York, 1901), p. 228.

35. *Colonial Records of Connecticut, 1636–1165*, p. 36. See also Rogers, "Municipal Corporations," p. 229.

36. These are printed in Howard, *Introduction to the Local Constitutional History*, pp. 68–72.
37. Howard, *Introduction*, pp. 86–88.
38. *Massachusetts Records*, vol. ii, p. 210. See also, Osgood, *American Colonies*, vol. i, p. 433.
39. Davis, *American Corporations*, p. 62.
40. Davis, *American Corporations*, p. 62.
41. Quoted in Davis, *American Corporations*, p. 63.
42. We must note here that in colonial America the term 'proprietor' was used in two different ways. One was proprietors of New England towns. These proprietors were the original grantees or purchasers of a town (township), which proprietors and their legal heirs, assigns or successors, together with those whom they chose to admit to their number, held in common ownership. See Akagi, *Town Proprietors of the New England Colonies*. The second use of the term was for Lord Proprietors who were granted large tracts of lands to establish colonies such as Pennsylvania (William Penn) and Maryland (Lord Baltimore).
43. Herbert L. Osgood, "The Proprietary Province as a Form of Colonial Government I," *The American Historical Review*, vol. ii (1897), p. 650.
44. Osgood, "The Proprietary Province as a Form of Colonial Government I," p. 655.
45. Davis, *American Corporations*, vol. i, p. 50.
46. Davis, *American Corporations*, vol. i, pp. 8–9.
47. Davis, *American Corporations*, vol. i, p. 9.
48. Davis, *American Corporations*, vol. i, p. 51; McBain, "The Legal Status of the American Colonial City."
49. *Documentary History of New York*, vol. i, p. 390; John A. Fairlie, "Municipal Corporations in the Colonies," *Municipal Affairs*, vol. ii (1898), no. 3, p. 344.
50. Fairlie, "Municipal Corporations in the Colonies," pp. 345–346.
51. Davis, *American Corporations*, vol. i, p. 53.
52. Kavenagh, *Colonial America*, vol. ii, pp. 1504–1508.
53. Fairlie, "Municipal Corporations in the Colonies," p. 347.
54. Davis, *American Corporations*, vol. i, p. 55.
55. James T. Lemon, *The Best Poor Man's Country: A Geographical Study of Early Southeastern Pennsylvania* (New York, 1972), p. 143.
56. Lemon, *Best Poor Man's Country*, pp. 118, 144.
57. Lemon, *Best Poor Man's Country*, p. 124, table 22.
58. Davis, *American Corporations*, vol. i, pp. 67–68.
59. Griffith, *History of City Government: the Colonial Period*, chap. vii.
60. Jensen, *Colonial Documents*, p. 251.
61. Jensen, *Colonial Documents*, 32A-B note, p. 248.
62. These can be discerned from the *Journal of the Commissioners for Trade and Plantations, 1704–1782* (Great Britain, Public Records Office (1920–1938), 14 vols. The commissioners were established in 1675, and the office later became the Board of Trade in 1696. The office was terminated in 1782 and was continued as The Colonial Office in 1801.
63. Greene, *Peripheries and Center*, p. 14.
64. Greene, *Peripheries and Center*, pp. 14–15.
65. Herbert L. Osgood, *The American Colonies in the Seventeenth Century*, vol. iii: *Imperial Control: Beginnings of the System of Royal Provinces* (New York, 1926).

66. Keith, *Constitutional History of the First British Empire*, p. 167.
67. Jensen, *Colonial Documents*, p. 44.
68. Osgood, *American Colonies in the Seventeenth Century*, vol. iii, p. 23.
69. For a detailed examination of this conflict see Jack P. Greene, *The Quest for Power: The Lower Houses of Assembly in the Southern Royal Colonies* (Williamsburg, 1963).
70. Leonard W. Labaree, *Royal Government in America: A Study of the British Colonial System before 1783* (London, 1930), p. 8.
71. Labaree, *Royal Government in America*, pp. 6–7.
72. Labaree, *Royal Government in America*, p. 30. An important portion of these instructions and some commissions are contained in Leonard W. Labaree, ed., *Royal Instructions of British Colonial Governors, 1670–1776*, 2 vols. (New York, 1935).
73. Labaree, *Instructions*, vol. ii, p. 542, section 774.
74. Labaree, *Instructions*, vol. ii, p. 542, section 774.
75. Labaree, *Instructions*, vol. ii, p. 542, section 774.
76. Labaree, *Instructions*, vol. ii, p. 542, section 774.
77. Labaree, *Instructions*, vol. ii, p. 542, section 774.
78. Labaree, *Instructions*, vol. ii, p. 540, section 769.
79. Akagi, *Town Proprietors of the New England Colonies*; Fries, *Urban Idea in Colonial America*; Reps, *Making of Urban America*.
80. H. L. Osgood, *The American Colonies in the Seventeenth Century*, vol. iii: *Imperial Control. Beginnings of the System of Royal Provinces* (London, 1926).
81. Griffith, *American City Government*, p. 107; Meinig, *Shaping of America*, vol. i, pp. 235–239.
82. Howard, *Local Constitutional History*, chap. iii.
83. Edward M. Riley, "The Town Acts of Colonial Virginia," *The Journal of Southern History*, vol. xvi (1950), p. 306; Reps, *Town Planning in Frontier America*, pp. 80–90.
84. Riley, "The Town Acts of Colonial Virginia," interprets this as "the dislike of the Virginians for town life," which I think conflates those who govern with those who are governed.
85. These pamphlets are little emphasized in literature. See, however, Reps, *Town Planning in Frontier America*, pp. 80–90; Fries, *Urban Idea in Colonial America*, pp. 122–125.
86. "Instructions to Berkeley, 1662," *Virginia Magazine of History and Biography*, vol. iii (1895–1896), pp. 16–17.
87. R. G., *Virginia's Cure: Or An Advisive Narrative Concerning Virginia* (London, 1662). Reprinted in Peter Force, ed., *Collection of Historical Tracts*, vol. iii, no. 15 (Washington, 1835), 19p.
88. R. G., *Virginia's Cure*, p. 3.
89. R. G., *Virginia's Cure*, p. 6.
90. R. G., *Virginia's Cure*, p. 6.
91. R. G., *Virginia's Cure*, p. 8.
92. R. G., *Virginia's Cure*, p. 10.
93. R. G., *Virginia's Cure*, p. 11.
94. R. G., *Virginia's Cure*, p. 13 (emphasis added).
95. R. G., *Virginia's Cure*, p. 14.
96. R. G., *Virginia's Cure*, p. 16.

97. R. G., *Virginia's Cure*, p. 16.
98. R. G., *Virginia's Cure*, p. 16.
99. "Virginia Colonial Records: Culpeper's Administration," in *Virginia Magazine of History and Biography*, vol. xiv (1906–1907), p. 364; Riley, "Town Acts of Colonial Virginia," p. 309.
100. Labaree, *Royal Instructions to British Royal Governors, 1670–1776*, vol. ii, no. 777 (1679), p. 545. These instructions remained in force between 1679 and 1705.
101. "Virginia Colonial Records: Culpeper's Administration," in *Virginia Magazine of History and Biography*, vol. xiv (1906–1907), p. 364.
102. William W. Hening, ed., *The Statutes at Large...of Virginia*, vol. ii, pp. 471–478.
103. See Riley, "The Town Acts of Colonial Virginia," for a list of places which were selected as sites for new towns; also see John W. Reps, *Tidewater Towns: City Planning in Colonial Virginia and Maryland* (Williamsburg, 1972), chap. iv.
104. Riley, "The Town Acts of Colonial Virginia," p. 312.
105. Reps, *Tidewater Towns*, p. 75.
106. "Memorandum of the Commissioners of Customs to the Lords of Trade and Plantations," *Calendar of State Papers, Colonial Series, 1681–1685*, p. 152.
107. Riley, "Town Acts of Colonial Virginia," p. 313.
108. *Calendar of State Papers, Colonial Series, 1681–1685*, p. 188.
109. Riley, "Town Acts of Colonial Virginia," p. 315.
110. John P. Kennedy and Henry R. McIlwaine, eds., *Journal of the House of Burgesses* (Richmond, 1905–1915), 13 vols. vol. ii, 1659/1660–1693, p. 444.
111. Francis Makemie, *A Plain and Friendly Persuasive to the Inhabitants of Virginia and Maryland for Promoting Towns and Cohabitation* (London, 1705). Reprinted in *Virginia Magazine of History and Biography*, vol. iv (1896–1897), pp. 252–271.
112. Makemie, *Persuasive*, p. 259.
113. Makemie, *Persuasive*, p. 260.
114. Makemie, *Persuasive*, p. 268.
115. Makemie, *Persuasive*, p. 269.
116. Makemie, *Persuasive*, p. 270.
117. Labaree, *Royal Instructions to British Royal Governors, 1670–1776*, vol. ii, no. 778 (1705). This instruction remained in force until 1707.
118. "An Act for Establishing Ports and Towns," in Hening, *Statutes at Large*, vol. iii, pp. 404–419. Also reprinted in Kavenagh, *Colonial America*, vol. iii, pp. 2354–2363.
119. Riley, "The Town Acts of Colonial Virginia," p. 320.
120. William P. Palmer, et al., eds., *Calendar of Virginia State Papers and Other Manuscripts* (Richmond, 1875–1893), 11 vols. vol. i, pp. 137–138; also see Riley, "The Town Acts of Colonial Virginia," p. 322, note 44.
121. H. R. McIlwaine, ed., *Executive Journals of the Council of Colonial Virginia* (Richmond, 1925–1930), 4 vols., vol. iii, pp. 576–577; also see Riley, "The Town Acts of Colonial Virginia," p. 322.
122. Fairlie, "Municipal Corporations in the Colonies," p. 349.
123. For example, the lieutenant governor of Upper Canada John Graves Simcoe defended his decision to build a capital city by stating that "it has been adopted as a principle, so to form the place for future Establishments in this Colony, as

to avoid the errors which the former settlements of the United States and Canadians have fallen into; and to second those advantages which nature seems to have pointed out; a central Capital, from whence should flow loyalty, attachment, and respect to the British Government and all those principles, qualities and manners which are of eminent use in decorating and strengthening such an attachment." *Simcoe Papers*, vol. iii (1794), p. 61.

124. Davis, *American Corporations*, vol. i, p. 69.
125. Davis, *American Corporations*, vol. i, p. 70.
126. These conflicts were analyzed by Greene, *Quest for Power*.
127. Griffith, *History of American City Government*, p. 52.
128. Griffith, *History of American City Government*, pp. 54ff; see also Fries, *Urban Idea in Colonial America*, chap. i.
129. Quoted in Griffith, *History of American City Government*, p. 63.
130. Griffith, *History of American City Government*, pp. 118–119; Teaford, *Municipal Revolution in America*, p. 36.
131. Griffith, *History of American City Government*, p. 52.
132. Griffith, *History of American City Government*, p. 52.
133. Griffith, *American City Government*, pp. 72–73.
134. Here our main sources are Frug, "City as a Legal Concept"; Ernest S. Griffith and Charles R. Adrian, *A History of American City Government: The Formation of Traditions, 1775-1870* (New York, 1976); and Teaford, *Municipal Revolution in America* and "The City versus State: The Struggle for Legal Ascendancy," *The American Journal of Legal History*, vol. xvii, 1973, pp. 51–65.
135. Griffith and Adrian, *Formation of Traditions, 1775-1870*, p. 34.
136. Teaford, "The City versus State," p. 51.
137. Frug, "City as a Legal Concept," pp. 1109–1113.
138. J. F. Dillon, *Commentaries on the Law of Municipal Corporations*, 5th ed. (Boston, 1911).
139. Griffith and Adrian, *Formation of Traditions, 1775-1870*, pp. 40–42.
140. Edwars A. Gere, "Dillon's Rule and the Cooley Doctrine: Reflections on the Political Culture," *Journal of Urban History*, vol. viii (1982), pp. 271–298.
141. Griffith and Adrian, *Formation of Traditions, 1775-1870*, pp. 34–39.

4

CITIES IN BRITISH NORTH AMERICA: A COLONIAL LEGACY

C ITIES in British North American history originated as cities without citizens: from the beginning, cities were never allowed to develop practices of citizenship (*de facto* rights and responsibilities). The British colonial apparatus was very calculating and deliberate in circumventing the development of such practices as town meetings, for as we have noted, the development of citizenship practices in corporate colonies in America was considered to have caused the rebellion of the thirteen colonies. But at the same time regular settlement through towns and cities was seen as essential to building colonies. To put it bluntly, the question of governance that the British colonial apparatus faced was how to build cities without citizens. This chapter focuses on how this question was posed and addressed.

The settlement of British North America spanned the period of transition from early modernity to modernity in Western European and English politico-legal institutions. But there were unique political conditions we can observe in British North American colonies. Before we proceed, let us briefly outline these conditions. To begin with, the colonies were acquired through conquest and diplomatic bargaining, which ended with the Treaty of Paris in 1763. As we have seen, the fact that the American colonies were not acquired by conquest, but had originated as settler communities with charter privileges, was of the highest significance for the problem of 'government at a distance'.[1] By contrast, British North American colonies were conquered and the existing liberties and customs of the conquered subjects (the French inhabitants of Québec) were open to interpretation, as it were, by the British colonial apparatus.[2] Hence, as Gordon Stewart has noted, between the 1760s and the 1790s British North America had the most extreme form of statist and centralist constitution.[3] So, the royal colonial constitution, the beginnings of which we traced in American colonies, was also introduced in British North America. Québec (1763), Nova Scotia (1749), New Brunswick (1784), Upper Canada (1791) and Lower

Canada (1791) were constituted as royal colonies with royal governors, appointed councils and representative assemblies.

Still, in the aftermath of the rebellion of the thirteen colonies, the administration was not yet decided as to whether, and if so how, British North America should be peopled. Between the 1780s and the 1820s, the British colonial apparatus was in a state of disarray and reorganization: in the minds of colonial administrators and governors, it was not at all clear or obvious that Britain was going to build a new empire of colonies from the 1820s onwards.[4] Instead, it was a period of questioning and reordering of priorities. The Board of Trade and Plantations was abolished in 1782 and was not replaced with the Colonial Office until 1801, and, as Buckner stated, "Until the 1820s, the Colonial Office had neither the expertise, the knowledge, nor the desire to supervise effectively the work of distant governors."[5] Hence, there was a considerable lack of continuity in colonial government, which now depended on painstaking correspondence between the secretaries of the State in Whitehall and the governors, even on minute matters. This is why many of the documents that relate to cities and towns in British North American colonies in the late eighteenth century consist of correspondence between the principal secretaries of the State and the colonial governors.

The undercurrent of concern that comes out of this correspondence is a fear of the recurrence of the rebellion. The consequences of this undercurrent for British North American political and legal culture were far reaching: the colonial governors and their councils formed a distinct colonial oligarchy and exercised unchecked power within the colonies, protected by the provisions of royal constitutions.[6] By 1828, when a select committee produced its report on government, there were rising constitutional and political problems in British North America: growing discontent within both English and French populations; the union of the Canadas which were divided in 1791; declining revenue for government and administration; and, the conflicts between executive councils and elective assemblies. These were some of the issues that were mentioned in the report.[7] And there was no clear idea as "to what degree the embarrassments and discontents which have long prevailed in the Canadas, had arisen from defects in the system of laws and constitutions established in these colonies."[8] But, by the late 1830s, clear ideas were emerging and the system of laws and constitutions was being reformed.

For British North America, in short, the period between the 1780s and the 1830s was one of tension and intensity. The tension between towns and the legislatures, which was a consequence of these unique political conditions, reached an intense point and forced the formation of new institutions and practices in British North America. This chapter focuses on this tension and the institutions that were introduced to address it—a tension that dominated colonial politics until the municipal corporations acts were passed in the 1840s and 1850s. Those readers who are familiar with the literature on the 'development' of British North American 'municipal institutions' will recognize that the organization of this chapter departs from established accounts of a steady progress toward 'municipal freedom' or 'free institutions'. Rather, a thematic organization is introduced around a tension between central authority and potential autonomies, which brings a different interpretation to bear on changes in this period—one which focuses on the political and legal measures that were introduced to contain this tension. The chapter begins with a discussion of the nature of the tension, and then examines a series of laws and institutions. The chapter ends with a discussion of the rebellions in Upper and Lower Canada as an indication of the failure of the measures that were introduced to contain the tension.

Colonial Cities Without Citizens: A Tension

Between the 1780s and the 1830s two themes predominate colonial political and legal discourse on cities. First, there was an antagonism toward towns on the grounds that they make possible the emergence of different and undesirable loyalties and *de facto* citizenship practices among the settlers. This theme has been noted and expressed time and again by a number of historians since the late nineteenth century. J. B. Bourinot, for example, noted that the statesmen "...appear to have quietly acquiesced in a state of things calculated to repress a spirit of local enterprise and diminish the influence of the people in the administration of public affairs. Indeed, we have some evidence that the government itself was prepared for many years to discourage every attempt to introduce into Canada anything that had so long existed in New England."[9] He also noted that this antagonism began as early as 1770 when a resolution was passed in Nova Scotia declaring all town meetings illegal.[10] Adam Shortt, displaying his liberal belief in British institutions, also noted that the colonial statesmen Haldimand, Dorchester and Simcoe "professed to fear another revolution as the natural and inevitable consequence of granting them British freedom; and in this they were probably not far astray, assuming that their views of what a colony should be are correct."[11] James Aitchison, in his more recent and comprehensive historical survey of municipal government in Upper Canada, joined the earlier historians by noting that "when the first townships on the upper St. Lawrence were surveyed in 1783, the surveyors were instructed not to call them townships but royal seigneuries, and to number, not name them. The intention was to consider them merely as divisions like the concessions and lots into which they were subdivided and thus to avoid any suggestion that they were to form units of local administration."[12] David William Smith, the surveyor general of Upper Canada, expressed this fear of town meetings quite succinctly: "...as I conceive these meetings to have been the cause of the late unhappy rebellion and must always be attended with riot and confusion...I think the majority of the people should never be called together but to choose their representatives for a House of Assembly."[13] William Smith, chief justice of Upper Canada, also expressed a similar sentiment when he said, "I trace the late revolt and rent to a remoter cause, than those to which it is ordinarily ascribed. The truth is that the country had outgrown its government...All America was thus...abandoned to democracy...and [to] little republics."[14] Of course, here 'democracy' and 'little republics' refer to practices of autonomous governance and citizenship. The rebellion of the thirteen colonies then influenced not only the early British North American culture in general but also attitudes toward towns, since they were thought to have played a decisive role in the rebellion.

The second theme has been less emphasized by historians: the necessity of governing through towns to induce loyalty and obedience amongst the subjects by requiring that the territories be settled in a regulated manner and that a population not be permitted to scatter throughout the territories. From the beginnings of settlement, British colonial statesmen urged settlement in specified and clearly delimited towns and townships for purposes of government. We have seen in Chapter Three that settlement in townships became an instrument of both administration and government in royal colonies in colonial America. The township was considered both as a unit of taxation and representation. We have also noted that in British North American colonies, Québec (1763) was divided into Upper Canada (1791) and Lower Canada (1791), and New Brunswick (1784) and Nova Scotia (1749) were constituted as royal colonies.[15] Similarly, the settlement in townships was considered as an instrument of administration and government in all British North American colonies.

When Edward Cornwallis was appointed governor of Nova Scotia in 1749, for example, his instructions included settling in townships and convening a house of assembly drawn from those townships.[16] The governor was also given full power and authority to "erect, raise and build cities, boroughs and towns."[17] Cornwallis showed a special concern for founding Halifax and developing it.[18] On August 20, 1749, Governor Cornwallis transmitted the plan of the town to the Board of Trade and Plantations, and he said, "...a great many acres have been cleared—the Town has been marked out, lots drawn and now everyone knows where to build his house, a great many houses are begun."[19] Although Cornwallis was instructed to constitute a house of assembly within the legislature "according to the usage of the rest of our colonies and plantations in America,"[20] it was not convened until October 2, 1758, the first in British North America.[21] Thus, Nova Scotia was governed through only an executive council and a governor, as in Québec between 1783 and 1791. But the Board of Trade was insistent on convening an assembly on the grounds that the authority without representation could not be legal and legitimate.[22] The board then proposed the division of the colony into townships and counties for government and administration. Hence, Nova Scotia was divided into the townships of Halifax, Lunenburg, Dartmouth, Lawrence Town, Annapolis Royal and Cumberland, as units of representation and taxation. When James Murray was appointed to govern Québec in 1763, his instructions, too, included laying out towns and townships. And, finally, when New Brunswick was settled in 1784 the governor was also instructed to lay out towns and townships.[23] The royal governments of British North American colonies, therefore, followed similar constitutional *and* settlement patterns in their beginnings as those royal colonies we traced in Chapter Three. The emphasis placed on the necessity of governing through towns was an established practice in royal colonies.

With that background, let us now focus on specific practices that operated with this idea and emerged in Québec and continued later in Upper Canada. Gilbert Stelter has argued how the colonial statesmen urged the formation of towns and cities for purposes of government,[24] and David Wood has discussed how new towns were conceptualized and planted by the colonial apparatus.[25] But still, an analytical treatment of this theme awaits us. On the basis of documents of the British colonial apparatus, the theme of the necessity of settling in towns and townships for purposes of governance can be summarized as follows: (i) we know that we have to populate this territory if we want to establish at once a political and an economic force (strength and wealth) in British North

America; (ii) we need loyal (in political terms of allegiance) and industrious (in economic terms of productivity) subjects; (iii) in order to achieve this, men must be given property so that while industriously improving their land, they will develop respect for the political authority that protects their property; (iv) the *compactness* and *togetherness* of this population is instrumental in terms of inducing appropriate habits, customs and attitudes among the subjects for forming political bodies for government; thus towns and townships are desired forms of settlement and their growth cannot be left to spontaneous or 'organic' development; and (v) authority cannot be legitimate without representation of these communities in the house of assembly.

But it was also known that concentration alone would not necessarily guarantee inducing loyalty to, and respect for, political authority: it was also capable of fomenting allegiance to other ideals, as the rebellion of the thirteen colonies had shown. British North America could not become the fourteenth colony: here arose a tension between these two themes of political and legal practice. Shortt isolated such a tension when he stated that "...we observe the conflict of the two rival American systems typified by New England and Virginia, the one seeking to vest in the people the election of their local officers and the regulation of their local affairs, the other seeking to confine these rights to the justices of the peace in Quarter Sessions, who again derived their positions from the Governor-in-Council."[26] I think the tension Shortt notes between the New England and Virginia systems is important because of his use of New England (corporate colonies) and Virginia (royal colony) as typifying decentralized and centralized forms of political and legal organization. We can see this tension as being an apprehension toward potential *de facto* powers that bodies politic might develop, which might make the government of subjects difficult. Let us now see in detail both themes and the tension that governed political and legal practice until the 1840s. This tension was apparent in the first incorporation of a city in British North America: Saint John, New Brunswick.

Saint John, New Brunswick: 1785

On April 30, 1785, a royal charter was granted to the inhabitants of the two districts on both sides of the Saint John River incorporating them into a city.[27] The inhabitants were loyalists who had arrived from New England colonies three years earlier.[28] A petition had been presented by the inhabitants to the new governor of New Brunswick, Thomas Carleton, with a "...promise that their prudent use of the liberties so to be granted them will justify the favour."[29] This petition indicates two important things at once: the acquaintance of the New Englanders with the institution of corporation and their recognition of the reluctance of the colonial authorities to grant it.[30] The charter, referring to the petition, stated that "the advantages to be derived from a charter, empowering [the people] to establish such ordinances as are requisite for the good government of a populous place are so obvious, they think it necessary only to hint at them."[31] The text of the charter does not further elaborate the reasons for incorporation, but an important letter by Governor Carleton makes some of the reasons explicit. The letter was dated June 25, 1785. It was addressed to the then Colonial Secretary Lord Sydney at Whitehall. Carleton wrote that "the sudden increase of Inhabitants at this port and the confusion incident to so novel a situation have induced me to comply with the general wish in granting them a charter of incorporation."[32] And he added that "...although every useful liberty is given to the citizens, there is a sufficient influence retained in the hands of Government for the preservation of Order and securing of perfect Obedience."[33] Now, what this reasoning demonstrates is twofold. The charter was granted as a compliance with the demands of the inhabitants. It appears that in the absence of such a demand the city would not have been incorporated while, at the same time, the purpose of the charter was to oblige the inhabitants to recognize the authority of colonial agencies. This is understandable because of the crisis of authority in the English State and the desire of British statesmen to ensure that the new ideas nurtured by the rebellion should not hold sway in British North America.[34] Carleton, for example, wrote that "the internal police of the city of Saint John...is organized by this Charter nearly on the same plan with that of the City of New York when under His Majesty's Government." By this he implied that the less-than-enthusiastic participation of New York City in the rebellion may have been due to its form of government.[35]

Let us now look at some of the details of this first charter: corporate rights and duties, constitution and delegated authorities. The charter constituted "the inhabitants, the Mayor, Recorder, Aldermen and Assistants [as] one body corporate and politic in deed, fact and name."[36] As a body corporate and politic, the inhabitants of the city of Saint John now possessed rights and duties which they did not possess as individuals. But this does not mean that all inhabitants of the city were considered as qualified inhabitants. Only freemen and freeholders were considered inhabitants and could participate in city politics. The freeholders were those who held real property in the city, and freemen were defined and admitted by the city council on the basis of not only property but also status, family and privileges. According to Acheson, freemen and freeholders made up about one fourth of the total population of the city.[37] The corporate rights of the city thus constituted stipulated perpetual succession and empowered the corporation to hold lands, to pass regulations and bylaws, to sue and be sued and to hold a common seal.

The charter ordained that the officials shall include a mayor, six aldermen, six assistants, one sheriff, one coroner, one common clerk, one chamberlain, one high constable, six constables and two marshals. Of these, the mayor, the recorder, the common clerk and the sheriff were to be appointed by the governor of New Brunswick. These appointments were already made by Carleton for the first term. The aldermen were to be elected by the qualified inhabitants from six wards that were specified in the charter. The mayor, the aldermen and the three assistants were constituted as the Common Council of the city with executive capacities within the corporation. For judicial purposes the city was also constituted as a county, which meant that the administration of justice did not require justices of the peace of a higher level. As we have seen, in English law the county was the main unit of the administration of justice and operated through Quarter Sessions of the justices of peace. From the charter we can see the "sufficient influence" that Carleton spoke about: the mayor and other important officials of the city were to be appointed by the governor.

As to the corporate powers and obligations of the city, its council was empowered

> to frame, constitute, ordain, make and establish, from time to time, all
> such laws, statutes, rights, ordinances and constitutions which to them,
> or the greater part of them, shall seem to be good, useful or necessary
> for the good rule and government of the body corporate...provided
> that such laws be not contradictory or repugnant to the laws or statutes
> of that part of our kingdom of Great Britain called England, or of our
> said province.[38]

It was also empowered to levy, assess and collect taxes for the purpose of government. A series of elaborate and detailed items were included in the charter specifying the target of such laws: regulations of the market, ordering the layout of the city, disposition of lands, assuring due observance of Sunday, watching the port and the harbour, and the building of houses of correction and workhouses. For this last purpose, council was also empowered "...to take up and arrest or order to be taken up and arrested all and any rogues, vagabonds, stragglers, idle and suspicious and disorderly persons...and to order all or any such [persons]...to be committed to a workhouse, there to remain and work...or else to the house of correction, there to receive such punishment, not extending to the loss of life or limb."[39] What this provision tells us is important: the sovereign authority to punish, correct and detain was delegated to the body corporate thereby functionally decentralizing certain aspects of State power. Within two years, on December 17, 1787, a house of correction was ordered by city council.[40] Council also ordained elaborate orders, rules and regulations for the operation of the house of correction. All this indicates that a clear distinction was made between punishment and correction, the importance of which we discussed at the end of Chapter Two.

From this brief look at the first charter of incorporation in British North America, we can glean a number of points and ask some questions. First, although the demand for incorporation came from the prominent inhabitants, the charter itself does not contain any provision that would encroach upon the royal prerogative, or, as the attorney general who confirmed the charter put it, the charter contained nothing "prejudicial to the interest of His Majesty."[41] The remark made by Carleton that "...although every useful liberty is given to the citizens, there is a sufficient influence retained in the hands of Government for the preservation of Order and securing of perfect Obedience..." demonstrates this interesting aspect of the charter of incorporation. For whose benefit was liberty given to the people? How did the concept of obedience seem not to conflict with liberty? What is the nature of liberty implied here? Second, the constitution of a body politic and corporate meant that some authority and tasks of the State were delegated to the corporation. Third, the explicit stipulation that the city of Saint John could enact local ordinances provided these be neither repugnant nor contradictory to higher laws and statutes indicates the subordinate nature of the body politic that was constituted. Fourth, and finally, the charter presupposes an accumulated experience in legal, administrative and political practices by calling for actions and arrangements that did not originate in British North America: workhouses, correction houses, regulation of markets, and so on. The distinction between punishment and correction, for example, made first in the charter and adopted in council, was a pillar of modern European jurisprudence around the turn of the nineteenth century. As a whole, then, the charter can be seen as an instrument that is at once responsive and restrictive: it envisages and foresees other patterns of life and conditions that *must* exist in a city as a body politic. In practice, there is no inconsistency between the two. On the contrary, the charter constitutes a city in so far as it is useful for the State, and without citizens.

Up until the 1830s no other cities were incorporated in British North America. This was not because there was a lack of a similar demand such as that which precipitated the Saint John charter. As was discussed, there were unauthorized town meetings (as in Adolphustown, Upper Canada), governor-initiated attempts (as in Niagara, Upper Canada) and local petitions for incorporation (as in Kingston, Upper Canada, and Halifax, Nova Scotia).[42] But the principle that all local communities were subject to centralized control and supervision remained intact until the 1830s and the 1840s.

Antagonism Toward Cities

This section will examine documents of the colonial apparatus that appeared between the 1790s and the 1840s, which demonstrated an antagonism toward local communities, and the legislation that resulted from this antagonism. Throughout this section we shall see how the British colonial apparatus was careful, deliberate and calculating in circumventing the development of *de facto* powers in bodies politic by retaining central control of, at times, mundane local matters such as the establishment of markets.

Township and Parish Officers Act, Upper Canada

The earliest act concerning local polities was passed on July 9, 1793, in Upper Canada, in which the practice of incorporating towns was used in a somewhat indecisive manner.[43] The interesting aspect of this act is that it replaced a bill that had proposed a limited form of town meetings. But Simcoe thought that in proposing this bill legislators seemed "rather to have a strong attachment to the elective principle for all Town affairs, than may be thought altogether advisable."[44] Simcoe somewhat revised his opinion and became resigned to the idea that "many well affected settlers were convinced that Fence Viewers, Pound Keepers and other petty officers to regulate matters of local policy would be more willingly obeyed, if named by the housekeepers, and especially that the collector of rates should be a person chosen by themselves...It was therefore thought advisable not to withhold such a gratification, to which they had been accustomed, it being in itself not unreasonable, and only to take place one day in the year."[45] Simcoe here conceded to town meetings in a limited form, recognizing some town meetings that had been already held in Adolphustown and Sidney, but at the same time being assured that this would only facilitate the obedience of town inhabitants in matters of policy.[46] The act provided that each town, township or parish should elect two town wardens to represent the inhabitants in the Quarter Sessions of the District in which it was located. But, as soon as a church was built in the town, the minister was empowered to choose another person to act as a town warden. The town warden or the church warden were defined as "a corporation to represent the whole inhabitants."[47] This act was repealed twice, in 1806 and 1808, and the word 'corporation' disappeared altogether from the new provisions.[48]

Simcoe and Portland on Corporations

On December 21, 1794, Simcoe asked Portland, the Secretary of State, for the authorization to incorporate the cities of Kingston and Niagara.[49] The Constitutional Act of 1791 had not conferred any power on governors to incorporate bodies politic, hence Simcoe was obliged to ask for authorization. Simcoe wrote, in an often-quoted famous passage, that "a principle on which I have considered this Government as most wisely established, and which I have never lost sight of in its Administration, has been to render the Province as nearly as may be a perfect image and transcript of the British Government and Constitution."[50] For this reason he thought these two cities had reached a stage where they should be bodies corporate and politic. He proposed that these corporations "should consist of a Mayor and six Aldermen, Justices of the Peace *ex officio*, and competent number of Common Council, to be originally appointed by the Crown, and that the succession to vacant seats might be made in such a manner as to render the Elections as *little popular* as possible; meaning such Corporations to tend to the support of the Aristocracy of the Country." Here we can see clearly the lineages between what Simcoe envisaged to create in Kingston and Niagara and the early modern corporations, close corporations with a governing body that perpetuates itself without elections.

How did Portland respond to Simcoe? On May 20, 1795, he wrote that the idea of delegating powers to corporations would tend to diminish the powers of the central colonial authorities.[51] These corporations, therefore, "may be disposed to use it in obstructing the Measures of Government, and in all events, will require to be courted and managed, in order to secure the right direction of the Influence thus unnecessarily given them." And Portland adds that "...I observe that your adoption of them arises from an idea, that by assimilating the modes of Government of the Province, to the modes of Government of England,

you will obtain all the beneficial effects which we receive from them—
Whereas to assimilate a Colony in all respects to its Mother Country, is
not possible, and if possible, would not be prudent."[52] Portland here
rejects the principle of creating a perfect image and transcript of the
English constitution in the colonies. He thinks colonial constitutions
should be suited to their peculiar circumstances because "the one may
have many Institutions, which are wholly inapplicable to the situation of
the other." Here, however, Portland does not provide any reason why
corporations would be unsuitable for the colonies. But the crux of the
matter becomes clear when he adds that there are some institutions
"...which we permit to continue here [in England] only because they
already exist, and are interwoven with other parts of the Government,
but which, perhaps, if we had a choice, we should not now be disposed
originally to introduce—Such, in the Opinion of many, are
Corporations, and separate Jurisdictions of all sorts." Now, Portland is
expressing here a common sentiment of the late eighteenth century not
only about the imprudence of creating a perfect image of the English
constitution in the colonies but also of corporations. The following letter
from Whitehall to Simcoe reveals that Portland was by no means alone
in his opinion:

> You suggest an idea of incorporation...the policy of such a measure
> after the experience we had at home...together with the conduct of the
> Mayor and Corporation of New York in the colonies is no longer a
> matter of doubt. Repeated experience has proved it to be a *most power-
> ful engine* in the hands of an unprincipled demagogue...The *prevailing
> opinion* is that charters do not tend to promote but rather to check
> trade and manufacture, they are useful for *purposes of police*—but more
> useful for the purpose of faction—it was one of the few subjects on
> which I spoke to Mr. Dundas—he did not approve of incorporations.
> Nor does your humble servant for reasons aforesaid.[53]

It is clear that creating or allowing "separate jurisdictions of all sorts"
was considered harmful to the authority that was being established in
British North America on the grounds that such jurisdictions or corporations would tend to foment disobedience and disloyalty. And the rebellion of the thirteen colonies formed a backdrop against which these
claims were justified. It is impossible to ascertain what would have happened if Simcoe had been authorized to incorporate Kingston and
Niagara and whether he would have incorporated other cities. Or, how
was he assured that the incorporations he proposed would not be
'misused' as was feared by Portland? At any rate, the incorporation of
cities was not to occur for another three decades, which, when set in

motion by the new liberal idea of colonialism in the 1830s, was, interestingly enough, the same as Simcoe's principle of creating the perfect image of the English constitution. But this idea appeared under different conditions and pressures and for different purposes than could be thought around the turn of the nineteenth century when the political climate was one of hostility toward local communities and their liberties.

Markets and Police Towns, Upper Canada

Another series of laws demonstrates that the powers to establish markets and police were entrusted to the justice of the peace in Quarter Sessions as opposed to town inhabitants. When the colonies were settled in the aftermath of the American rebellion, Upper and Lower Canada were divided into districts for the administration of justice and settlement. Each district was administered by quarterly sessions of appointed magistrates who gained and retained considerable control until the 1840s in affairs concerning towns and townships. Two of these controls were to establish markets and police in towns.

Markets. The right to establish and regulate markets within towns was conferred upon the justices of the peace of the districts of six towns in Upper Canada. In 1801, a market was established in Kingston by the legislature empowering the justices of the peace to make regulations.[54] Similar statutes were passed to establish markets in York (1814), Niagara (1817), Cornwall (1818), Perth (1822) and Amherstburg (1831).[55] In these statutes the power to regulate and to prescribe a fine for breach of regulations was given to the Quarter Sessions of the district in which the town was located. The legislation concerning markets is an indication of centralized authority for not allowing town inhabitants to concern themselves with collective regulation but to regulate them through appointed district authorities.

Police Towns. The first act to empower the justices of the peace to establish police was passed in 1816 for Kingston.[56] The second act was passed in 1817 and empowered the justices of the peace to establish and "to regulate the police within the towns of York, Sandwich and Amherstburg."[57] Such acts included the powers "to make, ordain, constitute and publish, such prudential rules and regulations as [the justices of the peace] may deem expedient...provided that such rules and regulations shall not be contrary with the laws and statutes of this Province." Another act was passed in 1819 that empowered the justices of the peace to establish and regulate police in Niagara.[58]

These five towns were designated "towns having a police established by law," or more briefly "police towns."[59] It is clear that in these early acts of market and police towns, the legislature was careful to retain power through the justices of the peace. The inhabitants of the towns were not allowed to possess any rights or liberties let alone conduct town meetings. The towns were held under centralized control. Here it should be pointed out, however, that the term 'police' did not then have the same narrow meaning we associate with it now. The term police has been used in our century primarily to denote a body of functionaries organized to maintain order and public safety, to enforce the law, and to investigate breaches of the criminal law.[60] But, as Michel Foucault has recently emphasized, things were not always this way. In European legal traditions, approximately between the 1690s and the 1860s, the police had the broader and less rigid function of the 'administering of things' such as morals, health and welfare of the subjects, regulation of conduct, relief of the poor and so on.[61] As we shall see below in the discussion of the boards of police, the term police in the phrase 'police towns' should be construed within that broader meaning. The police towns of Upper Canada were placed under the power of magistrates and as such were entities for the 'administering of things'. To put it differently, police towns were considered as polities for the administration of subjects. And these towns did not possess the liberties of incorporated bodies politic.

Boards of Police

Another series of laws was passed between 1832 and 1840 which established boards of police in nine towns in Upper Canada. With this, the institution of corporation was reintroduced in a quite distinct British North American pattern, which demonstrated continuing caution by the legislature toward the formation of bodies politic: only the members of the boards were incorporated as a body politic but not the town inhabitants. The boards of police also constituted a departure of policy from police towns that were controlled by the justices of the peace. The boards of police consisted of members elected from and by *qualified* town inhabitants.

The first incorporation of a board of police took place in 1832 in the town of Brockville, amply reflecting a new principle of establishing authority in local polities, that of delegating powers to an elected body.[62] The preamble of the act stated that "...from the great increase of the population of the Town of Brockville...it is necessary to make further provision than by law exists for the internal regulation thereof...that there shall be in the said Town a Board of Police...to be a body corporate and politic, in fact and in law, by the name of the President and Board of Police of Brockville." The rights and capacities of a corporation to perpetual succession, to sue and to be sued, to hold property, to have a seal and to make regulations were conferred on the board, whose main duty was to prevent vice and to preserve good order in the said town and "to make such rules and regulations for the improvement, good order and government of the said town as the said corporation may deem expedient, not repugnant to the laws of the Province, except so far as the same may be virtually repealed by this Act."[63] The members of the board of police would be elected. For the purposes of election the town was divided into two wards, the limits and bounds of which were stated. Each ward would then elect two members of the incorporated board. Once elected, the board was to appoint a fifth member. And then a president was to be chosen within the board.

The qualification to be a member of the board required that the town inhabitant be a freeholder or a householder paying a certain amount of rent per annum for his dwelling. A governing elite was formed whose obligation was to govern the town. The qualification to be a voter in the election required that the town inhabitant be a male householder, a subject of the king, and possessing a freehold estate. These qualifications for board membership and voting demonstrate the calculated restrictions that were put upon participation in town politics. The powers clause of the Brockville Act is worth quoting in full since this clause was repeated in all other incorporated boards of police:

That it shall and may be lawful for the said Corporation from time to time to establish such ordinances, by-laws and regulations, as they may think reasonable in the said Town, to regulate the License Victualling-houses and Ordinaries, where fruit, victuals and liquors, not distilled, shall be sold, to be eaten or drunk in such houses or groceries; to regulate Wharves and Quays; to regulate the weighing of Hay, measuring of Wood; to regulate Carts and Cartsmen; to regulate Slaughter-houses; to prevent the firing of any Guns, Muskets, Pistols, Squibs and Fireballs, or injuring or destroying Trees planted or growing for shade or ornament in the said Town; to prevent the pulling down or defacing of Sign-boards, or inscribing or drawing any indecent words, figures or pictures, on any building wall, fence or other public place; and generally to prevent vice and preserve good order in the said Town; to enter into and examine all Dwelling-houses, Ware-houses, Shops, Yards and outhouses, to ascertain whether any such places are in a dangerous state with respect to fires, and to direct them to be put in a safe and secure condition; to appoint Fire-Wardens and Fire-Engineers; to appoint and remove Fire Men; to make such rules and by-laws as may be thought expedient for the conduct of such Fire Companies as may be raised with the sanction of the said Corporation; to compel any person to aid in the extinguishment of any Fire; to require the Inhabitants to provide and keep fire-buckets and scuttles, the ladders to their houses; to stop, or authorize any other person to stop, any one riding or driving immoderately in any Street, or riding or driving on any Side-walk, or to inflict fines for any such offence; to regulate the Assize of the Bread; to prevent and abate and remove any nuisances; to restrain and prevent any horses, cattle or swine, from running at large; to prevent and remove encroachments in any Street, and to make such rules and regulations for the improvement, good order and government of the said Town as the said Corporation may deem expedient, not re-pugnant to the laws of this Province, except in so far as the same may be virtually repealed by the Act; and to enforce the due observance thereof by inflicting penalties on any person for the violation of any by-law or ordinance of the said Corporation, not exceeding one pound ten shillings.

The term 'Board of Police' may thus be misleading as to the functions which this board fulfilled. From this clause we can see that the modern concept of a police force, which means a body of trained officers en-trusted with the maintenance of public peace, covers only one of the many functions that the board of police had to fulfill in the early decades of the nineteenth century. The board of police, for example, was em-powered to regulate and alter the layout of the town if the public good required it, and it was provided that "if any person shall transgress the orders and regulations made by the said Corporation under the authority of this Act, such person shall for every such offence forfeit the sum which in every such order, rule, or regulation shall be specified."[64] On April 16, 1832, the board of police for the Town of Brockville intro-duced its first rules and regulations based on its act of incorporation.[65] The board of police then engaged in watching and steering the conduct of town inhabitants; the board appointed town wardens, who began to observe and inspect the habits and conduct of the town inhabitants.

Boards of police appeared in other towns in Upper Canada with almost identical clauses and provisions of incorporation: Hamilton (1833), Cornwall (1834), Port Hope (1834), Prescott (1834), Belleville (1834), Cobourg (1837), Picton (1837), and London (1840).[66] What these incorporated boards of police suggest is that the Upper Canada legislature was very cautious in conferring corporate capacities on towns: the boards of police had more duties and obligations than rights and liberties. Or, stated another way, these bodies politic were constituted so as to make them accept the delegated powers of the State; and, by empowering a qualified elite to govern through taxation, these commu-nities also relieved the State of the costs of governance.

Necessity of Governing Through Cities

As mentioned earlier, the concern about towns ran parallel to a concern with establishing them for purposes of government. Of course, these concerns are not and were not altogether separable from each other, and as already demonstrated, were closely related. We discussed in the previous section how the British colonial administrators carefully guarded against the formation of autonomous towns by keeping them in check. In this section, we will discuss a series of practices that were initiated to create bodies politic for government by the British colonial apparatus between the 1780s and the 1840s—the same period in which considerable hostility was developed toward the potential local autonomies. We have outlined earlier how British North American colonies were constituted as royal colonies and how towns and townships were established as polities for government and administration. Now let us focus on some details of these practices and their rationalities.

"The Scattered and Broken Fragments": Québec, 1783–1791

As Lord Dorchester observed retrospectively in 1793: "the Policy which lost those great provinces cannot preserve these scattered and broken Fragments which remain."[67] The rebellion of the thirteen colonies and the influx of disbanded soldiers and loyalists presented a new cluster of problems: the colonies of Québec, Nova Scotia and New Brunswick were confronted with the challenge of settling lands in a manner that was efficient and with people who were loyal.

Throughout the British colonial experience, the land was disposed in townships with free and common socage tenure, which meant that the 'settler' held the exclusive rights of title to land but paid rent.[68] The seigneurial land tenure, in contrast, did not confer such rights on 'habitants' who were bound with a contract to the seigneur—the person who received a large grant of land on the express condition that he concede lands to those who applied for them and whose rights and duties were laid down by the English State in minute detail.[69] The encounter with the established seigneurial regime of land tenure caused the British colonial apparatus a considerable concern. On December 7, 1763, the governor of Québec (James Murray) received detailed instructions calling for the adoption of the regime of townships, towns and free land tenure.[70] Within the span of a few years, however, the imposition of the township regime onto that of the seigneurial system was found impractical.

On July 2, 1771, the governor of Québec (Guy Carleton) received the additional instructions that revoked all previous articles related to land settlement and towns in the 1763 instructions.[71]

The governor of Québec, Haldimand, received an additional instruction from the Privy Council in July 16, 1783, stating that "Whereas many of Our Loyal Subjects Inhabitants of the Colonies and Provinces, now the United States of America, are desirous of retaining their Allegiance to Us, and of living in our Dominions, and for this purpose are disposed to take up and improve Lands in our Province of Québec...It is our Will and Pleasure, that immediately after you shall receive this Our Instruction, you do direct our Surveyor General of Lands for our said Province of Québec, to set aside and lay out such a Quantity of Land as you with the advice of our Council shall deem necessary and convenient for the Settlement of our said Loyal Subjects...who shall be desirous of becoming Settlers therein; such Lands to be divided into distinct Seigneuries or Fiefs."[72] Still, in this instruction Haldimand was asked to lay out the territory in units of seigneuries as opposed to townships, which reveals an indecisiveness on the part of the Privy Council. In 1784, Haldimand wrote a letter to the Deputy Surveyor General John Collins in which he stressed the pressing demand of 'business' for rapid land settlement. He indicated, however, that there was no strictly established rule so that, "the progress in this business will depend so much upon local circumstances and unforeseen contingencies that it would be in vain to offer any other than general instructions."[73] A year earlier, Haldimand had issued the first known instructions to survey a township in the province when he ordered John Collins to lay out lots in Cataraqui (now Kingston).[74] These instructions were still specific to a single case and within the span of a few years there was an increasing concern for establishing and regulating more effective land settlement practices.

In 1786, in response to months of intense inquiry, reflection and reconsideration of land settlement, Lord Dorchester stated in a letter to the secretary of State responsible for colonies that he was "as yet at a loss for any plan likely to give satisfaction, to a people so circumstanced as we are at present."[75] But he added that, "...what urges more immediately is an alteration in the tenure of lands to be granted by the Crown." By 1786 the land tenure system in Québec, with the exception of the earliest townships mentioned above, was seigneurial. Instead, he proposed to grant lands in free and common socage without any rent. He also cautioned that a grant should never be more than one thousand acres. Another proposal he made which became one of the most contentious issues of settlement afterwards was "...to reserve in every township of thirty thousand acres, five thousand to be granted only at a future day under the King's Special directions; These reserved parcels will enable His Majesty to reward such of His provincial Servants as may merit the Royal favour, and will also enable the Crown to create and strengthen an Aristocracy, of which the best use may be made on this Continent, where all Governments are feeble, and the general condition of things tends to a wild Democracy." Here Dorchester envisaged an idea that granting of lands could be used as a means of safeguarding against 'wild democracy'. The idea itself was a result of reconsidering the 'causes' of the problems of government the British colonial apparatus experienced in the thirteen colonies, particularly those arising from attempts at raising revenue. Now, in establishing a new colony with a 'proper' government of its population, it was thought unfit to adopt a policy "which may serve to excite animosities against the Crown."[76] Dorchester envisaged a complex land settlement plan in comparison to what was practiced in the thirteen colonies by granting lands in free and common socage, but also without rent, and combined with reserved lands for the crown for future use particularly in creating a landed aristocracy.

Upon reading this letter by Dorchester, Lord Grenville regretted that such an idea was not adopted before losing the thirteen colonies. He thought that "there is certainly great reason to regret, that this object has hitherto been overlooked, in the first establishment of all our Colonies: because, at that period, it would have been easy to have secured this point, by measures, similar to those which are said to have been adopted by Penn, in the original settlement of Pennsylvania; who, by reserving to himself, and to his heirs, a certain portion of Land, situated in the middle of every Grant made to individuals, secured a property, which could not but increase, in value, in proportion to the increase, of the Colony itself."[77] But Glenville thought that Lord Dorchester recommended this idea "...with a view of retaining the power of rewarding individuals, than with that of securing a revenue to the Crown, for the purposes of the Provincial Government."[78] Lord Grenville suggested instead to focus solely on the use of reserved lands as a source of revenue. The reserved lands could thus be used as a remedy for this problem perhaps in the long run. Meanwhile, these lands could be used to create a 'landed aristocracy' to foster the principles of allegiance to the Crown. This particular rendering of the notion of reserved lands, both as a diagnosis and as a means of preventing a potential repeat of the rebellion also prepared the conditions for regulated settlement. Grenville expressed this enthusiasm to Dorchester by stating that "if [this idea] had been adopted when the Old Colonies were first settled, [we] would have retained them to this hour in obedience and Loyalty. I confess that I am very particularly anxious to find myself sufficiently informed to be able to recommend to His Majesty, the adoption of some system of this nature...and as to the best mode of carrying it into effect, in the different Provinces under the King's Government in North America."[79]

From the early correspondence on settlement we can see that the immediate concern of the colonial apparatus was to people British North America rapidly with loyal subjects. The immensity of this task is often stated: millions of acres of land had to be opened up for settlement while simultaneously inculcating loyalty in the subjects, without any as yet established institution to coordinate settlement, lay out townships, guide settlers and establish authority among them. As a response to the rising problems of government and administration a land committee was established in 1787 within the governing council. It began to hold regular meetings on land settlement, the records of which contain significant thoughts on the necessity of governing through towns.

On January 25, 1788, the committee established the general rule that "the increase of people is the means of advancing the wealth and strength of any country, that therefore industrious men ought to be encouraged to come from all quarters to settle in this Province (more especially those who can bring effects along with them) provided they will take the oaths prescribed and are all well attached to the British Government."[80] But this attachment was not taken for granted; on the contrary, it had to be produced since "men will always be disposed to support that Government that protects them in their rights and where their property is in perfect safety."[81] In order to advance the wealth of the territory, it was not enough, therefore, to people it, but to people it with subjects who demonstrated their loyalty to the State. This was an important principle that established one of the most significant functions of this committee, namely, the processing of applicants (petitioners) for land. This process included examination of their 'pretensions', character and abilities to improve land, as well as judgment regarding the quantity and location of the land to be granted. In addition, the committee continued to establish further principles as the experience of processing applicants accumulated. The processing of petitioners by the land committee, however, became difficult administratively, as their numbers increased significantly. On December 29, 1788, in a land committee meeting, Lord Dorchester "informed the [Governing] Council that representations having been made to him on his late visit to the western districts of delay and expense being occasioned to many loyalists desirous of forming settlements in the upper country, from the want of authority on the spot for allotting lands for them, He had therefore to remedy that inconvenience [and] appointed the following boards in the Districts of Mecklenburg, Luneburg, Montréal and Nassau."[82] This was the first time the new districts were established for administration. In its meeting on February 17, 1789, the land committee established its first rules and regulations, which provided for the formation of land boards in each district "to be empowered to receive applications for grants of parcels of the waste lands of the Crown."[83] The land board for each district was required to "hold stated and periodical meetings made publicly known; to give free and easy access to petitioners; and to examine their loyalty, character and pretensions"[84] and after becoming "well satisfied of the safety and propriety of admitting the petitioner to become an inhabitant of this Province the Board administer to him the Oath of Fidelity and Allegiance; and then give him a certificate to the Surveyor General, or any person authorized to act as an agent."[85] In other words, the district land boards assumed functions that originated with the land committee of the governing council in dealing with land settlement. This transfer of functions to district land boards entailed a further codification of rules on townships and towns in an attempt to coordinate the proceedings of different land boards, and to assure consistency among their activities.

The emphasis on towns and the necessity of settling in townships surfaced quite strongly in these rules and regulations. "That the Surveyor General's Office for the purpose of combining the strength of the settlers and rendering them mutually assistant to each other, lay out the tracts or townships to be granted as nearly contiguous to each other as the nature of the country will permit, exercising all due care to give them certainty in the descriptions of their boundaries and locations, observing in each Township to lay out Town plots, Glebes and other spaces for public uses."[86] The plan of these townships and town plots was considered as a model to be uniformly applied throughout the territory. "The dimensions of every inland Township shall be ten miles square, and such as are situated upon a navigable river or water shall have a front of nine miles, and be twelve miles in depth, and they shall be laid out and subdivided respectively in the [prescribed] manner...and the Surveyor General's Office shall prepare accurate plans according to the above particulars, which shall be filed in the Council Office to be followed as a general model, subject to such deviations respecting the site of the Town and directions of the roads, as local circumstances may render more eligible for the general convenience of the settlers. But in every such case it shall be the duty of the Surveyor-General and his Agents or Deputy Surveyors to report the reasons for such deviation to the Governor and Commander in Chief for the time being with all convenient speed."[87] In the same meeting of the land committee in which these rules and regulations were drafted, a series of 'model township plans' were prepared for "further consideration and eventual adoption of one which seemed more expedient."[88]

To establish stricter guidelines to regulate the establishment of townships and towns, the committee issued "additional rules and regulations" on August 21, 1789:[89] (i) "The dimensions of every inland township shall be ten miles square and such as situated upon a navigable river or water shall have a front of nine miles and be twelve miles in depth"; (ii) "The town plot in every township shall be one mile square. In an inland township it shall be situated in the centre thereof and in a township upon a navigable river or water, it shall be in the centre of the front bordering upon the river or water"; (iii) "Every town lot shall contain one acre or less"; (iv) "Every township lot shall contain twenty-four acres or less"; (v) "Every farm lot shall contain two hundred acres more or less"; (vi) "There shall be a public square or parade in the centre of the town containing four acres more or less." Strict control was exercised in applying these rules and regulations: "inasmuch as local circumstances may sometimes render a deviation from the foregoing orders respecting the site of the town and the directions of the roads, more eligible for the general convenience of the settlers, the boards [were] authorized to direct such deviations therefrom in the said particulars, as the circumstances may require; but the surveyors shall, on no pretense whatever, make any deviation from the general orders, in these or any other respects, but by the written authority of the Boards."[90] The land boards were also instructed "for the exercise of due caution in the ordering of any such deviation from the general models respecting the sites of towns and the directions of roads, as may be authorized by the boards under the preceding article, it shall be the duty of the boards as often as one or more new townships are to be laid out, to call in magistrates [justices of the peace of the Quarter Sessions], the officers of the militia and other intelligent planters of the vicinity thereof of the district at large as the importance of the case may require; to assist in their deliberations respecting the aforesaid particulars; the majority of whom and of the members of the board present shall determine the necessity of the deviation proposed and the proper spot for the town, and the proper directions of the roads in every such township, and the board shall thereupon proceed to authorize and report the same as directed in the preceding article."[91]

The period between February 17, 1787, and December 24, 1791, when the land committee held significant meetings and established rules and regulations concerning the land settlement in British North American colonies, attests to the emphasis placed upon regular settlement by British colonial apparatus.

The New Towns of Upper Canada

When Québec was divided into the two provinces of Upper Canada and Lower Canada in 1791, Lord Dorchester was the governor and commander in chief of British North American colonies. On September 16, 1791, Dorchester received detailed instructions regarding land settlement and towns from the Privy Council. The thrust of these instructions endorses the experience accumulated in the period between 1784 and 1791. Since "nothing can more effectively tend to the speedy settling of Our said Province of Lower Canada, the Security of the Property of our Subjects and the Advancement of our Revenue, than the disposal of such Lands as are Our Property upon reasonable terms, and the establishing of a regular and proper method of Proceeding, with respect to the passing of Grants of such Lands. It is therefore Our Will and Pleasure, that all and every Person and Persons who shall apply for any Grant or Grants of Land, shall previous to their obtaining the same, make it appear that they are in a condition to cultivate and improve the same."[92] The theme of "a regular and proper mode of proceeding with land granting" was emphasized here but with one further qualification, that is, land grants were restricted to those who demonstrated the ability to improve the land speedily. Moreover, it was urged in these instructions that persons, before admission, make a declaration of obedience besides taking the usual oath of allegiance "in order to prevent any Persons disaffected to Us and Our Government from becoming Settlers."[93]

This emphasis on the character of the subjects as the target of government and its relation with land settlement was now firmly established in political and legal practice. John Graves Simcoe, upon his appointment as the lieutenant governor of Upper Canada in 1792, in accordance with the instructions of speedy settlement, proposed to circulate a proclamation to the thirteen colonies to encourage immigration to the Canadas. The secretary of the State, Henry Dundas, expressed his concerns about attracting any population: "...in the very Infancy of the Province under your Government such Emigrations would not be productive of all the good consequences...Population is often the effect, but never I believe was, or will be, the cause of the prosperity of any Country."[94] And he added, "I am well aware that what is true and applies in many instances, may not apply to a Country of the extent of Upper Canada; but an engrafted Population, (if I may so call it), to a great extent and outrunning, (as it must do), all those regulations, laws, usage, and customs, which grow up and go hand in hand with a progressive and regular Population, must I conceive in all cases be attended with a want of that regularity, and stability, which all, but particularly Colonial Governments, require."[95] The regularity and stability of a population as requirements of specifically colonial governments is an important qualification. Another, and perhaps more important one, is that a population, however regular and stable, is not the cause but the effect of prosperity, that is, the character, customs, usage, or, in other words, discipline of the population is constitutive of wealth: it is not enough that the population be large, dense and industrious; it must also be obedient, disciplined and controlled. The British colonial apparatus redefined and refined its target of governance, partly in response to the consequences of the American Revolution. Perhaps more than anyone else at the time, Simcoe was well aware of this as is clear from his prompt response to the above letter from Dundas. In this response he argued that he noticed the problem, but that if revenue was to be created from the reserved lands then the population increase must be immediate and rapid.[96] It appeared that the erection of towns would solve the problem of securing rapid population growth, while, and this is the point here, fully satisfying the requirement of obedience and governability. Town life was thought to induce "habits of Civilization and Obedience to just Government" and a "Spirit of Loyalty to His Majesty, and attachment to the British Nation."[97] The gradual crystallization of the specific notion of discipline prepared the conditions for reconsidering the relations among wealth, population and territory through which the town appeared as a solution.

Until this reconsideration, towns had figured as spots, locations within townships. This view was captured quite succinctly at an executive council meeting of Lower Canada in February 4, 1792. The committee stated

> that the Proclamation should also be silent, as to the Town Spots in the large Townships to be granted, Husbandry being the first object, and Village Settlements following as the Population by Farmers advances, and then in such locations as Accident or a coincidence of circumstances may direct: and for this reason, the Proclamation is so framed as

to reserve to the Government, the power of devoting a proportion for Villages, where the utility of the measure shall become apparent, and a Township to be created, shall be so well known, as to enable the Crown to provide for a close settlement in it, and to designate the Spot.[98]

On the need for 'immediate and rapid' population, and the importance of selecting 'progressive and regular' settlers, there was agreement.[99] But, leaving things to accident or circumstance, relegating town planting to secondary importance seemed improper to Simcoe.[100] In order to achieve this immediacy, population concentration and growth should not be left merely to agriculture in an organic manner as the above Lower Canada committee suggestion intimated.[101] Rather, towns must be the agents of this immediate and rapid settlement by obedient and controllable subjects. Thus, the erection of towns became a prominent practice as part of the problem of governance in the Canadas.

Use of Settlement Agents and Agencies

The settling and peopling of British North America was a deliberate intention of the colonial apparatus in the eighteenth century, which relied significantly on settlers procured from European countries.[102] The use of companies and agents to accomplish settlement was a widespread instrument.[103] But one problem of erecting towns was the absence of local authorities that would, on the one hand, sustain and enforce law and loyalty and, on the other, take care of matters that were local in character, such as the maintenance and building of roads, the regulation of markets and so on. In short, the colonial authorities lacked those institutions that extend the administration and government to towns effectively and efficiently. One early response to this problem was to entrust leaders or associates with settling and ordering towns.

William Berczy was a German settlement agent who procured German settlers in Hamburg for a settlement company in London for the Genesee territories in New York.[104] William Berczy was one of these agents who arrived in New York in 1792, and whose path converged with the events that were unfolding in British North America. His "Narrative" furnishes us with an interesting and detailed account of ideas that were embodied in the practices of settlement agents and their relations with the governor and the council, which he sketched around 1812.

In the preface, Berczy recounted that before the rebellion of the thirteen colonies there was hardly any population in Upper Canada and the population in Lower Canada was 'thin' and of French origin. After

1783 the British government, as Berczy continues, decided to open up Upper Canada for settlement. But the requirement that these territories must be settled rapidly meant that the government wanted a stronghold in "...the neighbourhood of an aspiring, growing and newly emancipated Commonwealth."[105] For the rapid peopling of territories the colonial administration relied on colonists from Europe and the granting of land in free and common socage. Berczy noted that "this mode of settling the British Provinces of the Continent of North America, was generally pursued from 1784 until 1792, when the proclamation of the 7th February of the same year was issued, and partly even till 1794, in which time the last transport of two vessels with 500 persons were sent out from England to North America, and these settlers established in Upper Canada."[106] Berczy, however, argues that this mode of peopling territories was costly and slow: "In order to take off from the British Nation that heavy burden and never-the-less to accomplish the necessary and desired purpose of promoting, even probably with more success, the speedy settlement of Canada, Government adopted the new plan of Granting lands in whole Townships or other large tracts." Berczy contends that the colonial administration "...foresaw that for the acceleration of the settlement, it was necessary that men of higher influence, of more property, than could possess the lower and generally indigent classes of men, should find it an object worth their attention, to lay out necessary pounds required for the introduction, and the support of new and beginning settlers."[107] These 'ideas of government' naturally led the "...private interest to cooperate with the public spirit in benefiting society at large."[108] What Berczy expresses here is how the creation of bodies politic for the government in British North America was accomplished by the colonial apparatus, by relying on influential leaders and proprietors to handle the immediate problems of the exercise of power in towns. Berczy then brilliantly observes the 'historical' conditions under which his life path converged with these events: "...these were the principles which the Government of Canada, insinuated to the applicants and contractors for Townships, and those were the *vehicles* by which not only these grantees of Townships, but the whole public of Canada and the United States were so deeply impressed..." and "under these circumstances, myself and a great many other persons in Upper and Lower Canada, were induced to trust to the promises and assurances held out by the Provincial Governments, respecting Grants of Townships of the waste lands of the Crown."[109]

In 1794, Berczy applied to the executive council of Upper Canada for a million acres of land. In May 1794, he was required to appear before the council. Simcoe expressed interest in Berczy's 'project' but one million acres was found so large a tract of land before Berczy "...had given proofs of [his] ability and punctuality in accomplishing [his] engagements in undertaking of such magnitude."[110] Upon this, Berczy promised to bring emigrants of more wealthy classes, in addition to those who now were in Genesee, and also good German settlers, from Pennsylvania and New York. Upon these promises Berczy was granted 64,000 acres of land *free of reserves*. He was also promised further grants of townships if he succeeded in this first project.

After this meeting, Berczy left for Genesee, but before he initiated the resettlement of his people he received a message from Simcoe "...by which [Berczy] was desired to wait once more upon him before [Berczy's] departure."[111] The message said that Simcoe wished to discuss with Berczy "some matters of consequence."[112] Berczy recounted:

> In this conference he acquainted me with the intention of the British Government to build Toronto, the new City of York, *which was to become the metropolis of Upper Canada*, and the seat of Government of the Province, he therefore proposed that I should exchange those lands which in conformity to my petition, the executive council had granted me between Lake Erie, and the River Thames (Latrenche) for a tract of equal extent situated on Yonge Street behind the intended seat of Government, in order to fix my first settlement in that district...he added that if I should thus assist Government by peopling this district, he shall himself authorize by his private instructions, and the power vested in him to promote equally my private interest in a more liberal and extensive manner, and as proof of it he offered to me at the same time, to add immediately to the first grant of 64,000 acres two Townships more, 90,000 acres of grantable lands if I would consent to the proposed plan of exchange and settlement.[113]

Berczy was impressed by the willingness of the governor and thought that "...he was convinced that not only I should sooner accomplish the desired object, but give to his Sovereign, at the same time, better and more loyal subjects."[114] After this meeting Berczy returned to the United States and explained his plans to his partners and people. He came back to Upper Canada within a month with more than what he promised to Simcoe, consisting of sixty-six heads of families. Upon his return, Berczy met with Simcoe again and reminded him about the two additional townships that he had been promised. Simcoe, according to Berczy, responded, "Yes Berczy, you deserve all my attention, not only have you accomplished in so short a time, more than you have promised, to the Provincial Government concerning the number of your settlers, but you are now ready to do us a service, very essential for the accomplishment of the views of the British Government." And Berczy added, "upon this the Governor sent for the Surveyor General [D.W. Smith] with the order to bring with him the map of the province."[115]

Additional townships were not the only rewards that were offered to Berczy's services. Berczy says, "At our meeting at York he manifested to me in the most flattering manner his satisfaction, and as a proof of his approbation he desired me to accept the commission of a magistrate in the district of York, and the commission of a Captain of the Militia, in order to embody my people, as well as the rest of the new neighboring settlers in a Militia Company." The rest of the Berczy 'case' or story, however, was not as straightforward as is so far recounted in his "Narrative." His settlement in Markham did not proceed with the speed he envisaged. Two additional townships that were promised were never granted to him. And, after Simcoe left, his settlers were questioned as to their legal status as alien property owners in Upper Canada for which Berczy had to visit London in 1799 to clarify the situation. At any rate, the Berczy case demonstrates one of the most significant instruments that were used in peopling British North America after 1792: settlement agents and agencies whose political use remains inadequately explored and warrants further research. The case really shows what was expected of local notables as agents of governance in the absence of local agencies. It, in turn, sheds some light on what kinds of obligations and responsibilities were imposed on local agencies.

The Birth of a Town: York

Another important case that demonstrates the necessity of governing through towns and cities was the founding of the Town of York (later Toronto). However, here our purpose is not to discuss all events leading up to the founding of York but to focus on a series of correspondence between Simcoe and Dundas, which was mentioned above and which formed the basis of discussion in the executive council of Upper Canada to found York. This correspondence spanned the period from 1792 to 1795. It embodies important ideas with regard to the necessity of governing through towns.[116]

In an executive council meeting held on April 6, 1796, this correspondence was laid before the committee members in working "to promote speedy establishment and welfare of the Town of York, its vicinity and dependencies."[117] The committee focused on two letters in particular that Simcoe had written to Dundas as Dundas had responded positively to both. In the first letter, which was written on September

16, 1793, Simcoe transmitted "the plan for the arrangement of future Townships in this Province which the Executive Council directed to be carried into execution as it seems to them to be properly calculated to enforce the Provisions for the reserves of the Church and the Crown."[118] At the committee meeting, mentioned earlier, model township plans were produced.[119] Simcoe informed Dundas that "in order to lessen the Expenses of Survey, the Council adopted the Plan No. 2 for a certain range of Townships which had been previously surveyed on the Borders of Lake Ontario, and which plan equally as the general one allots the due reservations."[120] This plan was also called a 'checkered plan'.

Simcoe also outlined various exceptions that had to be made in implementing this model plan. For example, the townships that had been laid out before this plan would be exempt from the allotment of the reserves. An important exception related to York: "The great importance that it appears to the Council to promote the erection of towns has also occasioned them to deviate from the general plan to assist the settlement at Toronto, or York."[121] Simcoe thought it was "expedient to reserve the whole of the Broken Fronts for Garrison purposes as well as to prevent the scattering of the Inhabitants in such situations as their Fancy or Interest might induce them, which would ever prevent that compactness in a Town, which it seems proper to establish." Simcoe also informed Dundas that "the reserves in Lower Canada being made in large Masses has occasioned some Persons to petition that the same system might be followed in this Province, but it did not seem expedient to the Council to make any alteration in the Plan they had maturely adopted." In another letter to Dundas on September 20, 1793, Simcoe sent "an actual survey of the harbour of York, later Toronto, the proper naval and military arsenal of Lake Ontario."[122]

In response to these letters Dundas stated, on March 16, 1794, that "the Plan for future Townships transmitted in your Letter of the same number and date with that which I have been answering, seems in placing the Reserves for the Crown and the Church, to have attended to the Spirit and Principles of the late Canada Act."[123] But he argued that "although there may be a good reason for making those Reserves in the Back Lands, in the particular Township of York, yet in that Township also, there should be a Reservation in the Front Concessions for the Glebe and Residence of the Clergyman, who shall be appointed the Rector under the Provisions of the Act." The secretary of State in Whitehall concerning himself with such minute matters shows the importance accorded to settlement affairs. Dundas further informed Simcoe that "it was at first proposed to make the Reserves in Lower

Canada in large Masses, but the same has been laid aside, in consequence of directions from hence." As to the question of "where to establish the chief naval station of the Province," Dundas was "of the same opinion with [Simcoe] that York is the most proper place for it."[124] In response to Dundas, on June 20, 1794, Simcoe wrote: "in the distribution of the front lots of the Town of York as it seemed to be probable that for a time this station would be the residence of the Government of the country, they were so laid out as to give one hundred acres to each of the officers of Government as an inducement to build a house in the town and a remuneration for its expense, but these grants I did not choose to make final until I understood your pleasure on the subject. A glebe and a residence for the clergyman were amongst such appropriations, but with the intention that such lands should be returned with the benefice."[125] Simcoe assured Dundas that his instructions would be attended to and "in the course of a few days a final ratification of the allotments will take place."[126] In another letter on June 21, 1794, Simcoe elaborated to Dundas his insistence on the location of troops: "...the most certain means of erecting Towns in this Province necessary in all respects for the establishment of the King's Authority and the general Welfare of the Province, is by the station of Troops in their vicinity, and selecting for that purpose places marked by natural advantages, the confluence of Rivers, the security of Harbours or the termination of Portages. The regiment that is annually cantoned in Lower Canada, on any opposite situation, would long before this, have given *Birth to a flourishing Town*, and not have left that Province without a vestige of its belonging to Great Britain, but the Garrison of Québec or factory of Montréal."[127] And he added: "It is therefore I conceive Wisdom to apply the means which Government must allow for the defence of this Colony in its Infancy to such purposes as may create a solid and permanent system, which would never spring up merely from Agriculture, and would be late indeed, if left to the culture of Mercantile Monopoly."

Simcoe thus conceived the erection of towns as agents of population increase and as the proper means of exercising political authority as opposed to leaving the emergence of towns to uncontrolled forces such as the vagaries of agricultural economics, trade or mercantile monopoly. In placing a great emphasis on the stationing of troops to erect towns, Simcoe used an instrument which was already under his control. The settlement of troops to erect towns was used as much for civil purposes as it was for the military ones. In a report he wrote to the Privy Council, he argued that "to place the Government of Upper Canada on solid foundations, [he had] always...esteemed it necessary that its seat of

Government should be removed from all immediate apprehension of danger."[128] The perception of external danger was, however, a secondary consideration for Simcoe to require a central seat of power in a town, for such a town

> also will lead, by possessing a natural and strongly marked boundary to that condensation of its inhabitants which will give to them in point of strength, a great superiority over their neighbors, who will probably for ages stretch out their settlements in a narrow line upon the margin of the Lakes and Waters opposite to the Province. It has therefore been adopted as a principle, so to form the place for future Establishments in this Colony, as to avoid the errors which the former settlements of the United States and Canadians have fallen into; and to second those advantages which nature seems to have pointed out; a central Capital, from whence should flow loyalty, attachment, and respect to the British Government and all those principles, qualities and manners which are of eminent use in decorating and strengthening such an attachment.[129]

After discussing these issues and considering in length the correspondence between Simcoe and Dundas, the executive council formed "a committee in order to take this statement into consideration..." and initiate procedures "to give effectual support to the growth and welfare of the Town of York."[130] The committee was directed to proceed with six instructions. From April 6 to May 28, 1796, the committee on York prepared recommendations for the erection of the town of York. These instructions and the committee's responses and recommendations were as follows.[131] "[i] To examine and report to His Excellency in Council upon all former proceedings of the Council relative to the settling the lands of the Crown in the Town and Township of York, and in their vicinity, and to state such parts thereof as shall seem just and expedient to be finally ratified and confirmed. For this purpose to call upon the Acting Surveyor General forthwith to lay before the Committee the several plans in his office of the Town and Township of York with a return of each and every assignment he has directed to make therein, and any documents in his possession relative thereto." The committee prepared a detailed schedule of all subjects who had been assigned lots in the Township of York since May 25, 1793. This information was based on the records in the Surveyor General's Office. The schedule included names of petitioners, original petitions filed, lot designation, concession and the recommendations and assignments prepared by the Acting Surveyor General David W. Smith. "[ii] To summon every person to whom a certificate or Order of Council has been given, or assignment has been made as a settler on Yonge Street, to appear of himself or his lawful agent before the Committee and to recommend the grant of lands to those who may seem duly entitled to the same." In compliance with this instruction, "the committee summoned every person to whom a certificate of Order of Council had been given, or assignment had been made as a settler on Yonge Street, to appear before the committee" and transmitted the results with recommendations. It appears that some persons had failed to improve their land and build houses in which case they were not recommended to occupy lots on Yonge Street.[132] The committee also recommended that "whenever Your Excellency in Council may judge proper to grant the prayer of a petition for a lot [on] either [Yonge or Dundas], the resolution thereon shall be so worded as to suspend an assignment thereof from issuing from the Surveyor's Office until Your Excellency in Council shall permit it, upon being satisfied that the applicant has built a house thereon and actually dwelled therein."[133] "[iii] To call upon the settlers in the Township of York and to confirm such grants therein as may be proper." "The Committee proceeded next to carry into execution the third article of the [instructions] by calling upon the settlers in the Township of York and confirming them in their possessions, agreeable to Excellency's directions." The names of those who appeared were included in the report. "[iv] To report what period, in the opinion of the Committee, ought to be allotted to each officer of the Government for the construction of a house in the front lots of the Town of York agreeably to a plan that shall be recommended by the Committee to His Excellency, provided such officers receive one hundred acres of land respectively in the first concession of the Township of York and adjacent to the town, in aid of the expense necessary to the erection of such an house conformably to the original principle." "The Committee [recommended] that every applicant for a town lot shall be obliged by his licence of occupation to lay down his house on a line which shall be marked for him by the Surveyor, which line in the front of the first range shall be retired twelve feet from the edge of the street in order to allow a space for palisades or other ornaments in front of the buildings at the pleasure of the occupant, and that the front of all the other back buildings shall be on an exact line with the side of streets."[134] "It is also recommended to allow three years for the completion of their plan before officers of Government shall be considered as having forfeited their claim to the 100 acres in the first concession." The names of persons who were assigned a town lot under the above conditions appear in the report. "[v] To assign such portion of land as may hereafter reimburse Government for the expenses incurred in the opening of Yonge Street." In response to this instruction, they recommended to reallocate a person (William Berczy) on Yonge street who had high value lands and sell the lands "for whatever sum they may bring, and the money applied for the expenses incurred in opening Yonge Street."[135] "[vi] To adjust such regulations as may be expedient and not burdensome, to give an architectural uniformity to the town, an object of very great importance in the establishment of a new province and to propose whatsoever may have a tendency to promote the welfare and speedy settlement thereof." As to this last instruction, the committee thought that this issue "has been already attended to in the previous recommendations of the Committee, and it only remains for them to suggest the propriety of appropriating certain blocks in suitable situations for a church, a gaol [jail], a court house and a market place."

The beginnings of the town of York tell us how detailed, calculated and elaborate efforts were used for the making of a town. From the character of subjects who occupied the town to its 'architectural uniformity', every detail of making a town a reality was thought of. The town was created as an agent of rapid settlement but also, and at the same time, it was created "in order to induce habits of Civilization and Obedience to just Government and to cherish the Spirit of Loyalty to his Majesty, and attachment to the British Nation."[136]

Tension Released:
Rebellions in Upper and Lower Canada

From the evidence adduced in the last section, it is apparent that as much as there was a fear of local liberties, there was also considerable effort to settle in towns and townships. There was no doubt in the minds of English statesmen, administrators and legislators that the formula of royal colonies required settlement in towns and townships at least with provisions for representation and taxation. The question was how to settle colonists in such communities and at the same time form allegiance amongst them to authority because it was also known from experience that local communities without close supervision developed other allegiances and loyalties—they became 'little republics'. This was the tension between the two themes of colonial discourse on cities: a tension between centralized authority and potential local autonomy.

And yet, the rebellions in both Upper and Lower Canada demonstrated that retaining central authority without diffusion of that authority had unpredictable or disastrous consequences. Without established local authorities, the centralization of power apparently polarized opposition. This argument was made very passionately and eloquently by Sydenham upon his appointment as the governor general of British North America in 1840. He went on to elaborate his point, which is worth quoting at length since it is one of the clearest statements by a British statesmen on the relations between the rebellions and the absence of municipal corporations:

> Owing to this [lack of a municipal system], duties the most unfit to be discharged by the general legislature are thrown upon it; powers equally dangerous to the subject and to the Crown are assumed by the Assembly. The people receive no training in those habits of self-government which are indispensable to enable them rightly to exercise the power of choosing representatives in Parliament. No field is open for the gratification of ambition in a narrow circle, and no opportunity given for testing the talents or integrity of those who are candidates for popular favour. The people acquire no habits of those self-dependence for the attainment of their own local objects. Whatever uneasiness they may feel—whatever little improvement in their respective neighborhoods may appear to be neglected, affords grounds for complaint against the executive. All is charged directly upon the Government, and a host of discontented spirits are ever ready to excite these feelings. On the other hand while the Government is thus brought directly in contact with the people, it has neither any officer in its own confidence in the different parts of these extended provinces from whom it can seek information, nor is there any recognized body enjoying the public confidence with whom it can communicate, either to determine what are the real wants and wishes of the locality, or through whom it may afford explanation.[137]

For Sydenham, under these conditions, the rebellions were almost inevitable. How could a territory be governed without certain techniques that could both effectively deal with the most minute matters and also allow people to participate in their own government? The legal and political measures formulated to contain this tension shortly before the rebellions can be seen as formative in the birth of the modern city as a corporation in British North America. For the establishment of institutions that conferred calculated powers on communities in order to contain the tension between the central authority and local autonomy went a long way to discipline (in the sense of inculcating habits in) colonists to participate in local politics within prescribed terms and conditions. These attempts also reveal that the British colonial apparatus began to demonstrate a recognition that initiating incorporated towns and cities was a means to govern the colonies effectively and efficiently. Lord Sydenham expressed this quite clearly when he said that he was convinced that "the misgovernment of [British colonies] is to be found in the absence of Local Government."[138] He was also convinced that the rebellions could have been avoided if the experiments in Upper Canada had been more successful, thoughtful and extensive.[139] By the 1830s then, with the release of tension between central authority and local autonomy, and with the transformations that were occurring in England, cities as corporations were being rethought and reconsidered. It is a noteworthy aspect of British North American history that one of its most intense periods is enveloped in rebellions—the successful rebellion of the thirteen colonies, which precipitated its beginnings, and the unsuccessful uprisings, which drew intense attention from British statesmen and legislators in the late 1830s. But the interpretation of the rebellions and the steps taken to deal with them differed between these periods. While in the 1780s the British colonial apparatus identified towns as causes of the American rebellion, in the 1830s it attributed the British North American rebellions to their absence. The difference in diagnosis is very important, and it signifies the difference between early modern and modern attitudes toward the city as a corporation. While the early modern attitude was concerned with restricting autonomous liberties that were defined by citizens, the modern attitude was confident in cities as apparatuses of governance created by law. When Sydenham was lamenting the absence of cities, he had in mind *modern* cities—cities with governing elites and their voters.

Now let us turn to the 1830s and the 1840s to see the birth of the modern city as a corporation in British North America.

Notes

1. Gordon T. Stewart, *The Origins of Canadian Politics* (Vancouver, 1986), p. 20.
2. See Instructions to Governor Murray, December 7, 1763, *Third Report*, article 51.
3. Stewart, *Origins of Canadian Politics*, p. 21.
4. The best and the most comprehensive account of this period is by Helen T. Manning, *British Colonial Government After the American Revolution, 1782–1820* (New Haven, 1933); see also John W. Cell, *British Colonial Administration in the Mid-Nineteenth Century: The Policy-Making Process* (New Haven, 1970) which contains a brief discussion of the organization of the Colonial Office in the 1800s; Klaus Knorr, *British Colonial Theories, 1570–1850* (Toronto, 1944) contains a discussion of the prevalent ideas in this period.
5. Phillip A. Buckner, *The Transition to Responsible Government: British Policy in British North America, 1815–1850* (London, 1985), p. 51.
6. The impact of this was one of the most popular periods of Canadian history: the family compact. See a recent account by Stewart, *Origins of Canadian Politics*.
7. "Report of the Select Committee on the State of the Civil Government in Canada," *Parliamentary Papers*, House of Commons, July 22, 1828. W. P. M. Kennedy, ed., *Documents of the Canadian Constitution, 1759–1915*, 1st ed. (Toronto, 1918).
8. Kennedy, *Statutes*, p. 350.
9. John George Bourinot, *Local Government in Canada: An Historical Study* (Baltimore, 1887), p. 26.
10. Bourinot, *Local Government*, "We have abundant evidence that at this time the authorities viewed with disfavour any attempt to establish a system of town government similar to that so long in operation in New England." On the 14th of April 1770, the Governor and Council passed a resolution that "the proceedings of the people in calling town-meetings for discussing questions relative to law and government and such other purposes, are contrary to law, and if persisted in, it is ordered that the parties be prosecuted by the attorney-general." p. 44.
11. Adam Shortt, "The Beginning of Municipal Government in Ontario," *Transactions of the Canadian Institute*, vol. vii, 1902, p. 410.
12. James H. Aitchison, "The Development of Local Government, 1783–1850" (unpublished Ph.D. dissertation, University of Toronto, 1953), p. 188. Also see C. F. J. Whebell, "Robert Baldwin and Decentralization, 1841–1849" and G. T. Glazebrook, "The Origins of Local Government" in Armstrong, F. H. et al., eds., *Aspects of Nineteenth Century Ontario* (Toronto, 1974).
13. D. W. Smith to Askin, October 2, 1792, *Simcoe Papers*, vol. i, p. 231.
14. Chief Justice William Smith to Dorchester, February 5, 1790, Kennedy, *Statutes*, p. 290.
15. Martin, *Empire and Commonwealth*, pp. 18, 19 note 3.
16. "Papers Relating to the First Settlement of Halifax, 1749–1756," in T. B. Akins, ed., *Selections from the Public Documents of Nova Scotia* (Halifax, 1869).
17. Instructions to Edward Cornwallis in Akins, *Selections*, p. 502.
18. "Letter from Governor Cornwallis relating to the First steps in the Founding of Halifax," *Report of the Public Archives of Canada* (Ottawa, 1939), pp. 47–49.
19. Akins, *Selections*, p. 574.

20. Akins, *Selections*, p. 499.
21. "Papers Relating to the First Establishment of a Representative Assembly in Nova Scotia, 1755–1761," Akins, *Selections*, p. 715.
22. Lords of Trade to Governor Lawrence, July 8, 1756, in Akins, *Selections*, p. 715.
23. Esther C. Wright, "The Settlement of New Brunswick: An Advance Towards Democracy," *Canadian Historical Association Report*, 1944, p. 55.
24. G. A. Stelter "Urban Planning and Development in Upper Canada," in W. Borah, J. Hardoy, and G. A. Stelter, eds., *Urbanization in the Americas* (Ottawa, 1980).
25. David J. Wood, "Grand Design on the Fringes of Empire: New Towns for British North, America," *Canadian Geographer*, vol. xxvi, 1982, pp. 243–255.
26. Shortt, "The Beginning of Municipal Government," p. 422.
27. *Canada's First City: The Charter of 1785 and Common Council Proceedings under Mayor G. G. Ludlow, 1785–1795* (Saint John, New Brunswick, 1962), pp. 3–46.
28. *First Report of the Commission on Municipal Institutions*, Ontario Legislative Assembly, Sessional Papers, no. 42, 1888, p. 26.
29. *Canada's First City*, p. 3.
30. *Canada's First City*, p. 3.
31. *Canada's First City*, p. 3.
32. The letter is transcribed in *Canada's First City*, p. 50.
33. *Canada's First City*, p. 50.
34. Carleton wrote: "I have on every occasion cautiously avoided publishing any ordinances-in-council which could lead to the belief of an intention to govern without an assembly, but I think on all accounts it will be best that the American's spirit of innovation should not be nursed among the loyal refugees by the introduction of acts of the Legislature for purposes to which the common law and the practice of the best regulated colonies, the Crown alone is acknowledged to be competent."
35. Gary B. Nash, *The Urban Crucible: The Northern Seaports and the Origins of the American Revolution* (London, 1986) documents the reluctant engagement of New York in the rebellion as opposed to Boston and Philadelphia. See pp. 39–43.
36. *Canada's First City*, pp. 4–5.
37. T. W. Acheson, *Saint John* (Toronto, 1985), p. 32.
38. *Canada's First City*, pp. 14–15.
39. *Canada's First City*, pp. 21–22.
40. *Canada's First City*, pp. 116–117.
41. *Canada's First City*, p. 45.
42. Adam Shortt, "The Beginning of Municipal Government in Ontario," *Transactions of the Canadian Institute*, 1902, vol. vii, p. 409; George M. Betts, "Municipal Government and Politics," G. J. J. Tulchinsky, ed., *To Preserve and Defend: Essays on the Nineteenth-Century Kingston* (Montreal, 1976); T. B. Akins, *History of Halifax City* (Halifax, 1895).
43. "An act to provide for the Nomination and Appointment of Parish and Town Officers within this Province," *Statutes of Upper Canada*, July 9, 1793, 33 George III, c. 2.
44. Simcoe to Dundas, quoted in Aitchison, *Development of Local Government*, p. 190.

45. Simcoe to Clarke, August 2, 1793, *Simcoe Papers*, vol. v, p. 197.
46. Aitchison, *Development of Local Government*, p. 189.
47. 33 George III, c. 2, clause vii.
48. 46 George III, c. 3 (1806); 48 George III c. 5 (1808).
49. Simcoe to Portland, December 21, 1794, W. P. M. Kennedy, ed., *Statutes, Treaties and Documents of the Canadian Constitution, 1713–1929* (Oxford, 1930), pp. 215–216.
50. Kennedy, *Statutes*, p. 215.
51. Kennedy, *Statutes*, p. 217.
52. Kennedy, *Statutes*, p. 217.
53. Osgood to Simcoe, January 30, 1795 (secret and most confidential), quoted in Aitchison, *Development of Local Government*, p. 548 (emphases added).
54. 41 George III, c. 3, *Statutes of Upper Canada*.
55. "An Act to empower the Commissioners of the Peace for the Home District, in their Court of General Quarter Sessions Assembled, to establish and regulate a Market in and for the Town of York," *Statutes of Upper Canada*, March 14, 1814, 54 George III, c. 15; "An Act to establish a Market in the Town of Niagara, in the Niagara District," 57 George III, c. 4.
56. 56 George III, c. 33, *Statutes of Upper Canada*.
57. "An Act to Establish a Police in the Towns of York, Sandwich and Amherstburg," *Statutes of Upper Canada*, April 7, 1871, 57 George III, c. 2.
58. "An Act for establishing a Police in the Town of Niagara, in the District of Niagara, and for other purposes therein mentioned," *Statutes of Upper Canada*, July 12, 1819, 59 George III, c. 5.
59. Aitchison, *Development of Local Government*, p. 553.
60. *Encyclopedia Britannica*, 15th ed., s.v. "Police," vol. xxv.
61. Michel Foucault, "The Political Technology of Individuals," in Luther H. Martin, Huck Gutman and Patrick H. Hutton, eds., *Technologies of the Self* (Amherst, 1988).
62. "An Act to establish a Police in the Town of Brockville, in the District of Johnstown," *Statutes of Upper Canada*, January 28, 1832, 2 William IV, c. 17. See also Canada (Upper Canada, 1791–1840) House of Assembly, *Report of the Committee of Conference on Brockville Police Bill* (York, 1832).
63. 2 William IV, c. 17, clause xviii.
64. 2 William IV, c. 17, clauses xv and xxi.
65. City of Brockville, Municipal Records, The Board of Police Meetings, Minutes of Meeting on April 16, 1832, Archives of Ontario (MS610).
66. "An Act to define the Limits of the Town of Hamilton, in the District of Gore, and to establish a Police and Public Market therein," *Statutes of Upper Canada*, February 13, 1833, 3 William IV, c. 16; "An Act to incorporate the Village of Prescott, and to establish an elective Police therein," March 6, 1834, 4 William, c. 27; "An Act to establish a Police in the Town of Cornwall, in the Eastern District," 4 William IV, c. 25; "An Act to define the limits of the Town of Port Hope, and to establish a Police therein," 4 William, c. 26; "An Act to establish a Board of Police in the Town of Belleville," March 6, 1834, 4 William IV, c. 24; "An Act to establish a Police in the Town of Cobourg, and to define the Limits of the said Town," March 4, 1837, 7 William IV, c. 42; "An Act to incorporate the Villages of Hallowell and Picton, by the name of the Town of Picton, and establish a Police therein," March 4, 1837, 7 William IV, c. 44; "An Act to

define the limits of the Town of London, in the District of London, and to establish a Board of Police therein," February 10, 1840, 3 Victoria, c. 31.

67. Quoted in H. T. Manning, *British Colonial Government After the American Revolution, 1782–1820* (London, 1933), p. 1. Lord Dorchester was the new title held by Guy Carleton after 1786. Dorchester became governor of Quebec in 1786 and governor-in-chief of Quebec in 1792, which by then was divided into two provinces as Upper and Lower Canada.

68. See R. C. Harris, *The Seigniorial System in Early Canada: A Geographical Study* (Wisconsin, 1966); M. Trudel, *The Seigniorial Regime, The Canadian Historical Association*, Booklet No. 6, (Ottawa, 1971); W. B. Munro, *The Seigniorial System in Canada: A Study of French Colonial Policy* (Cambridge, Mass., 1907); and D. A. Heneker, *The Seigniorial Regime in Canada* (Quebec, 1927). The term socage is feudal in origin in which the "socage tenant" of the land paid a rent in money or labour to the lord. In 1660 in England this form of land tenure was designated as "free and common socage" which recognized the right of title to land with quitrent (that is, without any other obligations). See William Holdsworth, *An Historical Introduction to the Land Law* (Oxford, 1927).

69. See W. B. Munro, *Seigniorial System in Canada*, and D. A. Heneker, *Seigniorial Regime in Canada*.

70. Reports of the Bureau of Archives for the Province of Ontario, *Third Report*, Alexander Fraser, ed. (The Legislative Assembly of Ontario, Toronto, 1905). It should be noted here that these instructions were not particular to Quebec; identical instructions were sent to newly formed governments of East and West Florida, Grenada.

71. Shortt and Doughty, *Documents*, Part I, pp. 422–423.

72. Shortt and Doughty, *Documents*, Part II, p. 730.

73. The letter is documented in Joseph J. Murphy, "Documentary History of the First Surveys in the Province of Ontario," paper read before the Association of Ontario Land Surveyors (Toronto, 1889).

74. These instructions are documented in W. F. Weaver, *Crown Surveys in Ontario* (Toronto, 1968), pp. 8–9. They are also included in Murphy, 1889, "Early Surveys."

75. Shortt and Doughty, *Documents*, Part II, pp. 947–948.

76. Shortt and Doughty, *Documents*, Part II, p. 811, note 2.

77. Anonymous Memoranda on Government, 1789 (probably Grenville), Shortt and Doughty, *Documents*, Part II, p. 986.

78. Anonymous Memoranda on Government, 1789, Shortt and Doughty, *Documents*, Part II, p. 986.

79. A Secret and Private letter from Grenville to Dorchester (October 20, 1789) on land and settlement policy in response to the letter from Dorchester to Sydney. Shortt and Doughty, *Documents*, Part II, p. 970.

80. Minutes of Land Committee Meeting, *Seventeenth Report of the Department of Public Records and Archives of Ontario*, Alexander Fraser, ed. (Toronto, 1928), p. 43.

81. *Seventeenth Report*, p. 43.

82. *Seventeenth Report*, 1928, Minutes of Land Committee Meeting, January 25, 1788, p. 11.

83. *Third Report,* 1905, Rules and Regulations for the conduct of Land Office Department, article iv, p. lxx.
84. *Third Report,* 1905, article v.
85. *Third Report,* 1905, article vi.
86. *Third Report,* 1905, article ix.
87. *Third Report,* 1905, article x.
88. These model plans are reproduced in the *Seventeenth Report.*
89. *Seventeenth Report,* 1928, Minutes of Meetings of the Land Committee, August 21, 1789, p. 62.
90. *Seventeenth Report,* 1928, article iv.
91. *Seventeenth Report,* 1928, article v.
92. Privy Council, Instructions to Lord Dorchester as Governor of Upper and Lower Canadas, A. G. Doughty and A. M. McArthur, *Documents Relating to Constitutional History of Canada, 1791–1818,*
93. Doughty and McArthur, *Documents,* p. 21.
94. Dundas to Simcoe, July 12, 1792, *The Simcoe Papers: The Correspondence of Lieutenant Governor John Graves Simcoe,* E. A. Cruikshank, ed. (Toronto: Ontario Historical Society, 5 vols. 1923–1935), vol. i, pp. 178–179.
95. *Simcoe Papers,* vol. i, p. 178.
96. Simcoe to Dundas, November 23, 1792, *Simcoe Papers,* vol. ii, p. 264.
97. Simcoe to Dundas, September 20, 1793, *Simcoe Papers,* vol. ii, p. 58.
98. Report of Executive Council Respecting Crown Lands (Lower Canada), Doughty and McArthur, *Documents,* p. 60.
99. Simcoe to Dundas, November 23, 1792, *Simcoe Papers,* vol. ii, p. 264.
100. Simcoe to Dundas, November 23, 1792, *Simcoe Papers,* vol. ii, p. 264.
101. Simcoe to Dundas, June 21, 1794, *Simcoe Papers,* vol. ii, p. 284.
102. Bernard Bailyn, *The Peopling of British North America: An Introduction* (New York, 1986); D. W. Meinig, *The Shaping of America,* vol. i, *Atlantic America, 1492–1800* (New Haven, 1986).
103. See Bernard Bailyn, *Voyagers to the West: A Passage in the Peopling of America on the Eve of the Revolution* (New York, 1986).
104. *William Berczy Papers,* Archives of Ontario (MS 526). The "Narrative" of William Berczy is transcribed, which contains 66 (double-spaced typewritten) pages of text and 240 pages of documents and other related material appended by William Berczy and referred to in the text. See John Andre, *William Berczy: Co-Founder of Toronto* (Toronto, 1967).
105. Berczy, "Narrative," p. 1.
106. Berczy, "Narrative," p. 2.
107. Berczy, "Narrative," pp. 2–3.
108. Berczy, "Narrative," p. 3.
109. Berczy, "Narrative," p. 3.
110. Berczy, "Narrative," pp. 8–9.
111. Berczy, "Narrative," p. 11.
112. Berczy, "Narrative," p. 11.
113. Berczy, "Narrative," p. 11 (emphasis added).
114. Berczy, "Narrative," p. 12.
115. Berczy, "Narrative," p. 13.

116. See Edith G. Firth, "Introduction," in *The Town of York, 1793–1815: A Collection of Documents of Early Toronto* (Toronto, 1962) for a detailed discussion.
117. Minutes of Executive Council Meetings, April 6, 1796. *Seventeenth Report*, 1928, p. 150.
118. *Simcoe Papers*, vol. ii. This letter is also reproduced in the aforementioned minutes of the Executive Committee meeting, *Seventeenth Report*, 1928, pp. 150–151.
119. *Third Report*, Minutes of Land Committee Meeting, February 17, 1789.
120. *Simcoe Papers*, vol. ii.
121. *Simcoe Papers*, vol. ii, p. 150.
122. *Simcoe Papers*, vol. ii, p. 56.
123. *Simcoe Papers*, vol. ii, p. 185.
124. *Simcoe Papers*, vol. ii, pp. 184–187.
125. Read in minutes of the Executive Committee meeting, *Seventeenth Report*, 1928, pp. 151–152.
126. *Seventeenth Report*, 1928, p. 152.
127. *Simcoe Papers*, vol. ii, p. 284.
128. *Simcoe Papers*, vol. iii (1794), p. 61.
129. *Simcoe Papers*, vol. iii (1794). As a result, in an Executive Meeting on 9th July, 1794, it was "resolved that the Town of York to be built conformably to the plan." *Simcoe Papers*, vol. ii, p. 313.
130. Minutes of the Executive Committee meeting, April 6, 1796, *Seventeenth Report*, 1928, p. 152.
131. *Seventeenth Report*, 1928, pp. 152–162.
132. *Seventeenth Report*, 1928, pp. 158–160.
133. *Seventeenth Report*, 1928, pp. 154–155.
134. *Seventeenth Report*, 1928, p. 161.
135. *Seventeenth Report*, 1928, p. 162.
136. *Simcoe Papers*, vol. ii, p. 58.
137. Sydenham to Russell, September 16, 1840, Kennedy, *Statutes*, p. 552.
138. Sydenham to a Friend, 1840, Kennedy, *Statutes*, p. 555.
139. Sydenham to John Russell, September 16, 1840, Kennedy, *Statutes*, p. 552.

5

BIRTH OF THE MODERN CANADIAN
CITY AS A CORPORATION

WITH all the concern of, fear from, and resulting legal and political measures introduced against a potential rebellion, the fact that some colonists took up arms against the prevailing system of government in both Upper and Lower Canada in 1837 and 1838 attests to at least one truth: at the dawn of modernity it was no longer possible to govern without *incorporating* subjects in their own government. And this required calculated, detailed, minute and elaborate legal and political institutions. It now became apparent that government through proclamation, edict and centralized control cost too much, both in economic and political terms. And such centralized government tended to polarize opposition and intensify the tension between central authority and the city. Yet it is often overlooked that the rebellions in Upper and Lower Canada centred on and ultimately exploded in the cities, Toronto and Montréal, which were then incorporated.[1] Interestingly enough, after the rebellions, both Montréal and Québec were denied the renewal of their corporate status which had expired in 1836, displaying an early modern attitude toward the city at the dawn of modernity.

I do not of course mean to suggest that the rebellions were somehow precipitated by a desire for city autonomy by 'citizens'. Rather, the political and constitutional issues of the 1830s and the 1840s revolved around colonial autonomy. The royal colony model with its governor, appointed council and elective assembly, as we mentioned, resulted in conflicts which were so intense that independence from Britain, once again, became an issue in the 1820s.[2] The governors and councils acted as colonial oligarchies, almost without any influence from the representative assemblies since the beginning of settlement. And a new class of colonial statesmen emerged who, under the English liberal precepts, began not only to question but also mobilize support amongst the colonists against the colonial oligarchies. Whatever differences of opinion existed among them, such statesmen as Robert Baldwin, John Arthur Roebuck, William Lyon Mackenzie and Joseph Howe were important agents in this transformation. Although corporations did not appear as an issue in these political and constitutional battles, after the rebellions, as we have seen, there was an almost instant realization that without cities as corporations it was impossible to govern territories. How did this change come about?

To assume that these conclusions were drawn by the British colonial apparatus only during and after the rebellions in the late 1830s would be misleading. As was discussed, the tension between the necessity of governing through towns and an antagonism toward them existed from the beginning of settlement; so did experiments (market towns, police towns, boards of police) to address the tension, which was mounting with the rise of population. Furthermore, this tension was not peculiar to British North America, and the matter was addressed by the new jurisprudence of the nineteenth century as was discussed in Chapter Two. The shifting concepts of law and politics in England in the 1830s were bound to influence colonial politics and policy: as we have seen, constitutional, penal and poor laws were being rethought; municipal corporations were comprehensively reorganized; new State institutions and departments were built; and new ideas were formulated with respect to colonies. By the 1830s the pressure was already mounting to rethink the colonies and to reorganize the colonial apparatus; a new idea of liberal colonialism was taking hold of the British colonial apparatus which was to have profound implications for the British North American politics and cities. A pillar of this new thinking was a new institutional response to the tension between liberty and authority. For these reasons, as Colin Read also argued, it is improper to think that the legal and political reforms that were introduced in British North America were caused in any simple sense by the rebellions.[3] But the rebellions prepared the grounds for the British colonial apparatus to introduce new institutions in the 1840s that had been elaborated in the 1830s.

This chapter focuses on the transformations in the concepts of government and politics in the 1830s and the 1840s and on how the modern city as an apparatus of governance was born in British North America under these complex circumstances. First, we focus on six special-act incorporations that occurred in this period and discuss the political principles that are embodied in these legal acts. Second, we focus on some essential aspects of the new liberal colonialism and its emphasis on 'municipal institutions' as apparatuses of governance in the colonies.

And, third, we analyze the first general acts of municipal corporations in Upper Canada, Lower Canada and Nova Scotia that constituted the modern city as the atom of the State within a graded municipal *system*—a system that both diverged from and preceded English and American systems that emerged later in the century. Once again, those readers who are familiar with literature on the development of British North American municipal institutions will recognize that the organization of this chapter departs from established accounts of a steady progress toward 'municipal freedom' or 'free institutions'. Rather, a thematic organization is introduced around a transformation from statist and centralist policies on bodies politic to calculated usage of them for the purposes of governance.

Let us now review the first incorporations in British North America and their political and legal properties before and during the rebellions. These cities were incorporated through special acts before the general acts of the 1840s and the 1850s and warrant a separate discussion because this accumulated experience formed the basis on which the later general acts were founded. Moreover, what is truly remarkable in this series of laws that constituted modern cities as corporations, and which is perhaps one of the most important thrusts of this book, is how the lineage of the legal and political principles they embodied can be traced to centuries-long practices that we discussed in Chapters Two and Three. We shall see, for example, how certain attributes of the city as a corporation that were articulated since the 1440s were used in these acts. Similarly, we shall see how certain political attitudes toward the city that were prevalent since the 1440s were embodied in them. In short, this chapter will help us underscore the English and American lineage of the cities that emerged in the 1830s and 1840s in British North America.

First Modern Cities in British North America

The first incorporated cities in British North America were Saint John (1785), Québec (1832), Montréal (1832), Toronto (1834), Halifax (1841), Kingston (1846) and Hamilton (1846). The time span that separated the incorporation of Saint John in 1785 from Québec and Montréal in 1832 can be seen as a cautious deployment of this legal and political institution, which was a result of the tension between an antagonism toward cities and their necessity for governance. To put it differently, until the 1840s the British colonial apparatus had not developed an effective response as to how to govern colonies through bodies politic without allowing them to develop *de facto* powers. Moreover, as we have seen, the Saint John charter was modelled as an early modern corporation rather than a modern one. Here we will discuss in detail the legislative acts that constituted these towns as modern cities in the 1830s and 1840s. We will also discuss the ideas that the law-making authorities held about the incorporations. The section will close with a discussion of the legal and political principles that emerged out of the first acts of incorporation in British North America.

Montréal and Québec, Lower Canada: 1832 and 1840

Montréal and Québec were first incorporated by a temporary ordinance in 1832. It is very interesting to note that anticipating the rebellions and being already nervous about the potential *de facto* powers, the colonial authorities built an expiration date in the ordinance: it was valid for four years after which time if it was deemed appropriate it would be renewed. But the Lower Canada Legislature refused to renew the incorporation when it expired in 1836, because of political agitation, which was to result in the rebellion of 1837.[4] Between 1836 and 1840 both cities were governed by the justices of the peace of their respective counties. In 1840, both cities were incorporated by separate ordinances but with identical clauses.[5] It is also very interesting to note that, contrary to the prevailing practices, the preambles to these ordinances made no mention of the earlier ordinances of incorporation. Rather, both ordinances were drafted as if they were the first in both Montréal and Québec. The Montréal ordinance states that

> for the better protection, care and management of the local interests of the inhabitants of the City and Town of Montréal, and for the Municipal Government and the improvement thereof, it is expedient that the said City and Town be incorporated…and that the inhabitants of the said City and Town of Montréal and their successors, inhabitants of the same, shall be, and they are hereby constituted a body corporate and politic.[6]

The same attributes as Saint John (perpetual succession, to hold lands, to pass regulations and bylaws, to sue and be sued and to hold a common seal) were conferred upon both Montréal and Québec. As in Saint John, the governor was to appoint the first mayor who was to hold office for about two years (until December 1, 1842). But unlike Saint John, the governor was also to appoint six aldermen and twelve councilmen, who were to hold office also until December 1, 1842. In other words, Montréal and Québec were still not entrusted with civic elections. Only after 1842 were elections to be held in a manner that was prescribed in the act. Yet the property qualifications in Montréal and Québec for aldermen and councillors, although somewhat reminiscent of Saint John, were exceptionally high, as we shall see, when compared with other incorporations in the same period. The aldermen had to own or rent property assessed at £1,000. The councilmen had to own or rent property at £500. It is difficult to estimate accurately but this qualification must have been even more restrictive than the 25 per cent of the city inhabitants that Acheson estimated for Saint John.[7] These provisions demonstrate that the legislature was very calculating in devising this act so as to retain considerable power in the governor with respect to governance of Montréal and Québec and limit the city politics to an elite group.

Both cities were empowered with a clause:

> that it shall be lawful for the said Council of the said city, at a meeting or meetings of the said Council, composed of not less than two-thirds of the members thereof, to make such by-laws as to them shall seem fit, for the good rule, peace, and government of the said city, and for raising, assessing, and applying such moneys as may be required for the execution of the powers with which the said Council is hereby invested, and for maintaining in the said city a good and efficient system of Police.[8]

As we can see, the similarities between the Saint John charter and Montréal and Québec ordinances are quite remarkable. But two differences stand out. First, whereas in 1785 the royal governor was reluctant to grant incorporation, in 1840 it was becoming an acceptable practice. Was it acceptable because the State policies became liberal in conferring 'autonomy', or because the State became confident in the practice of governing through cities? It seems possible that it was the former *because* of the latter. Second, Saint John was incorporated by a royal charter that was drafted and confirmed by the Privy Council in Whitehall; whereas Montréal and Québec were incorporated through acts of the Lower Canada legislature. What this difference indicates is that by the 1830s colonial legislatures were attaining powers to create corporations, which were not prescribed in their constitutions. This was to have lasting effects, as provincial governments during the debates on confederation in the 1850s were considered to have 'natural' and inalienable rights over municipal governments.

Toronto, Upper Canada: 1834

Since its incorporation as a city in 1834, historical accounts assumed that the incorporation of Toronto was inevitable, as every city that grew with commerce and population would be incorporated. Edith Firth, for example, said that by the 1830s "York's incorporation as a city was inevitable."[9] Similarly Careless states that by the 1830s "municipal change was in the offing."[10]

But Toronto's incorporation cannot simply be explained away by attributing inevitability to commercial and population growth. As we have seen in this book, the practice of incorporation was certainly well known before the 1830s. Saint John, New Brunswick was incorporated in 1785, and John Graves Simcoe had proposed incorporation for Kingston, York and Niagara in 1793. Moreover, the British colonial apparatus had practiced incorporation in colonial America, particularly in the late seventeenth and early eighteenth centuries.[11] What were the arguments for and against incorporation? What was expected from the incorporated city? To understand the incorporation of Toronto it seems necessary to do away with assumptions of inevitability, and instead answer these questions. Let us now look at (i) some arguments for and against incorporation; (ii) the role the new city was expected to play, and; (iii) practices that the city became engaged in after it was incorporated. We shall see that the meaning of concepts used in arguments for and against incorporation such as 'order', 'regularity', and 'peace', become clearer once we look closely at the Act of Incorporation as well as at practices initiated immediately after incorporation.

In 1826, eight years before the incorporation of Toronto, William Lyon Mackenzie, a member of the House of Assembly of Upper Canada, urged that "an act incorporating this city is much wanted...for the encouragement of order and regularity."[12] Two years later he asked: "Would it not be of the greatest advantage to our townsfolk if an act for the incorporation of this town (after the most approved principle now in operation in towns in Great Britain) could be passed into a law during the ensuing session of parliament?"[13] The remark on Great Britain is interesting in that it shows Mackenzie's close interest in the legal and political developments immediately before the Reform Act of 1832, and the Municipal Corporations Act of 1835. The first proposal of incorporation was made in that same year, and was drawn up by H. J. Boulton, then solicitor general of Upper Canada. When the bill was introduced in the House of Assembly, however, it faced opposition. A member of the assembly, Francis Collins, argued that "York is too *little* as yet for a

Corporation, commerce and manufactures must grow and attract a more dense and intelligent community, a community independent of, and too powerful for the tools of office, before a Corporation can be with safety established."[14] And he added: "Indeed it is almost too ridiculous to talk about turning such a paltry little dirty hole as Little York into a corporate city."[15] Collins, a year later, also added that "We have seen enough...grinding taxation of corporations in the old country to make us almost tremble at the name...this town is too young to bear the burden."[16] Collins here expressed the view that the size of the city is a precondition of incorporation. Mackenzie also opposed the bill on the grounds that it created a close corporation, that is, the bill provided an "unnatural union of extensive patronage with legislative, judicial, and executive powers in the same body of Individuals, without any check to prevent the natural disposition of man to abuse power for his own advantage," a view of the act that he maintained when it was passed in 1834.[17] Mackenzie here displayed a genuinely modern, liberal attitude toward the city as a corporation, rejecting the creation of the city as an early modern, close corporation; he was certainly not against incorporation of the city but its incorporation as an early modern city. We will later see the full development of this modern conception of the city as a corporation in the context of liberal colonial politics.

From these debates we can glean some points.[18] First, the debate on the incorporation of York began in the 1820s when the population of the town was less than two thousand inhabitants.[19] That means incorporation was not simply a status that came about when population grew but a well-known apparatus of governance among legislators, politicians and administrator. Second, although there was opposition to the proposed bill, there was no disagreement over the usefulness of incorporating the town of York as a city, for better government and order.

On March 6, 1834, the City of Toronto was incorporated.[20] The act stated the reason for incorporation as "the rapid increase of the population, commerce and wealth of the Town of York, a more efficient system of police and municipal government than that now established has become obviously necessary...[and] none appears so likely to attain effectively the objects desired as the erection thereof into a City and the incorporation of the inhabitants, and vesting in them the power to elect a Mayor, Aldermen and Common Councilmen." For purposes of elections, the city was divided into five wards. The mayor, aldermen, councilmen and inhabitants of the city were incorporated as a body politic with capacities of perpetual succession, to hold lands, to pass regulations and bylaws, to sue and be sued and to hold a common seal. As we shall see, the property qualifications for aldermen and councilmen, although moderate when compared with Montréal and Québec, were high when compared with Kingston, Hamilton and Halifax. The aldermen had to own or rent property assessed at £200; the councilmen, property assessed at £150.

The city council was empowered "to make all such laws as may be necessary and proper for carrying into execution the powers vested...for the peace, welfare, safety and good government," which included some sixty-four specified fields of power. Some of the more important of these fields were to enforce the due observance of the Sabbath; to erect and establish, and also to regulate and provide for the proper keeping of any jail or house of correction; to provide regulation for the health of the city and to establish a board of health; to establish and regulate a city watch, and prescribe the powers of the watchmen; and, to take up, arrest or order to be taken up all and any rogues, vagabonds and disorderly persons, to commit such persons to the house of correction or the workhouse and to provide the police in the city.[21] In a separate clause the city council was also empowered to regulate the layout of the city and to enter upon the grounds of any person or persons for the purpose of examining and surveying with a view to the laying out, altering and protracting of streets.[22] As to the administration of justice, the mayor and aldermen were designated as justices of the peace for the city and the jurisdiction was separated from the district in which the city was located. It was also provided that the city send one representative to the House of Assembly.

The city embarked on a number of measures: in 1836, in a council meeting, a letter was discussed on the importance of convincing people that a workhouse would be "a more permanent and extended mode of relieving the *industrious* poor and of supplying the means of employment, clothing and education."[23] The letter urged that the people of Toronto should support this plan, for it would lead to the employment of the poor and promote "the inculcating and encouraging principles and habits of industry and moral virtue." In 1837, a petition by the people of Toronto proposed to construct a House of Industry: "The chief objects to be subserved by the provision suggested for the relief of the poor will be the total abolition of street begging, putting down of wandering vagrants, and securing an asylum at the least possible expense for the industrious and distressed poor, objects which and admitted to be highly deserving the consideration of the public authorities, and essential to the comforts and happiness of the community at large."[24] Now the city was targeting the disciplining of people and normalization. After its construction, the Toronto House of Industry was considered a success and received grants from the House of Assembly.[25] As we have seen in Chapter Two, workhouses originated in England at the dawn of modernity as a means to discipline, to inculcate useful habits and to normalize people, replacing the old and suppressive measures of the poor laws. Here, with incorporation of a town into a city, we see the transposition of these institutions as a means of governance of the city. Weren't these corporate institutions and their uses known to those English statesmen, legislators, and administrators who urged the formation of cities as corporations?

The houses of industry were not the only institutions that were transposed for 'the community at large': penitentiaries, asylums, prisons and schools were built to deal with the problems of discipline and normalization. In 1835, a report of the select committee on prisons argued that crimes were related to poor education and discipline in childhood: "Every person that frequents the streets of Toronto must be forcibly struck with the ragged and uncleanly appearance, the vile language, and the idle and miserable habits of numbers of children."[26] The report inferred that it was probably the problem of the family *environment* in which these children were brought up. The logical conclusion of these observations was the formation of schools in which children received a uniform and formal discipline: in a circular to explain the draft of an act to establish a system of schools, it was argued that "the *steady and punctual* attendance of pupils at the schools is a primary and essential object to be secured in a system of schools."[27] The target was primarily the children of those poor families and "in order to secure the attendance at school of children of the poor, Corporations of some cities and towns in the United States have recommended and enacted...that no assistance be given to pauper parents whose children do not regularly attend school; nor to pauper children not attending school...The efficiency of instruction, discipline and frequent and thorough inspection of the rising generations of the radiating centers of our population" was of utmost importance: otherwise "hundreds of young children will be driven to practice idleness in the streets and thus in consequence, incur the risk of acquiring habits of vice and immorality."[28]

This brief review of the incorporation of Toronto demonstrates the types of practices and institutions the governing body of the city thus constituted was supposed to initiate. It also demonstrates how the fields of power that were defined in the incorporating charter operated by using authority. During the debates on incorporation, administrators, politicians and legislators had full knowledge of what kinds of practices a corporation would initiate once established. It is important to understand this knowledge to understand why Toronto and other cities were incorporated as modern cities.

Kingston, Upper Canada: 1838 and 1846

Kingston is an important case because it was incorporated in 1838 as a town and was subsequently incorporated into a city in 1846. This gives us a chance to discern differences and similarities between a town and a city as understood in legal and political practices before the Municipal Corporations Act was passed in 1849.

The 1838 act stated that "the incorporation of the town of Kingston, in consequence of its increase, has become advisable and necessary for the improvement and prosperity of the town."[29] Although the act constituted the town as a body politic and corporate, three aspects of such bodies politic were excluded. First, the corporate capacities did *not* include the right to perpetual succession, to hold lands, to pass regulations and bylaws, to sue and be sued and to hold a common seal. This means the town could easily be abolished with little legal complication. Second, the town was not fully separated from its district in the administration of justice in that some authority was kept in the Quarter Sessions of the Midland District. Third, and finally, the familiar clause that prescribed the erection and regulation of a workhouse and a house of correction was omitted from the act. Aside from these three aspects, the act constituted the town as a corporation in quite similar terms and conditions as the City of Toronto: similar fields of regulation such as the regulation of buildings and of markets were defined. The property qualifications for aldermen and councilmen were quite low when compared with Toronto. They had to own or rent property assessed at £60. The property qualification specified for mayor was also very low at £75. However, residence qualifications for mayor was ten years, and for aldermen and councilmen it was seven years. For electors, property qualification was £10 with a residence qualification of three months.

The incorporation act of 1846 that erected Kingston into a city included those clauses and provisions of a body politic previously excluded.[30] The act stated that "from the increase in the trade and population of the said Town it is found that the provisions of the said Act are insufficient, and it is expedient for the better protection and management of the local interests of the inhabitants that the said Town should be incorporated into a City." These insufficiencies were remedied by activating the three clauses mentioned above: the city now could have perpetual succession, hold lands, make regulations and bylaws, sue and be sued and hold a common seal; the mayor could act as a justice of the peace; and, the council could establish and regulate a police, establish and regulate workhouses, houses of correction and almshouses. Both property and residence qualifications for aldermen and councilmen were reduced. For aldermen, the property qualification was now £40 with residence requirement of four years. For councilmen, the property qualification was now £25 with residence requirement of three years.

From Kingston, we learn some subtle but important differences that were contained in the concepts of the town and the city: it appears that the town was considered still subordinate to another level of jurisdiction, which was the district; it lacked some of the powers of the city as a corporation; and, correction, discipline and punishment did not fall exclusively under the jurisdiction of a town but that of a city.

Hamilton, Upper Canada: 1833 and 1846

The interesting aspect of Hamilton is that it was first incorporated as a Board of Police in 1833, which, as discussed earlier, was a system governing some towns in Upper Canada from 1832 to 1840. This system was found insufficient, and after 1840 towns which had been incorporated as boards of police were incorporated as towns, or in the case of Hamilton, as a city.[31] A number of towns which had been incorporated as boards of police were incorporated as towns in 1846 and 1847 with special acts. With such an act the Cornwall Board of Police was incorporated as the Mayor and Town Council of the Town of Cornwall.[32] This act stated that the Board of Police was found insufficient, "and it is expedient for the better protection and management of the local interests of the inhabitants that the said Act should be amended." And it was added "that such change of the corporate name shall not be construed to make the said Corporation a new Corporation, but merely to continue the former Corporation with another name and with new powers."[33] Among some eighty additional powers and authorities to make, revise, alter and amend, administer and enforce by the town council, the most notable were to regulate the layout of the town; to regulate all markets and commercial houses; to prevent the sale of any intoxicating drink to any child; to prevent or regulate bathing or swimming; to enforce the Sabbath day; to prevent the pulling down or defacing of sign boards; to prevent and punish breaches of the peace, and generally to prevent and punish vice, drunkenness, profane swearing, obscene language and every other species of immorality, and to preserve good order in the town; to enter into and examine all dwelling houses, warehouses, shops, workshops, distilleries; to establish, endow and regulate one or more public schools; to promote and encourage literary, scientific and agricultural institutions; to regulate public hospitals; to establish and support a house of industry, and enforce labour and discipline in the same, and generally to make all such laws as may be necessary and proper for securing the peace, welfare, safety and good government of the said town. This special act was repeated for Hamilton (1846), Cobourg (1847), and London (1847), which had been incorporated as boards of police as we have seen above. On the other hand, in 1847 an act was passed which conferred limited corporate powers on those towns which had not yet been incorporated, thereby erecting them into corporate towns.[34]

The Hamilton act provided similar clauses for the constitution of cities as in Toronto and Kingston. But there were slight differences in at least three areas. The powers of the council to lay out streets were specified with more detail. A newly worded clause was added, "to prevent vice, immorality and indecency in the streets or other public places, and to preserve peace, health and good order...and to restrain and punish all vagrants, drunkards, mendicants and street beggars." And, finally, the governor general of Upper Canada was to appoint a police magistrate for Hamilton (who was also to serve as a justice of the peace).[35] The qualifications for aldermen, councilmen and electors were moderately low. The property qualification for aldermen and councilmen was £40 with residence requirement of two years. The elector had to own or rent property assessed at £5 with residence requirement of three months.

Halifax, Nova Scotia: 1841

Halifax was founded in 1749 but was largely settled by people who came from the New England colonies during and after the rebellion of the American colonies.[36] As in other British North American colonies there existed a tension between allowing *de facto* corporate autonomy and the necessity of settling in towns. We have alluded above to a 1770 statute in Nova Scotia where town meetings, which New England colonists were accustomed to, were declared unlawful. Similarly, attempts by a number of colonists settled in Halifax to incorporate the city were consistently resisted by the legislature and the governor-in-council: a petition in 1785 for the incorporation of Halifax as a town was rejected by the executive council as being neither 'necessary' nor 'expedient'.[37] In 1790 there was another attempt by the Speaker of the House of Assembly, who drafted an act of incorporation but which was not taken into consideration by the governor-in-council.[38]

In the 1830s the issue of incorporation resurfaced, without doubt owing to the atmosphere of political change in other British North American colonies. There were a number of petitions and counter-petitions for incorporation. On April 10, 1841, Halifax was incorporated as the first modern city in Nova Scotia by an act passed by the legislature.[39] The act of incorporation was similar to those we discussed above. The *governance* of the city was vested in the city council: the constitution of the city council, procedure for elections, qualifications of voters and councilmen, the ward system, an elaborate powers-clause designating fields of regulations and the institution of corporate powers (suing and being sued, to hold lands, to pass bylaws, to hold a seal) were designed in similar forms to other acts of incorporation in British North America.

There were, however, some differences. One was that the corporation was created for a five-year term, as opposed to in perpetuity, which suggests some feeling of experimentation on the part of the legislature.[40] Another was that the appointment of the mayor (which was to be made by elected councilmen) was subject to approval by the governor-in-council.[41] Also, the bylaws of the council were to be approved by the governor-in-council.[42] The qualifications for mayor, aldermen and councilmen were within the same range as in the cities of Kingston, Toronto and Hamilton. The property qualification for mayor and aldermen was £50 with residence requirement of one year. The property qualification for councilmen was £30 with one-year residence requirement. The property qualification for electors was very high at £20 with one month residence requirement.

Principles of Incorporation in British North America, 1832–1846

It will be useful now to outline the salient political principles embodied in the early legal acts of incorporation that created modern cities in British North America before we analyze a series of laws in which these principles became general formulae.

The act begins with an incorporating clause declaring that the inhabitants of the town or the city are constituted as a body politic and corporate. Then it grants corporate capacities of perpetual succession, to hold lands, to make and ordain regulations and bylaws, to sue and be sued and to hold a common seal. The act then defines the *territorial boundaries* of the town or city thus incorporated, followed by the powers vested for the governance of the city in the governing body of the corporation, styled as the town or city council. The governing body is composed of the mayor and aldermen or councilmen; the latter are elected from the wards of the city, which have prescribed boundaries.

The mayor is either chosen among the elected councilmen or directly by the voters. The corporation is divided into wards, and each ward elects one or more aldermen. The qualifications of both the voters and the governing body are specified by the act, which are, usually, that the voters and the members of the governing body shall be male freeholders, and residents, for a specified duration, within the limits of the corporation. The property qualifications differ for the voters and the governing body in being more limited for the latter. The property qualifications are carefully calculated to control participation in city politics. The mode of holding elections is always specified. The provision is made for the election of a mayor, and his duties are defined, among which the most important and symbolic is to act as a magistrate. The act contains a minute and detailed enumeration of the fields of power of the city council, which are often numerous and listed in one clause, the most important of which are the following: the authority to create debts; to levy and collect taxes; to appoint corporate officers; to enact ordinances of public health; to establish a police force; to establish a correction and punishment system; and, to administer justice. The act of a corporation is its constitution, and it gives all the authority and specific powers that the town or city possesses; the corporation cannot exercise powers and authority that are not prescribed by its constitution.

The act of incorporation also presupposes a number of political principles. First, the modern city as a corporation is created at the pleasure of the legislature, and while the legislature might, it need not, obtain the consent of the people of the city to be affected. The act of incorporation is not a contract between the State and the corporation. And the legislature can erect, change divide, and abolish a corporation, at its pleasure, as it deems appropriate. In some cases perpetual succession is even withheld. Second, the authority and power conferred on the modern city are not merely local in nature but supra local: the act of incorporation empowers the city council to exercise the authority and power of the State on the people by officers. And, third, the principle of franchise enables the legislature to legitimate the central authority and power to be exercised in towns. Now, it is on the basis of these legal and constitutional attributes that we call the modern city an apparatus of governance: it enables the State to govern larger bodies of people in a functionally decentralized manner, which can mobilize support for governance without the creation of an unwieldy bureaucracy. Or, to put it in other words, the incorporation of the city means the creation of a body politic with an elaborate and written document, forming and empowering a governing body to bear both the economic and political costs of steering the conduct of subjects toward accepted and useful pursuits. The city institutes fields of power in which the liberty to act is granted to the subjects only within the limits defined and rules specified, hence containing the tension between authority and autonomy. At the same time, the corporation empowers qualified inhabitants to participate in their own governance within the prescribed limits of politics. Overall, the legislature has at its own disposal an apparatus of governance that is very flexible and adaptable to differences in specific local political conditions. We have seen, for example, how these limits and rules were different in Montréal, Toronto, Halifax, Kingston and Hamilton.

If these were the 'internal' developments in the political and legal practice of incorporating cities, there were at the same time 'external' developments in colonial policy. These 'external' developments were equally important in the corporation becoming a *general formula* of governance in British North America. As we have seen, the 1830s was an important decade in England in terms of the emergence of new institutions among which the corporation loomed significant. An aspect of these changes was a changing conception of and attitude toward colonies, which was influenced by new liberal ideas of governance and legislation. It will be useful to outline the salient aspects of these changing conceptions of colonies before we turn to the beginnings of general legislation on corporations in British North America.

New Liberal Colonial Politics

A very different way of thinking about colonies became prevalent in the administration of colonies in the 1830s.[43] The changes in Britain were the crucible of a new empire of settlement.[44] After Adam Smith, whose principles on colonies critiqued mercantilism, and until the early decades of the nineteenth century, the colonial question remained unattended by political economists and administrators.[45] As Buckner remarked, "Until the 1820s, the Colonial Office had neither the expertise, the knowledge, nor the desire to supervise effectively the work of distant governors."[46] What was new in British colonial policy in the 1830s? We need to see that after 1815, with the increasing demographic pressure, the idea of "shovelling out the paupers" had become the central principle of colonial thought and practice. In response to increased possibilities of unrest, the "removing" of paupers and destitutes had become an attractive idea. It was thought that shovelling out the paupers "would cease to engender the desire of change; the ideas of relief and of revolution would lose their fatal connexion in the minds of the multitude."[47] The removal of people who were likely to cause some trouble therefore appeared as a bright idea, and it was proposed that "a well-regulated system of colonization acts as a safety-valve to the political machine, and allows the expanding vapour to escape, before it is heated to explosion."[48] In 1819, the Poor Law Committee pointed out strongly that the unemployed should be helped to find work overseas. Three thousand Scots and several thousand Irishmen, most of whom went to British North American colonies, received State assistance in the 1820s.[49] In 1826 and 1827, select committees were appointed to inquire into the problems of emigration and colonization.[50] The conclusions of the reports prepared by these committees were "in favour of the profit to be derived from the employment of capital in the cultivation of the fertile lands of the Colonies, as compared with the unproductive appropriation of capital at home in the employment of these paupers."[51]

In the 1830s, however, an important shift occurred in colonial thought.[52] In 1841, the *Westminster Review* declared that "recently the spirit of colonization, under a new impulse, has acquired an entirely new character. Emigration is no longer confined to the most wretched portion of the population—to the mere labouring masses...colonization has taken the place of mere emigration: the removal of society, not that of mere masses...A complete revolution in the state of opinion respecting emigration has in fact taken place."[53] The colonies were no longer thought of as depositories of excess and useless population but as places where British institutions and customs prevailed—and this was the 'new' aspect of the British colonial policies in the 1830s, in contrast to the period between the rebellion of the thirteen colonies and the 1820s. An empire conducted according to mercantilist principles offended new liberal values.[54] The reasons for this change are not very difficult to understand: we have seen the political, economic and institutional transformations that occurred in Britain in the 1830s. The change created a pressure for rethinking the constitutional principles of colonialism.

What was this new idea of liberal colonialism? Edward Gibbon Wakefield, who was one of the foremost political economists on colonies, made a distinction between central and municipal principles of colonialism.[55] Wakefield argued that the municipal principle was often misunderstood as being confined to cities; it was a principle of government, which could be used in other matters such as colonial government. The municipal principle was "a delegation of power by the supreme authority...and may be applied no doubt to the least important matters. It is indeed the principle of that infinite variety of corporations for special or limited purposes...which distinguish England and English America from the rest of the world...But whilst the municipal principle embraces the minutest subject, as to which the supreme authority may choose to delegate power, it admits of a delegation of the highest power *short of sovereignty or national independence.*"[56] What Wakefield is expressing here is the idea of corporations as subordinate bodies politic within the modern State. Wakefield wonders why such a constitutional instrument is not used in colonization. In fact, he argues, this principle was used in the thirteen colonies before the 1780s.[57] He admits that the principle is not new but was abandoned after the rebellion of the thirteen colonies. Instead, the British colonial administration adopted what Wakefield calls (following Jeremy Bentham) 'government at a distance'; he argues that this is the central principle, and as a principle of government it is too costly: "The manner of control appears to me to be of far more consequence than its nature or amount."[58] Through the municipal principle of local self-government colonies would be made useful to the State. The colonies would govern themselves on matters that affect them locally, and supra local matters would be left to the 'parent' State. In other words, the State promises the colonies peace in return for order. The State would say: "you must yourselves be the architects of your own fortunes. My government has made the way clear for you in the first instance: these are the limits of the colony; make yourselves a community; sustain yourselves, and *govern yourselves.* Trade with other nations, with all whom you wish, that you may; fight with other nations or yourselves, that you shall not. Such is my will, and to it I shall enforce obedience."[59]

But what were the uses of such colonies for the parent State? Wakefield answered this question: "Colonies are of value simply because they enlarge the productive territory of the nation that plants them; thus adding directly to the means of support at its command, and opening a wider field for its energies, as well by the advantages they hold out to the settlers who resort to them, as by the markets they create for the various industrial products which the manufacturing and commercial capacities of the old country furnish."[60] There are then three main uses of colonies: the extension of markets; the relief from excessive population; and, the enlargement of the field of production.[61] The last one was the most important because the field of production consisted of land, labour and capital. In the parent State there was an abundance of capital in need of expansion, and in the colonies there was an abundance of land. A balanced field of production would result in increased capital accumulation. This, combined with the expansion of markets and the relief of population, was then the essence of the call for the art of colonization that the political economists pushed for in the 1840s. Successful colonization required the removal of able bodied, young and preferably married people from the State to the colonies and the proper disposal of land in the colonies.[62] Now, to attract settlers the wages had to be high in the colony; and "in order to create and maintain a very high rate of wages in the colony, it [was] necessary, first, that the colonists should have an ample field of production; ample, that is, in proportion to capital and labour."[63] In order for the field of production to remain ample, the price for land had to be low enough to attract settlers and high enough to avoid the inducement for speculation of a land-owning class. Hence, the disposal of lands was an essential element in colonization, and this was of cardinal importance for the founding of towns.

The art of colonization urged that the field of production "should never be so large as to encourage hurtful dispersion; as to promote that cutting up of capital and labour into small fractions, which, in the greater number of modern colonies, has led to poverty and barbarism, or speedy ruin."[64] This urge is political as well as economic because the concentration of population secured political features in a population that made it viable for economic ends. Otherwise, "the scattering of people over a wilderness, and placing them for ages in a state between civilization and barbarism...would induce the evils of great dispersion."[65] What were those evils? "If the settlers plant themselves here and there in out-of-the-way spots, where, being distant from a market, and *from all that pertains to civilization*, they would fall into a state of barbarism."[66] In other words, the formation of communities in concentrated settlements induced habits of civilization. This idea, as we have seen, was not novel; but it became an important element of systematic colonization in an effort to expand the field of production.

What were the main elements of liberal colonialism? The purpose of colonization was no longer to shovel out the paupers but to transfer capital and labour from the mother State to the colonies, that is, to expand the field of production: (i) the transfer of capital and labour was not by simple emigration but by a calculated and complex transposition of all classes of people. "To colonize beneficially it is necessary that the higher and richer, as well as the employed, that all classes of society should emigrate together, forming new communities, analogous to that of the parent state";[67] (ii) the formation of political communities required the disposal of lands and land settlement should be regulated with a view to concentrate population; and, (iii) concentrated land settlement meant transposition of all those laws and governmental institutions that make communities self-governing bodies politic.

Throughout the 1830s and the 1840s numerous treatises, pamphlets and arguments were produced on this liberal idea of an empire of settlement. Whatever disagreements were held among political economists, administrators and statesmen, as Ward put it, "all of them believed that, whether or not the self-governing colonies remained in the empire for ever (or for a long time), they would remain Britain transplanted and continue British in outlook, civilization and attachment."[68] These ideas were to have significant effects in the British colonies and on how local matters of government and land settlement were approached. But we must add here that the abstract and general arguments put forward by reformers and political economists could not be easily implemented in the colonies. Secretary of the State for colonies, Glenelg, in his instructions to Governor Gosford, drew attention to this body of literature: "[The] inquiry to determine the principles upon which the uncleared territory could be most advantageously brought into settlement has engaged the serious attention of both speculative observers and of persons practically engaged in such affairs."[69] But he added, "Aware, as I am, how many are the sources of error to which speculations of this kind are liable, and how necessary it is for correction of such fallacies, to possess an intimate acquaintance with the scene in which such abstract principles are reduced to practice...for the guidance of local government in maturing [the] scheme of [settlement]."[70] James Mill later credited John Arthur Roebuck—whose acquaintance with Jeremy Bentham and John Stuart Mill made him aware of all those 'abstract' ideas—with developing the new ideas of colonial policy.[71] Roebuck wrote an important treatise on colonies in which he showed a capacity to combine abstract ideas with the practical conditions of British North America.[72] We will focus on this treatise since it also served Lord Durham in formulating his ideas.

Roebuck on Colonial Politics and Cities

Roebuck had spent part of his youth in Lower Canada and had received his education there. He was first elected to England's House of Commons in 1832 as a supporter of parliamentary reform, and three years later he undertook to represent the interests of the Lower Canada Assembly in England as its agent. Although his treatise *Colonies of England*[73] was not published until 1849, the manuscript was made available to Lord Durham when he was writing his *Report on the Affairs of British North America* (1839).[74]

Roebuck set out with the principle that "in many ways it may be useful to the mother country to have her people employing their energies and their capital in the formation of new communities."[75] The problem was how to build such communities. He considered the formation of a community very much in terms of the formation of bodies politic. There were three main units: *settlement,* which was the earliest condition; *province* was a mature settlement; and *system* was confederated provinces. In the transition condition of settlement the parent State was "omnipotent with regard to colonies and interference is acceptable."[76] However, as the new colony developed, "it should not (except in the way of requiring protection from foreign aggression) cost the mother country anything....The colony, then, is to maintain itself; maintaining itself, common justice requires that she should tax herself, and should manage her own money concerns."[77]

The first step in the formation of a colony was the survey, but "not merely to determine the boundaries of private property, but with reference to its political existence and government...territorial divisions are necessary for the purposes of government."[78] Territorial institutions such as counties and townships were indispensable because of the administration of justice through courts, representation, taxation and militia formation; also "every man in the new colony would, on the instant of his arriving, and becoming a settler, not only feel interested in the success of the new community, but in some measure responsible for it."[79] Territorial institutions were then instruments of inducing particular conduct in settlers: loyalty, sense of duty, industriousness, hope and responsibility. "A colony certainly cannot be planted without inhabitants...[but] success will undoubtedly be rendered more probable, than if a host of idle, decrepit, and ignorant persons, attempts to plant a settlement."[80] For this reason two problems remained: selection of settlers and their concentration in communities. Let us focus on the concentration of settlers and its benefits for the formation of colonies.

Roebuck remarked that in the art of colonization, as we have seen above, "great stress has been laid upon the evils of allowing of population to be *scattered* over the country."[81] Therefore, he defended the doctrine of sufficient price as "a scheme for the purpose of preventing this mischievous *scattering,* and by compulsion producing *concentration* and all its attendant benefits. The scheme consists of a rule by which a high upset price is affixed to all wild land offered for sale in the colony."[82] But how was the compulsion to concentrate to be created? How were humans to be induced to concentrate in communities? Roebuck maintained that concentration was not part of human nature but produced through subjection. He admitted that the settler "when brought into the subjection of our civilization, [is] like a wild animal confined in a cage—his waking hours are hours of misery, because of the narrow limits of his enforced home; and in his sleep, he dreams of the distant wilds which he has lost for ever, lives again his life of happy freedom, and wakes, to find himself in the miserable thrall of his narrow prison."[83] And he added:

> Why should we then suppose that any peculiar and magical effects are to be attributed to concentration; and why should we attempt, by legislative provisions, to enforce a concentration, which private interests would not induce? Why should we co-opt people within a rigid circle of restraint, who desire to follow the suggestions of their own hopes and anticipations—and, under the influence of this powerful stimulus, to brave all the difficulties of the wilderness, and to extend the arc of civilization, imperfect if you will, yet still far superior to anything which these wild regions ever yet knew. There may be loss, there may be folly, there may be disappointment—yet, after the struggle, there will be found a town, a district, a people of civilized beings, securely placed, and enjoying happiness which they could not hope for in their ancient state—and there will be seen to be the broad foundations of a thriving, self-supporting, and constantly improving community. These surely are great results, sufficient to compensate us for the petty inconveniences to which, undoubtedly, the inhabitants of every rising community are subject, in which land is cheap, and labour highly rewarded.[84]

Roebuck was trying to convince himself as much as the statesmen and administrators: the passionate and compelling voice that begins the passage with questions on concentration ends with quite dull, rational and pragmatic answers and reasons. The effect of untamed Nature on Roebuck should not be underestimated; contact with the awesome and compelling British North American wilderness must have aroused all the questions with which Roebuck began the passage.[85] Yet, with his second, civilized or domesticated nature, one that has been cultivated in him through the system of values, his reason takes over and commands him toward the end of the passage. Roebuck perhaps experienced the doctrines of natural law, which dominated juridical and political thought since the seventeenth century and which claimed that it was the nature of man that compelled him to coalesce in communities and submit himself to authority and rule: the social contract. He thought, however, as much as other governors and administrators, that if the settlers were not governed they would not concentrate and hence become less and less governable by existing rules and regulations. Therefore, man had to be confined in order to be useful to the State.

What Roebuck accomplished in this treatise was to simplify and popularize some of the more complex and abstract schemes of the art of colonization and Benthamite ideas, and to transform them into more concrete principles of colonial government. He also incorporated his practical knowledge of British North American colonies into his principles—something that political economists and reformers could not have done. When Lord Durham set out to write his *Report*, he apparently found this treatise useful.[86]

Durham on Municipal Institutions

These principles of the art of colonization were formulated by political economists, jurists and State administrators in one of the most important and effective reports in the history of the British colonial apparatus and of British North American colonies: Lord Durham's *Report* in 1839. Here is not the place to discuss the importance of the *Report* within the colonial administration.[87] There is no doubt that the *Report* was immensely influential in directing the course of affairs toward the municipal principle which already had been set in motion in British North America and embodied the essential principles of the new liberal colonialism. As John Russell, the secretary of State for colonies, stated in 1839, the bill that was introduced in parliament to unite Upper and Lower Canada embodied "the results of deliberate reflection on the various suggestions contained in the report of the Earl of Durham."[88] The immense influence of the *Report* can be partly attributed to its style: it clearly sets itself apart from and against the 'old' system of colonialism; arguments are often set against the background of England and of the United States. Now Durham could observe British North American colonies from the perspective of creating colonies as "perfect transcript images of the parent state" and articulate the principles of new liberal colonialism in this concrete case.

The theme that runs through the *Report* was that the municipal institutions were instruments through which the colonies could be drawn into the field of production of England. "In the British colonies," he said, there is no "effectual system of municipal government...The great business of the assemblies is, literally, parish business; the making of parish roads and parish bridges."[89] As Lord Durham himself admitted, he was less informed about Upper Canada than Lower Canada. For this reason, but also because Lower Canada was considered more problematic in the emergence of rebellions in 1837 and 1838, he often isolated the municipal conditions in Lower Canada. He observes that "Lower Canada remains without municipal institutions of local self-government, which are the foundations of Anglo-Saxon freedom and civilization; nor is their absence compensated by any thing like the centralization of France."[90] He is surprised to find that the territorial institutions of the province did not serve the purposes of governance but were mere judicial (districts) and electoral (counties) divisions and remain, "during the present suspension of representative government, …useless geographical divisions. There are no hundreds [medieval English institutions] or corresponding sub-divisions of counties."[91] By this, Durham meant that these districts and counties were not territorial institutions with duties, obligations and perhaps liberties, which were considered essential elements of towns; nor were they connected with one another in a system of government and jurisdictional obligations. As to the Eastern townships of Lower Canada, they were "inhabited entirely by a population British and American in origin; and may be said to be divisions established for surveying, rather than any other purposes. The Eastern townships present a lamentable contrast in the management of all local matters to the bordering state of Vermont, in which the municipal institutions are the most complete, it is said, of any part even of New England."[92]

The conclusion Lord Durham reached was that "the utter want of municipal institutions giving the people any control over their local affairs, may indeed be considered as one of the main causes of the failure of representative government, and of the bad administration of the country."[93] He reasoned that the lack of municipal institutions required the concentration of power; and that was an inefficient form of exercising power and also occasioned the formation of its polar opposite, that is, resistance and rebellion: "The true principle of limiting popular power is that apportionment of it in many different depositories which has been adopted in all the most free and stable states of the Union."[94] Now, by 'apportionment' Durham means the proliferation and diffusion of power as the true principle of limiting popular resistance and rebellion. Hence, "the establishment of municipal institutions for the whole country should be made a part of every colonial constitution; and the prerogative of the Crown should be constantly interposed to check any encroachment on the functions of local bodies, until the people should become alive, as most assuredly they almost immediately would be, to the necessity of protecting their local privileges."[95] If concentration of population was a precondition of the possibility of corporations, the municipal corporations were the preconditions of the proliferation and diffusion of popular power throughout the bodies politic. The compulsion to concentrate that was created within the population was only the beginning of the building of territorial institutions; municipal corporations were the cement that would keep the population in peace and order. Or, as Herman Merivale, a disciple of Wakefield, said: There was in the colonies "the urgent desire for cheaper and more subservient labourers—for a class to whom the capitalist might dictate terms, instead of being dictated to by them...In ancient civilized countries the labourer, though free, is by a law of Nature dependent on capitalists; in colonies this dependence must be created by artificial means."[96]

The importance of the *Report* from our vantage point is that Durham (with Wakefield and Roebuck) clearly identified that without the creation and proliferation of municipal corporations the colonies could not be governed. Or, as Robert Baldwin stated, "If it is the desire of the Mother Country...to retain the colony it can only be done either by force, or with the consent of the people...I take it for granted that Great Britain cannot desire to exercise a Government of the sword, and that she will therefore only govern the Canadas so long as she can do so with the concurrence of the People."[97] For such a government, modern legislation and municipal institutions were necessary.[98] As mentioned above, the *Report* resulted in a legislation that united the Canadas. When Sydenham was appointed governor of British North America in 1839, the modern principles of governance and municipal corporations were being transformed into practice.

Sydenham and a System of Local Government

Roebuck, Lord Durham or Wakefield were not the first to introduce the idea of a comprehensive system of local government. When Archibald Gosford was appointed governor of the Canadas in 1835, his instructions had asked for such a system. The secretary of State for colonies, Glenelg, stated in his instructions that "[the] inquiry to determine the principles upon which the uncleared territory could be most advantageously brought into settlement has engaged the serious attention of both speculative observers and persons practically engaged in such affairs...[and] I express my concurrence with the general views...for the guidance of the local government in maturing [the] scheme of settlement."[99] But Glenelg did not further elaborate as to how this system was to be formulated and established, nor did he refer Gosford to a source.

At any rate, upon his appointment as the governor general of British North America in 1839, Lord Sydenham was told by Lord John Russell, the secretary of State for colonies, that "the establishment of

Municipal Institutions for the management of local affairs, will be among the most important of the subjects to which your attention will be called."[100] Russell stated that the bill introduced in the British parliament for the Union of the Canadas included many suggestions of Lord Durham, among which was the introduction of municipal institutions. And, Russell added that, "on the importance of such institutions I need not enlarge. Your acquaintance with the system of municipal government in this country will point out to you that there is no mode in which local affairs can be so properly administered, and that they form, at the same time, the most appropriate means of training the great body of people to the higher branches of legislation."[101] This clear expression of the importance of municipal institutions as a means of both administration and governance is indicative of the influence of Durham's *Report*. The British colonial apparatus had never expressed the need and use of municipal corporations with such urgency and clarity.

When the Canadas were united under one legislature with an act passed in 1840, however, it did not include any provisions on municipal corporations.[102] It immensely disappointed Sydenham when he received a copy from Russell.[103] But, at the same time, this disappointment prompted one of the clearest statements on municipal corporations and governance by a colonial statesman. He stated that upon reading the *Report* he had been convinced that municipal institutions must become a part of the colonial constitution.[104] Yet after the opportunity of studying British North American colonies, he was now convinced that "the cause of nearly all the difficulty in the government of every one of them is to be found in the absence of any well-organized system of local government."[105] At the end of Chapter Four we saw the elaborate argument Sydenham put forward to prove this point. Here we need simply to note that his interpretation of the rebellions from the point of view of the absence of authorities in towns was beyond doubt one of the reasons for moving toward establishing municipal corporations: here, municipal institutions or local government are understood as a means to contain tension that is polarized in the absence of local authorities. But Sydenham was aware that in Upper Canada some incorporations existed at the time. (Montréal and Québec incorporations were suspended after the rebellions in Lower Canada.) However, they were by no means adequate and other colonies also needed such institutions. Sydenham believed that if a successful system was introduced first in the Canadas, New Brunswick and Nova Scotia would soon follow.[106] In a letter to a friend in which Sydenham expressed similar views, he also stated his often-quoted view that "the establishment of Municipal Government by

Act of Parliament is as much a part of the intended scheme of Government for the Canadas as the union of two legislatures, and the more important of the two."[107] Sydenham took seriously the importance of municipal corporations as apparatuses of governance. The result was an act, as Sydenham put it, where "one party hated the measure because it was to give power to the people; another because it placed that power under wholesome control by the Crown; a third because it deprived the members of the Assembly of all their past power of jobbing."[108] Let us now see the details of this first general municipal system in British North America.

The District Councils Act, Upper Canada

It was the District Councils Act of 1841 that set out to establish authorities in localities where such did not yet exist.[109] The act stated that the provisions did not affect the established rights, capacities or powers of the corporation or other authorities of towns and cities within which the board of police might be established, but that "all powers and authorities vested at the time of the passing of this Act in the justices of the peace for any district, and being of the nature of those hereby transferred from such justices to the district council, may be exercised by such district council within any such city, town, or village, as they might have been exercised by such justices if such Act had not been passed."[110] Therefore, although the act did not affect the corporate towns and cities, it also kept intact existing established power over any such corporate city or town by the justices of the peace of the district within which it was located.

The act provided that there should be a district council in each district or group of counties, to consist of a warden and councilmen and that "the inhabitants of each of the Districts...be a Body Corporate, and as such shall have perpetual succession, and a common seal, with power to break, renew, and alter the same at pleasure, and shall be capable in Law, of suing and being sued, and of purchasing and holding lands and tenements."[111] The warden was to be appointed from time to time by the governor. The township was authorized to elect two councilmen when the names of inhabitant freeholders and householders on the assessment lists exceeded three hundred; if less than three hundred, the township would elect one councilman. The district council was empowered to make and ordain rules and regulations for the undertaking of public works, taxation, administration of justice and establishment of schools.

On June 9, 1846, the act was amended to provide that "the Warden appointed or to be appointed by the Governor for each District, shall go out of office from the time when a Warden shall be appointed for such District...and thereafter it shall not be lawful for the Governor of this Province to appoint any person to be Warden of such District."[112] The warden now was to be elected from among the councilmen. This amendment may have been in response to some discontent among the inhabitants of townships as can be inferred from the debates in the legislative assembly, which contain several references to the district councils being unpopular.[113]

The District Councils Act, however, introduced a breach between how cities and towns, on the one hand, and districts, counties, townships and villages, on the other, were governed and regulated. There was no coordination among these numerous forms of local authorities established in cities, towns and the board-of-police towns, which were governed by special acts; and, counties, townships and villages, which were now governed by the District Councils Act. Although it was the first general act concerning local authorities, all other local authorities established by special acts remained. As we can see, the system of administration that this act established was highly centralized. The district councils were set up as local branches of the State administration by limited powers that were conferred on them and by designating a warden who was directly appointed by the governor (although that was changed later). The townships were designated as mere units of local representation: they could only send one or two representatives to a council whose powers were limited and specific and which were at a distance from the township. Overall, to designate the inhabitants of a territory, which could include numerous townships scattered over a hundred square miles and without any meaningful power, to participate in decisions as a body politic, was a very limited and peculiar style of incorporation, even in its modern forms. All this shows, as the municipal commissioners in 1889 recognized, is how much the legislature feared to entrust and to empower the people but nevertheless attempted to "establish local authorities."[114] But as Whebell has argued, it also shows something else which is important in this context: that the concept of district councils also emerged as a means to 'implant democracy' in the colonies.[115] As we argued above, in the political climate of the 1830s it was to be expected that the colonies would come under the focus of 'reformers', and the District Councils Act was one of the first outcomes of reformed policies of the British colonial apparatus. Therefore, as much as there was fear of empowering bodies politic there was also an attempt politically to incorporate colonists in their own governance. The liberal credo that to govern meant to steer the conduct of subjects with their willing compliance was fully consistent with what is called the 'devolution of power'.116 And both Durham and Sydenham were remarkably clear on this point. For this reason we must concur with Whebell that the beginnings of 'self-government' in British North America was not the outgrowth of local trends or popular desire but initiated by the British colonial apparatus.117

Modern City within a Municipal System

By the late 1840s, then, two processes were at work: an accumulated experience on addressing the problem of local communities through incorporating cities and towns, and a changing attitude toward colonies within the British colonial apparatus fuelled by new political and economic conditions in England and the rebellions in Upper and Lower Canada. British North American colonies had practiced some of the principles that came to be formulated by political economists and administrators in the 1830s and the 1840s. What the liberal colonial principles did was to make some of these practices of incorporation explicit and to give a solid purpose to those practices that were set in motion. The ideas that were expressed in thought on municipal institutions, systematic colonization, systematic land disposal, the township system of courts and so on came to be represented in institutional forms that approximated these ideas. The actual realization of ideas is less relevant than what they made possible in practice: the period of the 1830s and the 1840s marked the beginning of municipal corporations in British North America.

Upper Canada: Municipal Corporations Act, 1849

By the 1830s, as we have seen, a series of municipal institutions began to appear in the local communities of British North America, which established their objective to "provide good order and government and prevent vice." These institutions, such as the board of police, the board of health and the board of trustees (discipline and schooling) were modelled after their English counterparts but possessed peculiar characteristics as well. By 1849, on the eve of the Municipal Corporations Act, there were in Upper Canada three incorporated cities (Kingston, Hamilton and Toronto), six incorporated towns (Cornwall, Bytown, Dundas, Cobourg, London and Brantford), five incorporated boards of police (Brockville, Port Hope, Prescott, Belleville, Picton) and twenty-two incorporated district councils.

In 1849, the then attorney general of Upper Canada, Robert Baldwin, introduced a bill in the legislative assembly to consolidate and repeal all acts relating to municipal authorities under one general act whose "operation was intended to be both urban and rural; to embrace every community, townships, counties, etc."[118] The bill was predicated on the principle of abolishing all district councils and establishing a gradation of corporate powers in different communities. There was strong opposition to the bill in a series of debates in that year, mostly on the grounds that to combine urban and rural legislation was untimely and that since the district councils had just acquired some popularity it would be inefficient to introduce a new system in rural municipalities.

As a response to the opposition, Baldwin asserted that the principle of inducing people to govern themselves was a principle that was now adopted in State administration but which still did not have a strong expression in *general* legislation.[119] He added that the Upper Canadian legislature had shown "that they were acquainted with the necessity of giving to the people the management of their local affairs by passing [the Act of 1793]." But since then this principle was not completely realized because "it was at one time found necessary to stimulate the people in the exercise of the power vested in them; for an Act was passed providing that where the people did not avail themselves of that power, the appointment of Municipal Officers should rest with the Quarter Sessions...There was a clear disinclination in Upper Canada, as well as in Lower Canada, to take any part in the Municipal elections....[However], the experiments...of the people having the management of their local affairs in their own hands...had the effect of creating a School of practical statesmen, and taught them the importance of civil institutions."[120] Baldwin did not question the necessity of governance but recognized the importance of local institutions. This is a cardinal point, the significance of which is often overlooked. The new colonial liberalism, among whose proponents were Durham and Baldwin, critiqued centralized governance for its inefficiency and ineffectiveness. The centralized control in British North America, according to its liberal critics, looked powerful, but in practice it could not reach the depth of the political body and hence was too narrow and limited.[121] It also contained economic and political costs that time and again proved burdensome. To assume a direct relationship between the 1835 act in England and the 1849 act in Upper Canada would be misleading, because the 1835 Municipal Corporations Act was addressed to distinct problems of municipal corporations that had centuries-old liberties, privileges, customs and duties as was discussed in Chapter Two.

However, the 1835 act brought a certain uniformity among these corporations (178 out of some 600), and there is no doubt that the general political climate of liberalism and reform in England in the 1830s was influential in the 1849 Municipal Corporations Act in Upper Canada.[122]

The Municipal Corporations Act was passed on May 30, 1849.[123] The act established all inhabitants of villages, townships, towns, counties and cities as a body corporate and politic with certain conditions and endowed them with the essential attributes of a corporation: perpetual succession, to right to hold lands, to pass regulations and bylaws, to sue and be sued and to hold a common seal. But it graded these communities by conferring distinct powers and imposing distinct liabilities and duties. The township that had one hundred or more freeholders and householders was to be a body corporate and politic. The township council consisted of five members who were elected from the township wards and who chose a reeve. The township council was empowered to appoint township officers, to erect and maintain a town hall and common schools, to undertake public works, to regulate inns and taverns, to ascertain and to establish the boundaries of the township, and to raise and assess taxes for the execution of these duties. The village was to be a body corporate apart from the township in which it was situated and which had similar powers as those of the town council. "That whenever any Incorporated Village in Upper Canada, shall be found by the Census Returns to contain within its limits upwards of three thousand inhabitants, thereupon petition of the Municipality of such Village..." it could be erected into a town.[124] The town council, which was elected from its wards, had ten specified purposes and duties, the most notable of which were establishing and regulating a police; establishing and regulating one or more alms-houses for the relief of the poor and destitute; erecting, establishing and providing workhouses or houses of correction; and, regulating buildings.

The county council was composed of the town reeves of the incorporated townships, villages and towns that were situated in the county. The county warden was to be elected from the county councilmen. The county council also could define the limits of police villages, which were unincorporated villages governed by county council. The county was a unit of the administration of justice and coordination of public works among the townships, villages and towns.

The city council was independent from and unrelated to the other councils. The city was a county by itself and justices of the peace had no jurisdiction within the city. The threshold for a town to become a city was set at fifteen thousand inhabitants. The city council consisted of aldermen and councilmen, who were elected from the wards of the city. The city council was empowered for making laws necessary for carrying into execution the authority vested in the corporation for the peace, welfare, safety and good government of the city, provided that such laws were not repugnant to that of the province or England.

From this brief look at the salient provisions of the act, we can see that there was a clear distinction brought to different kinds of corporations and their councils. Also provided was a clear set of thresholds by which townships and villages could be erected into towns and cities. This gradation of corporate powers was the cornerstone of the act, which made possible a more efficient regulation of powers possessed by numerous localities.

Lower Canada: Municipal and Road Act, 1855

The first attempt to incorporate Montréal was made in 1827 or 1828. At that time Montréal contained more people of British origin than of French. In 1832, Montréal and Québec received charters of incorporation, both of which expired in 1836 at the height of the rebellion, and were not renewed. Lord Durham remarked on this by stating, "But the want of municipal institutions has been and is most glaringly remarkable in Québec and Montréal. These cities were incorporated a few years ago by a temporary provincial Act, of which the renewal was rejected in 1836. Since that time these cities have been without any municipal government; and the disgraceful state of the streets, and the utter absence of lighting, are consequences which arrest the attention of all, and seriously affect the comfort and security of the inhabitants."[125]

In contrast with Upper Canada, municipal corporations in Lower Canada were slow to grow, and in legislative and administrative debates French Canadians were always reproached for being slow in learning to "govern their own local affairs." In his often-quoted address to the legislature, Lieutenant Governor Sydenham was expressing this idea: "It is highly desirable that the principles of local self-government, which already prevail to some extent throughout that part of the province which was formerly Upper Canada, should receive a more extended application and that the people should exercise a greater control over their own local affairs."[126] This was reflected in the lack of special acts that were passed to incorporate localities. The first general ordinance on local and municipal authorities was passed in 1840 and it was almost identical to the District Councils Act of Upper Canada already described.[127] The ordinance provided that each of the districts so erected and constituted was to be a body corporate and have perpetual succession and a common seal and be capable of suing and being sued and holding lands and tenements. The district council was composed of a warden appointed by the governor and elected councilmen from townships and parishes. The district council was empowered to make and ordain rules and regulations concerning police and to undertake public works, assessment and taxation, administration of justice and establishment of schools.

Another ordinance in the following year provided that, on the warrant of the district, the inhabitant householders of the parishes and townships should be assembled annually to elect a clerk, three assessors who were to assess taxes imposed by the legislature or the district council, a collector, a surveyor and overseer of highways, overseers of the poor, fence viewers, drain inspectors and pound keepers.[128] This act also constituted all parishes and townships as bodies corporate and politic with specified limited powers.[129]

On March 29, 1845, both these ordinances were repealed and replaced with a general act that introduced the graded system of corporate powers and capacities, which we have seen in the Municipal Corporations Act of Upper Canada in 1849.[130] The act was divided into two parts: (i) parishes and townships; and, (ii) villages, towns and boroughs. The freeholders and householders who inhabited these territorial institutions were constituted as bodies politic with graded corporate capacities and obligations. An extremely interesting clause provided that "if any Parish, Township or Municipality shall refuse or neglect to elect Councillors in the manner herein before provided, the Governor shall appoint them *ex officio*, and the Councillors so appointed shall be subject to the same duties and penalties as if they had been elected at a general meeting."[131] This provision sent a clear message to the inhabitants of Lower Canada that municipal institutions would remain in effect despite their potential or real resistance.

But, in 1847, this act was repealed and all parish and township municipalities were abolished in Lower Canada and were replaced with county municipalities.[132] This act introduced a distinction between rural municipalities (counties and their constituent parishes and townships) and villages, towns and boroughs. The inhabitants of counties were constituted as bodies politic and corporate, represented by a county council that consisted of two councilmen chosen from each parish and township situated in the county. Again, if the township or parish failed to elect councilmen, the governor could do so. These county councils, from their own number, elected a chairman or mayor and appointed necessary officers, who were to hold office for two years.

The system was again changed, this time to its present form by an act in 1855, the Lower Canada Municipal and Road Act.[133] This act left the incorporated cities outside its field of application and refined the graded system of corporate capacities by constituting the inhabitants of counties, parishes, townships, towns and villages as bodies corporate and politic. The councils were composed of seven councilmen elected at an annual meeting of the qualified inhabitants. The mayor was elected by the councilmen from their own number. The mayors of these local municipalities comprised the county council and they elected one of the mayors to be warden of the county. Once again it was provided that if any of the councils failed to be elected, the governor could appoint councilmen.[134]

From these efforts of the United Canada legislature to impose on the Lower Canadian population local authorities and obligations, we can see that the people were rather reluctant to take up the institutions of local governance, and general legislation took some experimentation before it was settled. This caused incessant complaints levelled against them by governors and legislators. These institutions that emerged in 1855 were not at all an expression of popular will, nor were they products of spontaneous choices of the people: these institutions were imposed on the people to decentralize the burden of governance and increase its efficacy by incorporating people in its sphere of influence.

Nova Scotia: Municipal Government of Counties, 1855

Under British rule after about the 1750s, Nova Scotia was governed through the justices of the peace of Quarter Sessions appointed by the governor-in-council.[135] This system remained remarkably intact in view of the fact that a large portion of the settlers after the American Revolution had come from New England colonies. We have already mentioned how the Nova Scotia legislature and the governor-in-council were loath to permit town meetings. Until 1855 the incorporation of Halifax remained the only legislation that was passed with regard to corporations in the Nova Scotia legislature. It was only in that year that the inhabitants of the counties of Annapolis, Yarmouth, King's and Queen's were incorporated as bodies politic and corporate and were placed under municipal government.[136] Halifax was excluded from the scope of this legislation.[137] The act constituted county councils to be composed of elected councilmen from townships in a somewhat analogous form to that of Upper and Lower Canada district councils. This act was followed by two further acts in 1856 that approximated a municipal system similar to those of Upper and Lower Canada. First, townships were constituted as bodies politic with limited corporate power and liabilities.[138] Each county or district incorporated was under obligation, "without delay, to proceed to lay the county or district off in so many and such municipal townships as shall be most convenient."[139] And second, the 1855 act was amended to apply to all other counties in the province. With these stipulations and with general legislation, the gradation of corporate powers in local communities as integral parts of governance took root in Nova Scotia.

Birth of the Modern Canadian City
as a Corporation

By way of concluding this chapter, let us touch upon three concepts that we can now question: 'autonomy', 'self-government', and 'municipality'. First, let us discuss the concept of autonomy. As John Taylor points out: "The birth of autonomous local government in Canada has usually been traced to the events of the 1840s, in particular to the Baldwin Municipal Act of 1849, and parallel legislation in Nova Scotia, and somewhat later, in Québec."[140] This book casts considerable doubt on this widely held interpretation because the shifts that occurred during the 1830s and the 1840s, as we have seen, were not from an absence of autonomy to its birth, but were shifts in the specific kind of governance that was conferred on the cities and towns as corporations by the legislatures—from statist and centralist policies to calculated techniques of power. The British colonial authority did not disappear or even diminish in the 1840s. It devolved and penetrated into the cities and towns more effectively and efficiently. Nor were cities restored to citizens: cities certainly did not emerge as autonomous associations of citizens. We argued in this book that Western culture has rich and vivid histories of *autonomous* (i.e., sovereign) cities. And it now seems reasonable to suggest that that term must be reserved for those histories. There is nothing autonomous or sovereign about the cities and towns that were instituted in the 1830s and the 1840s. They were not autonomous in the proper historical sense of that concept. Recall here what Wakefield said about the power of municipalities—"short of sovereignty." Moreover, whatever right and liberties that were conferred upon towns and cities, as we discussed in Chapter Two, they were not conferred upon people as a whole but on *governing bodies*. Recall here how Sydenham lamented the absence not of autonomy but of local authorities, that is, bodies authorized to govern localities. Also recall what Durham said about local authorities: local bodies were authorized to exercise governing privileges, which they would protect; he said establishing local authorities was simply the apportioning of power. The question then is not about whether modern cities are or are not autonomous but rather about what specific kind of governing rights and obligations they possess and *who* is vested with these powers. The power of the modern city *government* is not necessarily inconsistent with the power of the central authority and laws that create it. This constitutes perhaps the most distinctive element of the modernity of the city in contrast to the early modern and the medieval corporations.

We must recognize that the liberal concept of self-government lay beneath the development of the modern city as a corporation, which was not a voluntary desire on the part of 'citizens'. Was the modern city an outcome of the "genius of the English race to be concerned in the government of themselves," as Baldwin wrote to Durham?[141] Well, the English can certainly take pride in inventing the institutions to make people govern themselves at the command of authority, as Albert White so aptly described, whether that means self-determination by people is another question.[142] The analyses conducted in this book suggest that the modern principle that "people should manage their own affairs" was not reached out of some abstract affection for citizenship nor as a result of a popular, grassroots movement that agitated for local self-government. Nor was it an insight of some self-evident political philosophy. As we have seen in this study, political philosophies and legal theories were never anterior to or independent from practical struggles, but they always emerged from such struggles and were functional in them. The concept of self-government in British North America was introduced by statesmen, legislators, practical men in search of office, and overall by 'men of knowledge.' And they insisted on the institution of corporations in the hope and belief that such bodies politic would make the governance of the colonies more *efficient* and *effective* by reaching to the depths of the new society. So, the self-government that emerged in British North American colonies in the 1830s and the 1840s was neither spontaneous nor necessarily popular. It was induced, encouraged, and taught by statesmen, officials, administrators and 'men of knowledge.' The cities were constituted as corporations for better governance of the colonies: if it was not believed that constituting corporations would improve overall governance they would not have been initiated. The early period between the 1780s and the 1830s makes this abundantly clear.

Finally, we must question the relationship between the 'municipality' and the city. As we have seen, it was only in the 1840s and the 1850s that counties, townships and villages were granted corporate capacities, although *limited*, through the 'municipal corporations' acts in Upper and Lower Canada, which also constituted basic models for other provinces. At about the same time, the American law of municipal corporations also constituted villages, townships and counties as 'municipal corporations'. The Municipal Corporations Act of 1835 in England, in contrast, was applicable only to cities. The modern city differs from other municipal corporations in the wider rights (and liabilities) that are conferred upon it and also in being the historical precursor of other municipal corporations: the first corporate bodies in British North America were also cities.

It is not usually acknowledged that the term 'municipal corporation' was introduced into the Anglo-American legal systems only in the 1830s, and that before that time the act of constituting a community as a corporation was often equated with the creation of a city. According to the *Oxford English Dictionary*, before the nineteenth century the term 'municipal' was not in common use, and when used it meant, very interestingly, pertaining to the internal affairs of a State.[143] This was the case both in England after the fifteenth century and in colonial America. To complicate matters further, legal historians often used the term 'municipal corporation' as if it had been used before the nineteenth century. But the introduction of the term in that period had in fact marked something significant about the modernity of the city. The city was now considered as an internal affair of the State along with other territorial institutions such as the county. The city as a corporation in modernity is a creation of law, and that is why it is considered a municipality along with other agencies of State administration. We must recognize that the city as an autonomous corporation does not share the same lineage with other municipal corporations such as county, township, district, village, region, which, as we have seen, originated as territorial institutions of State administration. By contrast, the city as a corporation originated as a sworn association of citizens. The 'modernization' of the city as a corporation historically meant its *incorporation* into State administration as a *municipality*—a territorial institution.

Notes

1. Colin Read, *The Rebellion of 1837 in Upper Canada* (Ottawa, 1988), p. 17.
2. See Baldwin to Glenelg, July 23, 1836, Kennedy, *Statutes*, p. 329.
3. Read, *Rebellion of 1837 in Upper Canada*, pp. 19–22.
4. Municipal Commission, *First Report*, p. 25.
5. *Lower Canada Ordinances*, "An Ordinance to Incorporate the City and Town of Quebec," 3 & 4 Victoria, c. 35 (1840); "An Ordinance to Incorporate the City and Town of Montreal," 3 & 4 Victoria, c. 36 (1840).
6. 3 & 4 Victoria, c. 36, preamble.
7. Acheson, *Saint John*, chap. ii.
8. 3 & 4 Victoria, c. 35, clause xli.
9. Firth, *Town of York*, "Introduction," p. lxxii.
10. J. M. S. Careless, *Toronto to 1918*, p. 51.
11. See Griffith, *American City Government: Colonial Period*.
12. York, *Colonial Advocate*, March 30, 1826; see also Edith G. Firth, *The Town of York, 1815–1834: A Further Collection of Documents of Early Toronto* (Toronto, 1966), p. 270.
13. York, *Colonial Advocate*, December 18, 1828; Firth, *Town of York*, p. 278.
14. York, *Canadian Freeman*, January 1, 1829; Firth, "Introduction" in *Town of York*, pp. lxxiii–lxxiv.
15. York, *Canadian Freeman*, January 1, 1829; Firth, *Town of York*, p. 280.
16. York, *Canadian Freeman*, November 11, 1830; Firth, *Town of York*, p. 284.
17. Toronto, *Colonial Advocate*, March 20, 1834; Firth, *Town of York*, p. 300.
18. See Firth, *Town of York*, "Introduction," pp. lxviii–lxxix.
19. "Population Returns," Appendix M, *Journals of the Legislative Assembly of the Province of Canada*, vol. ii, 1842. See for comparison with other cities' populations G. A. Stelter, "Urban Planning and Development in Upper Canada," in W. Borah, J. Hardoy and G. A. Stelter, eds., *Urbanization in the Americas* (Ottawa, 1980), p. 147.
20. "An Act to extend the limits of the Town of York; to erect the said Town into a City; and to incorporate it under the name of the City of Toronto," *Statutes of Upper Canada*, 4 William IV, c. 23.
21. 4 William IV, c. 23, clause xxii.
22. 4 William IV, c. 23, clause xxiii.
23. City of Toronto, *Council Papers*, Letter to the Council, 1836, Archives of Ontario, MS385.
24. City of Toronto, Citizens' Committee, *Petition for House of Industry, Council Papers*, 1837, Archives of Ontario, MS385.
25. R. C. Smandych and S. N. Verdu-Jones, "The Emergence of the Asylum in 19th Century Ontario," in Neil Boyd, ed., *The Social Dimensions of Law* (Scarborough, Ontario, 1986), pp. 166–181.
26. Quoted in Smandych and Verdu-Jones, "Emergence of the Asylum in 19th Century Ontario," p. 173.
27. City of Toronto, Education Office, *Circular to explain the Common School Act and its Purposes* by E. Ryerson, Chief Superintendent of Common Schools, 1848, Archives of Ontario, MS385.

28. City of Toronto, Education Office, *Circular to explain the Common School Act and its Purposes* by E. Ryerson, Chief Superintendent of Common Schools, 1848, Archives of Ontario, MS385.

29. "An Act to Incorporate the Town of Kingston, under the name of the Mayor and Common Council of the Town of Kingston," *Statutes of Upper Canada*, March 6, 1838, 6 Victoria, c. 27.

30. "An Act to Incorporate the Town of Kingston as a City," *Statutes of Upper Canada*, May 18, 1846, 9 Victoria, c. 75.

31. "An Act to alter and amend the Act incorporating the Town of Hamilton, and to erect the same into a City," *Statutes of Upper Canada*, June 9, 1846, 9 Victoria, c. 73.

32. "An Act to amend the Act of Incorporation of the Town of Cornwall, and to establish a Town Council therein, in lieu of a Board of Police," *Statutes of Upper Canada*, June 9, 1846, 9 Victoria, c. 72.

33. 9 Victoria, c. 72, clause ii.

34. "An Act to confer limited Corporate Powers on the Towns and Villages of Canada West, not specially incorporated," *Statutes of Canada*, July 28, 1847, 10 & 11 Victoria, c. 42.

35. 9 Victoria, c. 73, clause xlii.

36. T. B. Akins, *History of Halifax City* (Halifax, 1895).

37. D. J. H. Higgins, *Local and Urban Politics in Canada* (Toronto, 1986), p. 37.

38. Akins, *Halifax*, p. 88; Higgins, *Urban Politics*, p. 37.

39. "An Act to incorporate the Town of Halifax," *Nova Scotia Statutes*, 4 Victoria, c. 55.

40. 4 Victoria, c. 55, clause lxxxiv.

41. 4 Victoria, c. 55, clause lvii.

42. 4 Victoria, c. 55, clause lii.

43. Richard Pares, "The Economic Factors in the History of the Empire," *Economic History Journal*, vii (1937), pp. 119f.

44. John Manning Ward, *Colonial Self-Government: The British Experience, 1759–1856* (London, 1976), p. 211.

45. Helen T. Manning, *British Colonial Government After the American Revolution, 1782–1820* (New York, 1933).

46. Buckner, *Transition to Responsible Government*, p. 51.

47. Robert Torrens, "A Paper on the Means of Reducing the Poor Rates," *Pamphleteer*, x, 1817, p. 524.

48. Torrens, "A Paper on the Means of Reducing the Poor Rates," p. 524.

49. Ward, *Colonial Self-Government*, p. 221.

50. Knorr, *British Colonial Theories*, p. 269.

51. Quoted in Knorr, *British Colonial Theories*, pp. 275–276.

52. Ward, *Colonial Self-Government*, pp. 209–246; Winch, *Classical Political Economy and Colonies*, pp. 144–168; Knaplund, *James Stephen and the British Colonial System, 1813–1847*, pp. 252–280.

53. "Emigration: Comparative Prospects of Our New Colonies," *Westminster Review*, xxxv, 1841, p. 132.

54. Winch, *Classical Political Economy and Colonies*, p. 144.

55. Edward Gibbon Wakefield, *A View of the Art of Colonization* (London, 1849). Wakefield was engaged in numerous experiments in colonization in New Zealand, Australia and British North America. He was an unofficial consultant

for Lord Durham in 1838 and was the author of Appendix B in Lord Durham's *Report on the Affairs of British North America*. The Appendix dealt with the issues of land disposal for systematic colonization.

56. Wakefield, *Art of Colonization*, pp. 226–227 (emphasis added).
57. Wakefield, *Art of Colonization*, pp. 226–227.
58. Wakefield, *Art of Colonization*, p. 276.
59. Roebuck, *Colonies of England*, pp. 102–103 (emphasis added).
60. Edward Gibbon Wakefield, "Sir Charles Metcalfe in Canada" (1844), article reprinted in E. M. Wrong, *Charles Buller and Responsible Government* (Oxford, 1926), p. 348.
61. Edward Gibbon Wakefield, *England and America* (London, 1833), page references are to the edition in his *Collected Works*, M. F. L. Pritchard, ed. (Auckland, 1969).
62. Wakefield, *England and America*, pp. 500ff.
63. Wakefield, *England and America*, p. 538.
64. Wakefield, *England and America*, p. 538.
65. Wakefield, *England and America*, pp. 552ff.
66. Wakefield, *Art of Colonization*, p. 433 (emphasis added).
67. William Molesworth addressing the House of Commons in 1848, in H. E. Egerton, ed., *Selected Speeches of Sir William Molesworth on Questions Relating to Colonial Policy* (London, 1903), p. 112.
68. Ward, *Colonial Self-Government*, p. 211. Ward expresses this more elaborately, which is worth quoting in length: "The new idea of great colonies of settlement was strongly apparent in Britain from the 1840s on, and was materially different from any earlier way of thinking about the empire. Colonies were still regarded as part of an imperial system of commerce, although for many people the system was becoming free trade, not protection, preference and privilege. Colonies were also still regarded as subordinate to Britain and believed to be a vital element of her strength and prestige. The new aspect was confident expectation of a great imperial destiny, in which the colonies of settlement would be extensions of Britain overseas, peopled from the British Isles, reproducing vital parts of British polity and society, developed with British capital, under some British control (economic as well as political), and sharing in British culture, civilization, and government. Even if they became independent they would remain British in character and attachment." p. 236. See also Phillip A. Buckner, *Transition to Responsible Government*, pp. 290–324.
69. Glenelg to Gosford, July 17, 1835, Kennedy, *Statutes*, p. 405.
70. Glenelg to Gosford, July 17, 1835, Kennedy, *Statutes*, p. 405.
71. James Stuart Mill, *Considerations on Representative Government*, in *John Stuart Mill: Three Essays* (Oxford, 1975), p. 403.
72. Robert E. Leader, ed., *Life and Letters of John Arthur Roebuck* (London, 1897), p. 28.
73. John Arthur Roebuck, *The Colonies of England: A Plan for the Government of Our Colonial Possessions* (London, 1849).
74. Roebuck was the first to envisage the idea of a federation of provinces in British North America. See William Ormsby, *The Emergence of the Federal Concept in Canada, 1839–1845* (Toronto, 1969).
75. Roebuck, *Colonies of England*, p. 13.
76. Roebuck, *Colonies of England*, p. 115.

77. Roebuck, *Colonies of England*, pp. 123–124.
78. Roebuck, *Colonies of England*, p. 114.
79. Roebuck, *Colonies of England*, pp. 121–122.
80. Roebuck, *Colonies of England*, pp. 129–130.
81. Roebuck, *Colonies of England*, p. 134.
82. Roebuck, *Colonies of England*, p. 134.
83. Roebuck, *Colonies of England*, p. 135.
84. Roebuck, *Colonies of England*, p. 141.
85. "The wild country, its great rivers, the vast scale upon which everything was framed, made on me a profound impression. The freedom in which we lived, the thorough liberty of going where we liked, the new scenes, brought with them a sort of enchantment." Robert E. Leader, ed., *Life and Letters of John Arthur Roebuck* (London, 1897), pp. 20–21.
86. Charles Buller says this in his account that he wrote in 1840: "Sketch of Lord Durham's Mission to Canada in 1838," in "Durham Papers," *Report of the Public Archives*, A. G. Doughty, ed. (Ottawa, 1924), p. 358.
87. See Ged Martin, *The Durham Report and British Policy: A Critical Essay* (Cambridge, 1972); a close reading of the text has been accomplished recently by Janet Ajzenstat, *The Political Thought of Lord Durham* (Kingston, 1988).
88. Russell to Sydenham, September 7, 1839, Kennedy, *Statutes*, p. 516.
89. Durham, *Report*, p. 92.
90. Durham, *Report*, pp. 98–99.
91. Durham, *Report*, p. 114.
92. Durham, *Report*, p. 114.
93. Durham, *Report*, p. 113.
94. Durham, *Report*, p. 287.
95. Durham, *Report*, p. 287.
96. Quoted by Karl Marx, *Capital: A Critique of Political Economy*, vol. i: *A Critical Analysis of Capitalist Production* (New York, International Publishers, 1967; original publication 1867), p. 770.
97. Baldwin to Glenelg, July 23, 1836, *Report of the Public Archives*, Arthur G. Doughty, ed. (Ottawa, 1924), pp. 329–330.
98. Baldwin to Glenelg, July 23, 1836, Doughty, *Report*, p. 331.
99. Glenelg to Gosford, July 17, 1835, Kennedy, *Statutes*, p. 405.
100. Russell to Sydenham, September 7, 1839, Kennedy, *Statutes*, p. 519.
101. Russell to Sydenham, September 7, 1839, Kennedy, *Statutes*, p. 519.
102. "An Act to re-unite Provinces of Upper and Lower Canada, and for the Government of Canada," *Statutes of Canada*, 3 & 4, Victoria, c. 35.
103. Sydenham to Russell, September 16, 1840, Kennedy, *Statutes*, pp. 551–554.
104. Sydenham to Russell, September 16, 1840, Kennedy, *Statutes*, p. 552.
105. Sydenham to Russell, September 16, 1840, Kennedy, *Statutes*, p. 552.
106. Sydenham to Russell, September 16, 1840, Kennedy, *Statutes*, p. 552.
107. Sydenham to a Friend, 1840, Kennedy, *Statutes*, p. 555.
108. Sydenham to his Brother, August 28, 1841, Kennedy, *Statutes*, p. 563.
109. "An Act to Provide for the better internal Government of that part of this Province which formerly constituted the Province of Upper Canada, by the establishment of Local and Municipal Authorities therein," *Statutes of Canada* (1841–1867), August 27, 1841, 4 & 5 Victoria, c. 10.
110. 4 & 5 Victoria, c. 10, clause lxii.

111. 4 & 5 Victoria, c. 10, preamble.
112. "An Act to amend the laws relative to District Council in Upper Canada," *Statutes of Canada*, June 9, 1846, 9 Victoria, c. 40, clause iv.
113. Elizabeth Gibbs, ed., *Debates of the Legislative Assembly of United Canada, 1841–1867*, vol. viii (1849), part ii, pp. 1573–1578.
114. Second Report of the Municipal Commission, *Sessional Papers*, no. 3, Legislative Assembly of Ontario, 1889, p. 50.
115. C. F. J. Whebell, "The Upper Canada District Councils Act of 1841 and British Colonial Policy," *The Journal of Imperial and Commonwealth History*, vol. xviii (1989), pp. 185–209.
116. Whebell, "The Upper Canada District Councils Act of 1841," pp. 204–205.
117. Whebell, "Upper Canada District Councils Act of 1841," p. 203. Without doubt the British colonial apparatus accumulated experience in creating incorporated localities in colonial America (as Griffith demonstrated in his study on de jure corporations) which influenced the colonial experience that unfolded in British North America. See Griffith, *History of American City Government*, p. 52.
118. Gibbs, ed., *Debates of the Legislative Assembly of United Canada, 1841–1867*, vol. viii (1849), January 30, 1849, part i, p. 364.
119. Gibbs, *Debates*, vol. viii (1849), March 27, 1849, part ii, p. 1574.
120. Gibbs, *Debates*, vol. viii (1849), March 27, 1849, part ii, p. 1574.
121. Stewart, *Origins of Canadian Politics*, p. 44.
122. See Whebell, "Robert Baldwin and Decentralization, 1841–1849."
123. "An Act to provide, by one general law, for the erection of Municipal Corporations, and the establishment of Regulations of Police, in and for the several Counties, Cities, Towns, Townships and Villages in Upper Canada," *Statutes of Canada*, May 30, 1849, 12 Victoria, c. 81.
124. 12 Victoria, c. 81, clause lxxix.
125. Durham, *Report*, p. 115.
126. Upper Canada, *Journal of the House of Assembly, 1841*, p. 8
127. "An Ordinance to provide for the better internal government of this Province, by the establishment of Local or Municipal Authorities therein," *Ordinances of Lower Canada, 1841*, 4 Victoria c. 4.
128. "An Ordinance to prescribe and regulate the election and appointment of certain Officers, in the several Parishes and Townships in this Province, and to make other provisions for the local interests of the Inhabitants of these divisions of the Province," *Ordinances of Lower Canada, 1841*, 4 Victoria, c. 3.
129. 4 Victoria c. 3, clause xviii.
130. "An Act to Repeal Certain Ordinances therein mentioned, and to make better provision for the establishment of Local and Municipal Authorities in Lower Canada," *Statutes of Canada*, March 29, 1845, 8 Victoria, c. 40.
131. 8 Victoria, c. 40, clause xvi.
132. "An Act to make better provision for the establishment of Municipal Authorities in Lower Canada," *Statutes of Canada*, July 28, 1847, 10 & 11 Victoria, c. 7.
133. "Lower Canada Municipal and Road Act," *Statutes of Canada*, May 30, 1855, 18 Victoria,, c. 100.
134. 18 Victoria, c. 100, clause xxxvi.
135. J. M. Beck, *The Evolution of Municipal Government in Nova Scotia, 1749–1973* (Halifax, 1973).

136. "An Act for the Municipal Government of Counties," *Statutes of Nova Scotia*, 18 Victoria, c. 49, 1855.
137. 18 Victoria, c. 49, clause lxxxix.
138. "An Act for the Municipal Government of Townships," *Statutes of Nova Scotia*, 19 Victoria, c. 11, 1856.
139. 19 Victoria, c. 11, clause i.
140. John H. Taylor, "Urban Autonomy in Canada: Its Evolution and Decline," in G. A. Stelter and A. F. J. Artibise, eds., *The Canadian City: Essays in Urban and Social History* (Ottawa, 1984), p. 491; see also Higgins, *Local and Urban Politics*, pp. 60–63; Crawford, *Municipal Government in Canada*, chap. ii.
141. Baldwin to Durham, August 23, 1838, Doughty, *Report*, p. 328.
142. White, *Self-Government at the King's Command*.
143. *Oxford English Dictionary*, 2nd ed. (Oxford, 1930).

6

CONCLUSION: PAST AND PRESENT

THE city as a sworn association of citizens that was organized as a *de facto* corporation emerged in the twelfth century in Europe. It was a distinctive institution which embodied traditions of Germanic folklaw, Christian practices and Roman law.[1] Its emergence coincided with revival of trade after the collapse of the Roman Empire. Although cities as fortifications and courts were founded before the twelfth century, mainly in the tenth and eleventh centuries by lords and kings, the cities that emerged during the twelfth century were autonomous associations of merchants and artisans that seized power from lords and kings and declared themselves as legitimate governing authorities. These *de facto* corporations exercised powers, made laws, created institutions, in short, governed themselves. The city as an autonomous corporation owed little to the past, although citizens were inclined to use Roman legal language to define their newly founded institutions: mayors, councils, congregations, and seals.[2] The city also owed nothing to the popes, emperors, princes, kings, or lords. The city declared itself as a sovereign corporation, and federations and leagues of sovereign cities were formed particularly in Germany, France and Italy.[3] The coexistence of multiple sovereignties or autonomous polities did not pose any problem for cities or lords and kings (and their jurists) who simply had to live with them. The cities of the twelfth century were cities with citizens in two senses. First, the law that prevailed in cities stipulated that a villein's or serf's unchallenged residence in a city as a citizen for a year and a day precluded any claim on him by a former lord.[4] Second, and more importantly, citizens as members of the city as a corporation had liberties of law making, regulation and administration as a collective, and practicing these liberties defined the sphere of citizenship. To put it differently, in the medieval power configuration and law, citizenship and liberty became synonymous.

But another institution that emerged at the same time and challenged the autonomous city was the kingship, which derived from the same traditions as the city. The kingdoms of Europe from the twelfth century onwards consolidated large territories under their rule and increasingly became hostile to cities but were enamoured by the revenue the cities generated for their war machines. Autonomous cities were the seedbed of merchants and artisans, trade and industry. Hence, a tension emerged between the kingdoms and the autonomous cities. But, for reasons that still confound historians, the kingdoms of Europe evolved into powerful monarchies and ultimately into modern States.[5]

Against such powers, to which they undoubtedly contributed, the autonomous cities of Europe could not resist. By the seventeenth century the autonomous city had become the subjugated handmaiden of the great absolutist States, which monopolized the means of rule in their territories. Among the most fascinating aspects of this transformation is the emergence of political and legal discourse about the city (treatises, theories, enactments, legislation, edicts, proclamations, practices, inquiries, surveys), which amply reflected the tension between the city and the State, and which has been the focus of this book. By the fifteenth century the political and legal discourse on the city reached the conclusion that corporate power not prescribed by the king was neither legitimate nor legal. It also reached a clear conception of what a corporation was and what legitimate powers it could exercise: *de jure* corporation. This was the legal invention of the early modern city as a corporation. According to this conception the corporation was an abstract and subordinate body politic. It was abstract because the obligations and liberties of the people who made up the corporation were distinct from individual obligations and liberties. For example, when a corporation was created, it was thought to have perpetual succession, an attribute that separated the existence of the city from its citizens in the eyes of royal law. Similarly, a corporation could appear before the court and hold landed property distinct from its individual members. It was also abstract because its properties and its very existence were the creation of law—royal law. These *de jure* characteristics became the basic attributes of an incorporated city in the early modern era. Any group of people who might gather and define themselves as a corporation, exercising powers that were not prescribed by law, was declared illegal, and in time, became unthinkable. By the eighteenth century, European kings and their functionaries (lawyers, historians, jurists) had rewritten the history of autonomous corporations, claiming that cities had always been created by the kings. This was a time of edicts and proclamations and the cities had to obey. They even had to accept their own histories rewritten by royal historians. Cities became separate from their citizens; citizenship was dissociated from liberty. It was also in the early modern city that the mayor became a ceremonial figure, who was now called lord mayor, and city councils began to organize processions and pageantry as well as feasting and liveries to keep citizens 'busy', 'well-regulated', and 'ordered'.[6]

The rudiments of the modern conception of the city as a corporation had been developing since the late seventeenth century. Faced with a demographic and economic upswing, the kings paid more attention to and encouraged the development of a discourse on the art of government. The ordering, regulating, and using of cities and their corporate oligarchies emerged as powerful instruments of governance in the early modern era. If in the twelfth century the kings were enamoured by the economic use of the city, the early modern legislators in the late-seventeenth and eighteenth centuries were enamoured by the political use of the city in inculcating useful habits in people: a great series of State legislation—poor laws—was by and large enforced by cities. But, by the nineteenth century it was impossible to govern the politically and economically complex European States with repressive legislation. Rather, the modern 'enlightened' legislation combined, on the one hand, positive rules and, on the other hand, apparatuses of governance, to increase the usefulness of the subjects to the State. By the nineteenth century the modern city as an apparatus of governance had proven useful in two ways. First, it relieved the State from the economic cost of undertaking political governance by delegating powers to governing bodies. Second, it incorporated the city within a system of continuous and rational governance along with other territorial institutions of State administration and governance such as counties, regions, townships, and villages.

The English colonial experience derived and also diverged from this pattern. When American colonies were opened up for settlement during the seventeenth century, for a number of complicated reasons the English State was not quite sure what to do with those distant territories. During this 'momentary' absence of royal authority, new local autonomies emerged in colonial America that haunted the rest of the British colonial history. This was the first divergence: while at home the autonomous city was subjugated, in colonies, new autonomous polities emerged. However, toward the end of the seventeenth century the English State wanted to use the colonies for its wealth and benefit. The question of how to govern distant colonies—government at a distance—was an entirely new question for political and legal discourse, which was never resolved. But in the process, the English State built up a colonial apparatus and invented new institutions among which royal cities figured prominently. Colonial American experience suggests that when State authority fails to make its presence felt, autonomous communities develop, that is, people with common interests tend to gather amongst themselves and organize their own political existence. There were certainly parallels with the medieval exercise of citizenship. Similarly, it also shows that loyalty and allegiance to the State were not universal human attributes but were produced through government. To put it bluntly, those people who organized their own political existence according to their own interests and concerns did not feel loyal to an abstract notion of a nation thousands of miles away. That kind of allegiance had to be inculcated through governance.

These were more or less the conclusions reached by the colonial apparatus and its statesmen, administrators and legislators who invented the royal colony with its appointed governor and council and elected house of assembly. The royal colony was anxious to create royal cities (close corporations) for exercise of colonial authority. By the time of the American Revolution, the number of royal colonies had reached eight and the royal cities twenty-four to thirty-five—clearly not enough to resist those 'little republics'. Not surprisingly, the early American Republic displayed considerable hostility towards royal cities and their oligarchic governing bodies. This was the second divergence: while in England there were considerations on how to integrate the city in a system of governance, in the early Republic the doctrine of absolute supremacy of state legislatures was being developed. Hence, the colonial period bequeathed two paradoxical legacies to American cities: municipal home rule, which derived from the citizenship practices that emerged in corporate colonies, and the rule of state supremacy (Dillon's Rule), which emerged in reaction to colonial oligarchies in royal cities.[7]

Meanwhile, the British colonial apparatus concentrated its efforts on settling British North America—Upper Canada, Lower Canada, Nova Scotia and New Brunswick. The colonial apparatus developed an ambiguous attitude toward cities as corporations. On the one hand, it was determined to prevent the emergence of autonomous practices of citizenship, for it had reached the conclusion that among the reasons for the rebellion of the thirteen colonies was acceptance of such practices as town meetings. But, on the other hand, it needed cities to speed up settlement for effective government. The question that the colonial apparatus confronted was, in short, how to build cities without citizens. In response to this question, the colonial apparatus initiated a series of institutions such as boards of police, police towns, and special incorporations. But in the 1830s and 1840s, with the sweeping changes in concepts of government and colonies in England and Europe, modern cities were instituted in British North America.

By the 1850s the basic institutional features of the modern city had taken shape in British North America. The modern city became an essential unit in a municipal system whose characteristics have, so far, remained remarkably intact.[8] And very similar systems have been established in other provinces that joined the British North American confederation.[9] If the analyses undertaken in this study are tenable we must conclude that the birth of the modern city was neither self-evident nor inevitable; it happened in the course of complex struggles, intricate balancing of partly incompatible aims, and above all, it happened within the context of broad historical changes. The British colonial practices of government had been evolving since the 1660s in colonial America; they reached a new threshold of sophistication in the 1830s and the 1840s in British North America.

The emergence of the city as a modern corporation in Canadian history must be associated with the rise of modern governance, a mode of exercising power that relied less on a punitive and negative system of law and more on institutional and enabling law. The centralized and statist policies of the colonial apparatus between the 1780s and the 1830s had not succeeded in containing the tension between the desirability of granting some local rights and the imperative of asserting central authority. The rebellions in 1837 and 1838, once again, taught the British statesmen and administrators this lesson. By contrast, the modern program of governance, resting mainly on a system of enabling legislation, managed to contain this tension by conferring upon local corporations the authority to govern 'their own affairs', by specifying the domains in which the corporations must establish institutions, by setting basic parameters and criteria. Or, in other words, modern municipal law forged an effective balance between local autonomy and central authority by constituting the modern city as an apparatus of governance. The modern city became an apparatus of governance inasmuch as it was encouraged and empowered to steer the conduct of its people towards accepted and useful pursuits. In this capacity, the modern city thus has legal, as well as political components. Let us highlight here some of the most important principles—principles that by and large we take for granted, but which, as I argued in this book, are anything but self-evident. They embody centuries-long legal practices and the political struggles out of which these practices arose. Seemingly self-evident 'legal' principles, such as why the city should have a council, elections, wards, or why it is constituted as a corporation with obligations and responsibilities, embody very significant political principles that have been lost in the abyss of time.

Consider, for example, the legal principles involved in the creation of a corporation with a name, with perpetual succession and with powers to hold property, to sue and be sued, and to pass bylaws. What do these attributes tell us? Above all, they signify the separation of the city as a corporation from its inhabitants, where an elected governing body is thereby authorized to act on behalf of the qualified inhabitants as a whole because these powers are delegated to the corporation and not to any of its individual members or to any member of its governing body. The governing body is constituted through local elections and on the basis of specified property and residence qualifications. The latter gave legislatures considerable power to influence the composition of local councils beyond the direct appointment of the first council of a newly incorporated city. We have seen how the property qualifications for mayor, aldermen, councilmen and their electors were adjusted carefully from one city to another to influence the composition of the governing body. Another set of legal components, therefore, has to do with the requisite qualifications for voters and electoral candidates. Although in British North America the property qualifications were moderately low in comparison with British municipal franchise in 1835, the practice itself reveals that not everybody was thought fit to participate in elections. Here is another capacity of the modern city as an apparatus of governance: by adjusting the property qualifications the legislature could determine the level of participation in the body politic.

What was the authority of the governing body? It could sell and buy property, appear before a court and pass bylaws to regulate, directly or indirectly, the conduct of the people with binding authority. The governing body exercises these powers as the executive of the corporation, authorized by a superior legislature ('from above') and by the qualified people ('from below'). Hence, the source of the authority of the governing body is twofold. First, it is the legislature that creates the modern city as a corporation and that empowers its governing body. And, second, it is the qualified inhabitants that elect those who form its governing body. But the latter source could authorize the governing body to exercise *only* those powers that are prescribed by the former. By contrast, as we have seen, the source of authority in the medieval corporation rested largely with the citizenry, whereas in the early modern city it was the State that seized the authority to create and govern corporations. We can see the intricate legal balance thus reached in the modern city between autonomy and authority. But the modern city as a corporation still retained the early modern principle of separation of the city from its citizens: the city was governed by a separate body. While in the autonomous city, citizens decided amongst themselves who belonged to the city and who was to govern, in the early modern city it was the State administration that appointed a governing body to exercise power over citizens. Both the early modern and modern cities were cities without citizens; if citizens were 'subjects' in the former they became 'voters' in the latter. The modernity of the city as a corporation consists in rules specified by the State within which a governing body authorized by the voters (whose qualifications are determined as citizens of the State) exercises its franchised rights and fulfills its governmental obligations.

As for the political principles, the modern city functions as an apparatus of governance by virtue and through continuous operations of specific fields of power that the governing body of the city is both enabled and enjoined to establish. First, there was the requirement to build and operate a system of penitentiaries, correction houses, houses of industry, court houses, and schools, all of which were set with the explicit purpose of disciplining (in the sense of inculcating 'useful' habits) certain segments of the population. Second, the birth of the modern city is clearly coterminous with the introduction of techniques ensuring a continuous presence and exercise of authority. As we have seen, the early function of police was less one of law enforcement than one of continuous watch and positive encouragement of proper conduct. Before full-time police forces had been established, constabulary forces consisted of unpaid and obliged labour, thus amply reflecting the principle of self-government as obligation. Third, cities were obliged to introduce 'public health' regulations which had more explicit social and moral functions and connotations than their more recent counterparts have for us today. Fourth, the governing bodies were empowered to introduce measures and practices to regulate the physical layout of cities and the use of lands within their boundaries. Orderly, uniform, and well-regulated city layout was considered to have positive effects on the conduct of the people.

If the modern city was an apparatus of governance, what was the role of citizens and citizenship? The function of a corporation as an agency to regulate and administer the internal concerns of a locality in matters peculiar to the place incorporated, and not common to larger jurisdictions, is only one aspect of the modernity of the city. The other side, which is more difficult to acknowledge but is thoroughly embodied in modern legislation, is that it is the purpose and practice of the legislature to make use of the apparatus of incorporation to exercise powers, to perform duties and to execute functions that are not local or municipal in their intent or scope but, in fact, serve the State at large. The fields of power discussed above, which the governing body is obliged to constitute, express general State policies by and large. Similarly, the meaning of autonomy in modernity is altogether different. If by that term one means the liberty of citizens to make decisions about the conditions of their city, independent from State or other external prerogatives, clearly this is belied by the mere fact that many obligations of citizens were and are specified by the State. The rights granted to corporations are by no means unconditional or unspecified; powers are always specified and qualified with the clear understanding that if the governing body goes beyond the powers thus granted, the corporation can be punished. To conclude, beneath the arrival of 'democracy' and 'responsible government' in British North American colonies in the 1840s, tirelessly announced by liberal historians, there emerged a tight network of institutions for discipline, continuous presence of governance and policing, the core of which was the modern city as a corporation.

If these are the conclusions we can draw from the birth of the modern Canadian city as a corporation set against the background histories of England and America, what comparisons and contrasts can we make with regard to corporations in England and America that would shed some light on the modernity of the city in general? British North American political and legal conditions, although circumscribed within broader English and American conditions, still diverged from them and formalized novel institutions. Perhaps the most striking and influential among these was the general *graded* municipal corporations acts we discussed above. At the time these acts were passed, neither England nor any of the states in the American Republic possessed similar counterparts. In England, the Municipal Corporations Act (1835) was addressed to the problem of close corporations and of industrial cities; it was applicable only to 178 cities. It was not until 1882 that the remaining boroughs were constituted as modern municipal corporations. And it was not until 1888 and 1894 that England instituted a municipal system similar to that of the 1840s in British North America. Similarly, in the early American Republic all incorporations were accomplished by special acts of state legislatures and it was not until the late nineteenth century that general acts were being passed. Furthermore, legal and political thought in the American Republic was mostly preoccupied with the question of the royal cities, the governing oligarchies created in them during the colonial period, and the rethinking of the relations between the cities and state legislatures. By contrast, the problems of close corporations and of *de facto* corporations did not exist in British North America. From the very beginning, the carefully calculated statist policies succeeded in circumventing autonomous practices of citizenship. Therefore, the practice of establishing a graded municipal system was an original synthesis of two contemporary developments. First, of course, the developments in English corporate law constituted a precedent. And, second, the early American legal practice that incorporated localities such as villages, counties and townships with special-act charters also constituted a model.[10] The modernity of the city was thus first fully crystallized in British North America, where the city became an apparatus of governance within a system of municipalities as early as the 1840s. More research is needed to explore the modernity of the city as a corporation by focusing on colonial societies.[11]

Finally, if the modern cities as corporations are cities without citizens, what lessons can we draw for governing our cities today? To draw lessons from an overview of centuries-long development of the city as a corporation is an extremely difficult if not a risky undertaking, for the usefulness of appropriating history in broad sequences, as discussed earlier, is not in finding 'solutions' to 'problems' that confront us at present but in questioning limits within which we think about those problems, and in formulating a new set of questions. To think about the modern city as a corporation requires questioning limits that have been bequeathed to us from a centuries-long legal and political discourse. We cannot think about issues such as autonomy, citizenship, and self-government without knowing and questioning such limits. The modern experience of citizenship has unfolded within these limits. Exercising our citizenship, for example, is understood in modernity by and large as the 'right' to choose from political candidates who run for civic positions. Accordingly, city politics means influencing either the composition or the agenda of the city council as the governing body. But why is the council the governing body of the city? Why is the act that governs the city drawn up by legislators and not citizens? Why is the city as a corporation separated from its inhabitants? Why are cities as political communities feared? Why are practices of citizenship treated with skepticism? Why is the city considered a creation of law? Why is the city considered a subordinate community? I have suggested if not convincing at least forceful answers to these questions, which should serve as an historical background to various studies of the city as a political institution.

A royal commission that inquired into municipal corporations in Ontario released its reports in 1888 and 1889. After laborious historical comparisons and contrasts with other Western municipal systems such as in Great Britain, the United States, Germany and France, the commissioners concluded that "the Ontario municipal system when compared with those we have thus briefly described must appear vastly superior to them all in simplicity, symmetry, and sufficiency."[12] Yet the commissioners stated that "as we have derived all our institutions, political and municipal, directly or indirectly from Great Britain, we endeavoured to trace the growth and development of municipal institutions in that country, and to ascertain whether it is likely to be beneficial to us could be gathered from its experience or example. We found the task very difficult and not very profitable."[13] A century later, under very different conditions and with different purposes, a similar historical inquiry is now published by an author who disagrees with the commissioners. About its usefulness the reader will be the judge.

Notes

1. Black, *Guilds and Civil Society*, pp. 53–65.
2. Huppert, *After the Black Death*, p. 19; Gierke, *Community in Historical Perspective*, p. 35.
3. Gierke, *Community in Historical Perspective*, chap. vi.
4. Reynolds, *English Medieval Towns*, p. 100.
5. Charles Tilly, *Coercion, Capital and European States, A.D. 990–1990* (London, 1990).
6. Reynolds, *English Medieval Towns*, p. 180.
7. Griffith and Adrian, *Formation of Traditions, 1775–1870*, pp. 34–39; Edwars A. Gere, "Dillon's Rule and the Cooley Doctrine: Reflections on the Political Culture," *Journal of Urban History*, vol. viii (1982), pp. 271–298; Frug, "The City as a Legal Concept," p. 1094; Jon C. Teaford "The City versus State: The Struggle for Legal Ascendancy," *The American Journal of Legal History*, vol. xvii, 1973, pp. 51–65.
8. Aitchison, "Municipal Corporations Act of 1849"; G. E. Hall, "Municipal Government's 100th Anniversary," *Municipal World* 59, 1949, pp. 369–374.
9. Crawford, *Municipal Government*, chap. ii.
10. Griffith and Adrian, *Formation of Traditions, 1775–1870*, pp. 34–39.
11. See, for an example of comparative research in this field, David Hamer, *New Towns in the New World: Images and Perceptions of the Nineteenth-Century Urban Frontier* (New York, 1990).
12. "First Report of the Commission on Municipal Institutions appointed by the Government of the Province of Ontario," *Sessional Papers*, no. 42, 1888, p. 30.
13. "First Report," p. 4.

APPENDIX 1
ANGLO-SAXON ORIGINS OF
ENGLISH CITIES

We have occasionally referred to the uniqueness of English cities during the twelfth and thirteenth centuries. Compared with European cities, especially with the Italian city republics and French communes, they were more integrated within the English State and had more restricted autonomy. This appendix surveys a literature that addresses this issue. It is important to understand the subsequent development of the English law of cities as corporations. The period that this literature largely focuses on is Anglo-Saxon England before the Norman Conquest, roughly between the ninth and late eleventh centuries. It was in this period that we observe, on the one hand, the emergence of counties and townships and, on the other, the founding of new cities (new *burhs*).

Counties and Townships

What were the origins of such English territorial institutions as counties and townships? This was the question that troubled institutional and legal historians in the late nineteenth century. Although by and large this question was motivated by an urge to establish the national identity of the English, especially its 'democratic' institutions, very useful research was accomplished.

The constitutional historian William Stubbs was first to point out a shift in the late ninth and tenth centuries, which he called "territorialization of power."[1] By this he meant that the kings began to divide and subdivide their territories into units through which they extended and focused their power. Similarly, the kings began to exercise their rule with territorial jurisdiction. The shift was concomitant with the consolidation of numerous kingdoms by Wessex: until the late ninth century the English had been divided among a number of kingdoms, which were often at war with each other. By the tenth century interregnal conflicts were practically over. All the kingdoms except Wessex had been subsumed by either the West Saxon kings or the Vikings, and during the following decades the kings of Wessex extended their authority over nearly all the territory hitherto thought of as English.[2] It can be argued that the invention of some form of royal administration through communities must be both cause and consequence of this consolidation: Stubbs stated that "the tendency toward territorial union [did not proceed] from any consciousness of national unity or from any instinct of self-government. Nor can it be attributed solely to the religious unity, which rather helped than originated such a tendency. This tendency resulted not so much from the striving of the peoples as from the ambition of the kings."[3] In other words, it is reasonable to suggest that the territorial institutions emerged as instruments of royal power.[4]

Although the origins of counties and townships remained a controversial issue, there seems to be agreement on this point among constitutional and legal historians. Maitland devoted a full chapter in *The History of English Law* to what he called land communities. He concluded that "men are drilled and regimented into communities in order that the state may be strong and the land may be at peace. Much of the communal life we see is not spontaneous. The community is a community, not because it is a self-sufficient organism, but because it is a subordinate member of a greater community...The communities are far more often the bearers of duties than of rights."[5] John E. A. Jolliffe identified the "conversion of the older organization by kindreds into that matrix of the medieval and modern society, the territorial community" as the most profound change in the tenth century.[6] He argued that with the emergence of these territorial institutions "the essentials of the territorial state were laid down." More recently, Henry Loyn brought economic and social considerations to bear upon the emergence of these juridical political formations.[7] He emphasized the connections between the royal exaction of revenues and creation of such communities. The growing wealth of trade and the increasing demand for defence must have pressured the kings to increase revenues.[8] The first regular and permanent land tax known in the West (the geld) was introduced in the early eleventh century.[9] The geld undoubtedly signified the territorialization of power and presupposed a growing efficiency of monarchical administration based on territorial institutions.[10] And, in a recent and important study of communities in early medieval Europe, Susan Reynolds concluded that few of the communities she surveyed could be considered "pure communities in the sense that their activities were entirely voluntary, reciprocal, and unmediated. By the tenth century European society was much too complex, rich, and unequal, and much too committed to ideas of hierarchy, to have been able to cope with statelessness."[11]

To summarize, what made such institutions territorial was that they were composed of a group of people whose communities were not based on relationships of blood or kinship (as was the predominant relation between the seventh and the ninth centuries in Germanic tribes and kingdoms) but on relationships of land proprietorship and jurisdiction of royal law. In other words, the emergence of royal government (imposing a particular conduct on people) and administration (integration and coordination of human activities) coincided with the founding of territorial institutions in the late ninth and tenth centuries. This period in Anglo-Saxon England saw profound changes, which were defined as the territorialization of power, that is, relations among people were organized around belonging to a territorial institution and possessing land. These territorial institutions constituted a network of obligations and duties that crisscrossed and overlapped each other and imposed enormous burdens. On the one hand, territorial institutions were entities of jurisdiction for the administration of royal law, and on the other hand, they made possible the spread of the king's authority through a system of bonds and obligations.[12] The imposition of taxes, formation of militia for the king when asked, enforcement of authority and royal law and collection of information when needed were all accomplished through territorial institutions.

This use of territorial institutions for royal administration led Albert B. White to propose a seemingly contradictory thesis: *Self-Government at the King's Command*, which stated that "English kings, working in what they believed to be their own personal interest, so used the English people in government, [and they] laid upon them for centuries [of royal] burdens and responsibilities."[13] From all this we can suggest that territorial institutions of the tenth century cannot be considered as organic or spontaneous associations of people either of Germanic or other origin. Rather, counties and townships were founded for the broad purposes of the kingdom, and as instruments of royal administration.

Burhs or Boroughs

More important from our perspective, historians also debated the origins of cities, which were called *burhs* in Anglo-Saxon dialect. Although the debate about the origins of *burhs* was even more controversial, it was agreed that their emergence was closely associated with successive Anglo-Saxon kings' willingness to found them for government, defence, and economic purposes.

It seems the late ninth and tenth centuries were a period of immense town founding in Anglo-Saxon England: there appeared a series of fortresses and fortified towns. *Burhs* embodied both kinds of places— a stronghold for the king and a place of administration (i.e., the royal court jurisdiction and a jurisdiction of taxation).[14] It was also a place in which a market was held. The borough was a new kind of institution whose members were not bound together by feudal, proprietary or agricultural ties: in the boroughs a group of people was formed whose principle of cohesion was a new form of land tenure, which allowed alienable plots.[15] What kind of community was the borough then? The borough was a 'wrought' community. As Maitland expressed: "In the ancient boroughs [before the Norman Conquest] there is from the first an element that we must call both artificial and national. The borough does not grow spontaneously; it is made; it is wrought; it is 'timbered'. It has a national purpose; it is maintained 'at the cost of the nation' by the duty that the shire owes to it."[16] Maitland contended that this was manifest in the *Domesday Book,* where all commissioners found a town in each county, and the town lay outside the general system of land tenure. In the midst of warlike England, within the borough there reigned a special peace and a special land tenure.[17] The establishment of a market was not spontaneous either: it was a definite legal act. The market in the borough was established by law. Each county was to have a borough (often in the middle), and each borough was to have a market (often in the middle, too).[18] The markets were strictly regulated.[19]

The contemporary archaeological and historical research tended to confirm the wrought and timbered borough Maitland came across in late Anglo-Saxon documents.[20] We have already mentioned the recent study of Reynolds. An archaeologist Martin Biddle stated that "the principal result of much of the recent work has been to show that the term 'fortress' formerly used to describe these *burhs* is misleading. It suggests an exclusively military function and obscures the variety of places actually involved...in the main these *burhs* were not fortresses, but fortified towns."[21] The hitherto neglected nature of Wessex *burhs* was that they "were organized and apportioned for permanent settlement where military effectiveness was to be founded on economic viability and a growing population."[22] Another archaeologist David Hill also made the point that "the king founded forts or founded towns—towns did not grow out of forts nor did they appear spontaneously."[23] Wessex *burhs* were deliberate and planned royal foundations laid out as new towns.[24] That remarkable set of documents known as the *Burghal Hidage* from the second decade of the tenth century reveals a series of deliberate and planned *burhs*.[25] These documents list thirty-three *burhs* and state how many hides (unit of land for taxation) belong to each. A medievalist F. M. Stenton pointed out that the *Burghal Hidage* embodied a strategic plan for the defence of Wessex based on a series of fortified towns.[26] At the end of one of the documents the logic is disclosed: "For the maintenance and defence of an acre's breadth of wall 16 hides are required. If every hide is represented by one man, then every pole of wall can be manned by 4 men. Then for the maintenance of 20 poles of wall 80 hides are required, and for a furlong 160 hides are required by the same reckoning as I have stated above."[27] Hill compared the figures derived from this logic with actual built walls and found a surprising degree of accuracy.[28] What the *Burghal Hidage* discloses is that the foundation of a series of *burhs* could only be made viable by the existence of a permanent population, which required some inducement to encourage people to settle in these planted towns.[29] Morley Hemmeon long ago argued that the peculiar land tenure of boroughs, burgage tenure, must have existed in Anglo-Saxon England although it remained uncodified.[30] The burgage tenure allowed town residents to hold lands alienable at money rents.[31] From this it can be suggested that the burgage tenure may have originated under the pressure to encourage people to settle in planted *burhs* of Wessex.[32]

The Wessex *burhs*, it seems, were a complex scheme of settlement that required the invention of a series of juridical, political, economic and social techniques and ideas. Both Stenton and Loyn emphasized the increasing importance of the ecclesiastical sphere in the secular affairs of the kingdom in the late ninth and tenth centuries. More recently, Biddle argued that the planned towns of Wessex were also important within the European context: "As we can see at present they were also a watershed in European urban revolution. Nowhere else north of the Alps at this date, or perhaps for another centuries, was so extensive an effort of town plantation to be undertaken on royal initiative and on so clearly regulated a basis." He added: "The very fact that the setting up of towns on this scale was then contemplated is an indication of the expectations men then held of their potential success."[33]

By briefly reviewing the historical and archaeological literature on the Anglo-Saxon origins of English cities, I wanted to draw attention to three facts that are important in understanding the development of corporation. First, the royal origins of counties and cities had a subsequent effect on allegiances of English medieval cities in the twelfth century, when the emerging citizens (merchants and artisans) were more aligned with royal interests. Hence, within a relatively more centralized royal administration, as citizens their aspirations for autonomy never reached the levels of European cities. Second, and perhaps more important, this review makes the emergence of English boroughs as powerful corporations in the twelfth century all the more remarkable since the citizens had to reckon with a more deeply entrenched and centralized State administration than their European counterparts. Finally, the city as a sworn association or corporation of citizens in the twelfth century owed little to its royal origins. Often, merchants and artisans seized power from the lords or kings and declared their independence. The origins of the autonomous city as a corporation, therefore, are different from counties and townships, which originated as territorial institutions of royal administration.

Notes

1. Stubbs, *Constitutional History*, i, chap. vii.
2. Reynolds, *Kingdoms and Communities*, p. 262.
3. Stubbs, *Constitutional History*, i, pp. 187–188.
4. We must note that recent historical scholarship has been critical of finding the *origins* of such institutions in either Germanic tribes or Romanic settlements. We must separate these two problems of absolute origins (which often turns out to be futile) and emergence (which is important). See Reynolds, *Kingdoms and Communities*, introduction.
5. Maitland, *History of English Law*, i, p. 688.
6. J. E. A. Jolliffe, *The Constitutional History of Medieval England* (London, 1937), p. 57.
7. Henry R. Loyn, *Anglo-Saxon England and the Norman Conquest* (London, 1962). Also see F. M. Stenton, *Anglo-Saxon England*, 2nd ed. (Oxford, 1947).
8. See Henri Pirenne, *Economic and Social History of Medieval Europe* (New York, 1937) on the growth of trade in the tenth century.
9. Loyn, *Anglo-Saxon England*, p. 305.
10. Loyn, *Anglo-Saxon England*, p. 313.
11. Reynolds, *Kingdoms and Communities*, p. 2.
12. Maitland, *The History of English Law*, p. 527.
13. Albert B. White, *Self-Government at the King's Command* (Minneapolis, 1933).
14. Maitland, *Domesday Book and Beyond*, p. 193. See also an excellent article by F. Keutgen (on whom Maitland relied), "Medieval Commune," *The Encyclopedia Britannica* (Cambridge, 1910; 11th edition), vol. vi, pp. 784–791.
15. Maitland, *Domesday Book and Beyond*, pp. 191, 203.
16. Maitland, *Domesday Book and Beyond*, p. 219. The use of "national" here is apparently exaggerated and anachronistic. Maitland may have used it to underscore the broad context in which *burhs* of Anglo-Saxon England were founded as opposed to organic or spontaneous "growth" which is often implied for the first emergence of towns in the tenth century.
17. Maitland, *Domesday Book and Beyond*, p. 185.
18. Maitland, *Domesday Book and Beyond*, p. 193; Jewell, *English Local Administration*, p. 60.
19. Such strict regulation throughout the kingdom first occurs in the laws of King Athelstan in the tenth century: "We declare...that there shall be one coinage throughout the king's dominions and that there shall be no minting except in a port...In Canterbury there shall be seven minters; four of them the king's, two, the archbishop's, one, the abbot's. In Rochester, three; two of them the king's, and one, the bishop's. In London there shall be eight, in Winchester, six, in Lewes, two, in Wareham, two, in Dorchester, one, in Exeter, two, in Shaftesbury, two, in each other *burh*, one." Quoted by Stenton, *Anglo-Saxon England*, p. 519.
20. See John H. Williams, "A Review of Some Aspects of Late Saxon Urban Origins and Development," Margaret L. Faull, ed., *Studies in Late Anglo-Saxon Settlement* (Oxford, 1984), pp. 25–34.
21. Martin Biddle, "Towns," David M. Wilson, ed., *The Archaeology of Anglo-Saxon England* (London, 1976), p. 124. Let us note that our focus here is mainly Wessex *burhs* during and after the late ninth and tenth centuries with the

emergence of other territorial communities. Biddle also suggests very useful ideas in rethinking the problem of origins of towns with which we are not dealing here.

22. Biddle, "Towns," p. 125; Martin Biddle, "The Evolution of Towns: Planned Towns before 1066," *The Plans and Topography of Medieval Towns in England and Wales*, M. W. Barley, ed., Council for British Archaeology Research Report No. 14, 1976, pp. 19–31; Colin Platt, "The Evolution of Towns: Natural Growth," Barley, *Plans and Topography of Medieval Towns*, pp. 48–56.

23. David Hill, *Atlas of Anglo-Saxon England* (Toronto, 1981), p. 143.

24. Martin Biddle and David Hill, "Late-Saxon Planned Towns," *Antiquaries Journal*, 1971, vol. li, pp. 20–85.

25. A. J. Robertson, *Anglo-Saxon Charters* (Cambridge, 1939), pp. 246–248; also see David Hill, "The Burghal Hidage: The Establishment of a Text," *Medieval Archaeology*, 1969, xiii, pp. 84–92.

26. F. M. Stenton, *Anglo-Saxon England* (Oxford, 1947), pp. 261–262.

27. Hill, "The Burghal Hidage," pp. 90–91.

28. Hill, *Atlas of Anglo-Saxon England*, p. 85. Here I find the question of the city posed in stark simplicity and precision; in fact, it makes one wonder what lineages must exist between this reckoning and the political arithmetic of the seventeenth century. Loyn observed this astutely: "The Burghal Hidage stands alone in importance and it is doubtful even now if we have realized its full significance in relation to the development of royal government as well as in the more urban field."

29. Biddle and Hill, "Late Saxon Planned Towns," p. 83.

30. Morley DeWolf Hemmeon, *Burgage Tenure in Medieval England* (Cambridge, Mass., 1914), p. 158. Stenton, *Anglo-Saxon England*, also emphasized this: "It is clear, in fact, that all the essential features which distinguished the burgess tenure of the middle ages had been developed in the Old English borough, and although no more precise term than *burgware*, "inhabitants of a borough" or *portmenn*, "townsmen" had been found for men holding burghal plots on these terms, *Domesday Book* was recognizing a genuine tenurial distinction when it described them as *burgenses*," pp. 522–523.

31. Loyn is quite bold in his assertion: "On the question of tenure it is certain that the essential characteristics of later borough tenure were present in the late Anglo-Saxon England, above all the holding of tenements at money rent with freedom to alienate or sell. It is probable that such tenure originated in conscious royal policy," p. 143.

32. Stenton, *Anglo-Saxon England*, provides a clue in this direction by saying, "it is highly probable that...settlers had been encouraged by the king to take up plots on easy terms as his tenants," p. 332.

33. Biddle, "Towns," p. 134

APPENDIX 2
AMERICAN COLONIES AND CITIES

The legal status of colonies and cities listed here is compiled from the following sources. (For full citations, see Bibliography.) Andrews, *The Colonial Period of American History*; Kavenagh, *Foundations of Colonial America* (documents); Thorpe, *The Federal and State Constitutions, Colonial Charters and Other Organic Laws* (documents); Osgood, *The American Colonies in the Seventeenth Century*; Ernest Griffith, *The American City Government: The Colonial Period*; James Lemon, *The Best Poor Man's Country*.

MASSACHUSETTS Charter of incorporation (1628); order-in-council to issue a *quo warranto* against Massachusetts (1683); surrender of charter (1684); commission of Edmund Andros as Governor of the Territory and Dominion of New England (1686); royal charter (1691).

RHODE ISLAND Royal charter of incorporation (1664).

CONNECTICUT Royal charter of incorporation (1662).

MAINE Proprietary charter to Ferdinando Gorges (1622); annexation to Massachusetts (1658).
Acomenticus Borough charter by the proprietor Gorges (1641); 'city' charter (1642); charter revoked by the Massachusetts Bay Company (1652).

NEW YORK Proprietary charter to the Duke of York (1664); becomes a royal colony (1699).
New York City Confirmation of Dutch charter (1664); charter from Governor Dongan (1686); charter from Governor Cornbury (1708); charter from Governor Montgomerie (1730).
Albany An example of a town that had acquired most of the rights of an incorporated borough by a succession of grants prior to actual issuance of a royal charter (1686).
Westchester Royal charter (1696) from Governor Fletcher.
Lansinghburgh Royal charter (1771).

NEW JERSEY Proprietary charter (1665); becomes a royal colony (1702).

Burlington Incorporated by Act of the Assembly—according to power delegated by the proprietors (1693); royal charter (1733).

Salem Incorporation from Governor Andros (1678).

Perth Amboy Erected as a town (1680); royal charter from Governor Hunter (1718).

New Brunswick Royal charter (1730).

Elizabeth Royal charter (1740).

Trenton Royal charter (1745).

PENNSYLVANIA Proprietary charter to William Penn (1681).

Germantown Proprietary charter (1689); forfeited for failure to function (1707); petition from inhabitants for re-instatement not granted.

Philadelphia Some evidence of a borough charter (1684); proprietary charter (1691).

Chester Proprietary charter (1701).

Bristol Proprietary charter (1720); increased powers by Act (1745).

Lancaster Proprietary charter (1742).

Reading County town (1748).

York County town (1741).

Carlisle County town (1752).

Easton County town (1752).

DELAWARE Transfer from the Burgomasters of Amsterdam (1663); annexation to Pennsylvania (1682); charter restored by Penn (1701).

Newcastle Charter from Governor Keith (1724); annulled by Governor Gordon (1726).

Wilmington Proprietary charter (1739).

MARYLAND Charter to the proprietor Lord Baltimore (1632).

St. Mary's proprietary charter (1667 or 1670); incorporation by an Act of Assembly (1708).

Annapolis Incorporation by an Act of Assembly (1696); charter from the Governor (1708).

VIRGINIA Proprietary charter by the crown (1606); royal charter as a joint stock company (1609); royal charter to give the company the power to elect a governor and a council (1612); the first house of burgesses (1619); the second assembly (1621); the last assembly under proprietorship (1624); royal commission to regulate Virginia affairs (1624); *quo warranto* before King's bench (1624); appointment of royal governor (1628); surrender of Virginia to the Commonwealth of England (1651); the royal commission (1677).

Williamsburg Town Act (1698/9); incorporation as a 'city' authorized by the assembly (1705); incorporation by royal charter.

Norfolk One of the towns included under the Act of 1705; this act was revoked; royal charter (1736).

NORTH CAROLINA Proprietary charter (1665); becomes independent proprietary colony (1720); becomes royal colony (1729).

Bath Erected as a town (1705); borough town by Act of Assembly (1715).

New Bern Erected as a town (1715); borough town (1723); royal patent 1760).

Edenton Borough town (1722); royal patent (1760).

Wilmington Erected as a town (1735); borough town (1739); royal patent (1760); royal charter (1763); charter surrendered (1767); reinstatement under consideration by Governor Martin (1774).

Brunswick Erected as a town (1745); borough town (1754); charter repealed and reissued by governor (1755).

Halifax Borough town (1757); royal charter (1760 and 1764).

Salisbury Governor's charter (1765).

Hillsborough Governor's charter (1770).

Campbelton Governor's charter (1772); abolished (1774).

Tarborough Governor's charter (1772).

SOUTH CAROLINA Proprietary charter (1665); becomes a royal colony (1720); surrenders charter (1729).

Charleston Charter by assembly and governor (1722); disallowed by Lords justices (1723).

Georgetown Royal incorporation (1732).

GEORGIA Proprietary charter (1732); becomes a royal colony (1742).

Savannah Incorporation (1733).

Frederica Incorporation (1735).

BIBLIOGRAPHY

Government Documents

Great Britain

Great Britain. *Parliamentary Papers*, 1828, no. 569, "Report from Select Committee on the Civil Government in Canada," 359pp.

Great Britain. *Parliamentary Papers*, 1839, no. 3, Durham, John George Lambton, 1st Earl, 1791–1840. "Report on the Affairs of British North America, from the Earl of Durham," Her Majesty's High Commissioner, February 11, 1839.

Great Britain. *Parliamentary Papers*, 1835, vol. xi, "First Report from the Select Committee of the House of Lords appointed to inquire into the Present State of the Several Gaols and Houses of Correction," pp. 1f.

Great Britain. *Parliamentary Papers*, 1835, vol. xi, "Second Report from the Committee of the House of Lords on Gaols and Houses of Correction," pp. 495f.

Great Britain. *Parliamentary Papers*, 1835, vol. xii, "Third Report from the Committee of the House of Lords on Gaols and Houses of Correction," pp. 1f.

Great Britain. *Parliamentary Papers*, 1835, vol. xii, "Fourth and Fifth Reports from the Committee of the House of Lords on Gaols and Houses of Correction," pp. 157ff.

Great Britain. *Parliamentary Papers*, 1840, vol. xi, "Select Committee on the Health of Towns."

Great Britain. *Parliamentary Papers*, 1842, vol. x, "Report from the Committee on Buildings Regulation and Improvement of Boroughs," pp. 161ff.

Great Britain. *Parliamentary Papers*, 1842, vol. x, "Select Committee on the Improvement of the Health of Towns," pp. 349ff.

Great Britain. Parliamentary Papers, 1845, vol. xviii, "Second Report on the State of Large Towns and Populous Districts from the Royal Commission."

Great Britain. Public Records Office, *Acts of the Privy Council, Colonial, 1613–1783*, W. L. Grant, and James Munro, eds., 6 vols. (1908–1912).

Great Britain. Public Records Office, *Calendar of State Papers, Colonial Series, 1574–1738*, London, 44 vols. (1870–1939).

Great Britain. Public Records Office, *Journal of the Commissioners for Trade and Plantations, 1701–1782*, London, 14 vols. (1920–1933).

Great Britain. *Statutes at Large.*

Great Britain. "Report from His Majesty's Commissioners for Inquiring into the Administration and Practical Operation of the Poor Laws," London, 1834.

British North America

Canada (1841–1867), *Statutes.*

Canada (1841–1867), Legislative Council. *Debates of the Legislative Assembly of United Canada, 1841–1867*, Elizabeth Gibbs, ed., 9 vols.

Lower Canada (1791–1840), *Ordinances.*

New Brunswick, *Revised Statutes*, 4 vols. (1786–1836, 1837–1845, 1846–1849, 1849–1853).

Nova Scotia, *Statutes*, 1758–1867.

Ontario. Bureau of Archives. *Report*, A. Fraser, ed., no. 3, 1905. Toronto, Legislative Assembly of Ontario. Documents relating to the formation of Land Boards; Rules and Regulations of the Land Boards; Proceedings of the District Land Boards.

Ontario. Bureau of Archives. *Report*, A. Fraser, ed., no. 17, 1928. Toronto, Legislative Assembly of Ontario. Grants of Crown Lands in Upper Canada, 1787–1791; Land Books A and B: Proceedings of the Land Committee.

Ontario. Bureau of Archives. *Report*, A. Fraser, ed., no. 18, 1930. Toronto, Legislative Assembly of Ontario.

Ontario. Bureau of Archives. *Report*, A. Fraser, ed., no. 19, 1931. Toronto, Legislative Assembly of Ontario. Grants of Crown Lands in Upper Canada, 1796–1797; Land Books B and C: Proceedings of the Land Committee.

Ontario. Bureau of Archives. *Report*, A. Fraser, ed., no. 20, 1932. Toronto, Legislative Assembly of Ontario. Grants of Crown Lands in Upper Canada, 1796–1798; Land Books C and D: Proceedings of the Land Committee.

Ontario. Bureau of Archives. *Report*, A. Fraser, ed., no. 21, 1933. Toronto, Legislative Assembly of Ontario. Minutes of the Court of General Quarter Sessions of the Peace for the Home District, 1800–1809.

Ontario. Bureau of Archives. *Report*, A. Fraser, ed., no. 22, 1934. Toronto, Legislative Assembly of Ontario. Minutes of the Court of General Quarter Sessions of the Peace for the London District, 1800–1809, 1813–1818.

Ontario. Legislative Assembly. *Sessional Papers,* no. 42. 1888. First Report of the Commission on Municipal Institutions.

Ontario. Legislative Assembly. *Sessional Papers,* no. 13. 1889. Second Report of the Commission on Municipal Institutions.

Public Archives of Canada, *Documents Relating to Constitutional History of Canada, 1759–1791,* Adam Shortt and A. G. Doughty, eds., 2 vols., Ottawa, 1918.

Public Archives of Canada, *Documents Relating to Constitutional History of Canada, 1791–1818,* Arthur Doughty and A. M. Duncan, eds., Ottawa, 1914.

Public Archives of Canada, *Documents Relating to Constitutional History of Canada, 1819–1828,* Doughty, Arthur and N. Story, eds., Ottawa, 1935.

Upper Canada (1791–1840), *Consolidated Statutes,* proclaimed and published under the authority of the Act 22 Victoria, c. 30, 1859.

Upper Canada (1791–1840), *Statutes.*

Upper Canada, Legislative Council. Journal and Proceedings of the Legislative Council of the Province of Upper Canada, 1792–1823 (2 vols., Ontario, Bureau of Archives, *Reports,* A. Fraser, ed., nos. 7 and 12, 1910 and 1915).

Upper Canada, House of Assembly. Journal of the House of Assembly of Upper Canada, 1792–1823 (5 vols., Ontario, Bureau of Archives, *Reports,* A. Fraser, ed., nos. 6, 8, 9, 10, 11, 1909–1914).

Upper Canada, House of Assembly. Committee of Conference on Brockville Police Bill, Report. Upper Canada, House of Assembly. *Journal. Appendix,* 1831/32.

Upper Canada, House of Assembly. Select Committee in favour of House of Industry. Report. Upper Canada, House of Assembly. *Journal. Appendix,* vol. i, 1839/40.

Upper Canada, House of Assembly. Select Committee on petition of the mayor, aldermen and common councilmen of the City of Toronto. Report. (Request for Act of Incorporation be made perpetual.) Upper Canada, House of Assembly. *Journal. Appendix,* vol. i, 1839/40.

Published Archival Documents

Andrews, Charles M. 1913. *Lists of Reports and Representations of the Lords of the Trade, 1660–1782,* American Historical Association, Annual Report, vol. i, pp. 321–406.

Armstrong, Frederick H. 1967. *Handbook of Upper Canadian Chronology and Territorial Legislation,* London, Canada: Lawson Memorial Library, The University of Western Ontario.

Attenborough, F. L., ed. 1922. *Laws of the Earliest English Kings*, Cambridge: Cambridge University Press.

Ballard, Adolphus, ed. 1913. *British Borough Charters, 1042–1216*, Cambridge: Cambridge University Press.

Ballard, Adolphus and James Tait, eds. 1923. *British Borough Charters, 1216–1307*, Cambridge: Cambridge University Press.

Bell, K. N. and W. P. Morrell, eds. 1928. *Select Documents on British Colonial Policy, 1830–1860*, Oxford: Clarendon Press.

Brigham, Clarence S., ed. 1911. *British Royal Proclamations Relating to America, 1603–1783*, American Antiquarian Society, Transactions, vol. xii, Worcester: Massachusetts.

Chalmers, G., ed. 1914. *Opinions of Eminent Lawyers on Various Points of English Jurisprudence*, 2 vols., London.

Cruikshank, E. A., ed. 1923. *The Correspondence of John Graves Simcoe with Allied Documents*, 5 vols., Toronto: Public Archives of Ontario.

———. 1934. *The Settlement of United Empire Loyalists in 1784*, Toronto: Ontario Historical Society.

Downer, L. J. 1972. *Leges Henrici Primi*, Oxford: Oxford University Press.

Firth, Edith, ed. 1962. *The Town of York, 1793–1815: A Collection of Documents*, Toronto, University of Toronto Press.

———. 1966. *The Town of York, 1815–1834: A Further Collection of Documents*, Toronto: University of Toronto Press.

Greene, Jack P., ed. 1970. *Great Britain and the American Colonies, 1606–1763*, Columbia, South Carolina: University of South Carolina Press.

Harlow, Vincent and F. Madden, eds. 1953. *British Colonial Developments: Select Documents, 1774–1834*, Oxford: Clarendon Press.

Henderson, G. F. 1967. *Federal Royal Commissions in Canada*, Toronto: University of Toronto Press.

Innis, H. A. and A. R. M. Lower, eds. 1930. *Select Documents in Canadian Economic History, 1783–1885*, Toronto: University of Toronto Press.

Jensen, Merrill, ed. 1955. American Colonial Documents to 1776, English Historical Documents, vol. ix. London.

Kavenagh, William Keith, ed. 1973. *Foundations of Colonial America: A Documentary History*, 3 vols., New York.

Keith, Arthur B., ed. 1918. *Selected Documents on British Colonial Policy, 1763–1917*, London: Oxford University Press.

Kennedy, W. P. M., ed. 1918. *Documents of the Canadian Constitution, 1759–1915*, 1st ed., Toronto: Oxford University Press.

Labaree, Leonard Woods, ed. 1935. *Royal Instructions to British Colonial Governors, 1670–1776*, 2 vols., New York.

Macdonald, William, ed. 1899. *Select Charters and other Documents Illustrative of American History, 1606–1775*, New York, Macmillan.

Madden, F. and D. Fieldhouse, eds. 1985–1987. *The Foundations of a Colonial System of Government*, vol. i: *"The Empire of the Bretaignes," 1175–1688*, Westport, Connecticut, 1985; vol. ii: *The Classical Period of the First British Empire, 1689–1783*, Westport, Connecticut, 1985; vol. iii: *Imperial Reconstruction, 1763–1840*, Westport: Connecticut, 1987.

Pronay, Nicholas and John Taylor, eds. 1980. *Parliamentary Texts of the Later Middle Ages*, Oxford: Clarendon Press.

Robertson, A. J., ed. 1925. *The Laws of the Kings of England from Edmund to Henry I*, Cambridge: Cambridge University Press.

———. 1939. *Anglo-Saxon Charters*, Cambridge: Cambridge University Press.

Stephenson, Carl and F. G. Marcham, eds. 1937. *Sources of English Constitutional History: A Selection of Documents*, New York.

Tawney, R. H., ed. 1924. *Tudor Economic Documents: Being Select Documents Illustrating the Economic and Social History of Tudor England*, London: Longmans.

Thorpe, F. N., ed. 1909. *Federal and State Constitutions, Charters and other Organic Laws, 1492–1908*, 7 vols., Washington.

Tierney, Brian, ed. 1964. *The Crisis of Church and State, 1050–1300*, New York, Prentice-Hall.

Political and Legal Treatises and Works

Alberti, Leo Battista. 1755. *Ten Books on Architecture*, trans. James Leone, London.

Anonymous. 1635. *Essay on Laying Out Towns*, Massachusetts Historical Society, Collections, vol. i (Series 5). Boston, 1861.

Bentham, Jeremy. 1776. *Emancipate Your Colonies!*, in his *Works*, John Bowring, ed., vol. iv, London, 1838–1843.

———. 1780. *An Introduction to the Principles of Morals and Legislation*, J. H. Burns and H. L. A. Hart, eds., London, 1970.

———. 1787. *Panopticon or the Inspection House*, in his *Works*, John Bowring, ed., vol. iv, London, 1838–1843.

————. 1787. *Pannomial Fragments, Works,* John Bowring, ed., vol. iii, London, 1838–1843.

————. 1832. *Constitutional Code, Works,* John Bowring, ed., vol. ix, London, 1838–1843.

Bethel, Silingsby. 1679. *An Account of the French Usurpation upon the Trade of England,* London.

Blackstone, William. 1768. *Commentaries on the Law of England.* London.

Blenerhasset, Thomas. 1610. *The Plantation in Ulster,* New York, 1972.

Bodin, Jean. 1576. *Six Books of Commonwealth,* M. J. Tooley, ed., Oxford, 1955.

Botero, Giovanni 1588. *The Greatness of Cities,* London.

————. 1589. *Reason of State,* London.

Bouchette, Joseph 1815. *A Topographical Description of the Province of Lower Canada,* London.

————. 1831. *The British Dominions in North America,* 2 vols., London.

————. 1832. *A Topographical Dictionary of the Province of Lower Canada,* London.

Brady, Robert. 1704. *An Historical Treatise of Cities & Burghs or Boroughs; showing their original whence, and from Whom they Received their Liberties, Privileges, and Immunities; What they were, and What Made and Constituted a Free Burgh, & Free Burgesses,* London.

Buchanan, James. 1834. *Official Information for Emigrants Arriving at New York,* Montréal.

Coke, Edward Sir. 1634. *The Institutes of the Laws of England.* London.

Coules, F. and W. Ley. 1641. *An Abstract of the Laws of New England as they are now Established,* London: Paules Chain.

Davenant, Charles. 1698. *Discourses on the Public Revenues and the Trade of England,* 2 vols., London.

Dunlop, William. 1833. *Statistical Sketches of Upper Canada for the use of Emigrants,* London.

Durham, Lord. 1837. *Report on the Affairs of the British North America,* C. P. Lucas, ed., 3 vols., Oxford: Clarendon Press, 1912.

Eburne, Richard. 1624. *A Plain Pathway to Plantations,* Louis B. Wright, ed., Ithaca, New York: Cornell University Press, 1966.

Frank, J. P. 1779. *A System of Complete Medical Police,* Erna Lesky, ed., 6 vols. (1779–1790). Baltimore: Johns Hopkins University Press.

Gourlay, Robert F. 1822. *Statistical Account of Upper Canada,* London.

Gray, Hugh. 1830. *An Inquiry into the Causes and Remedies of Pauperism*, London.

Hakluyt, Richard. 1584. *Discourse Concerning Western Plantations*, London.

Hobbes, Thomas. 1651. *Leviathan*, Harmondsworth: Penguin, 1968.

Joseph, Frank John. 1889. *The Municipal Manual*, Toronto: Boswell and Hutchison.

Lewis, George C. 1841. *An Essay on the Government of Dependencies*, London.

Locke, John. 1690. *Second Treatise of Government*, C. B. Macpherson, ed., Hackett Philosophical Classics, 1980.

Madox, Thomas. 1726. *Firma Burgi, Or an Historical Essay Concerning the Cities, Towns and Boroughs of England*, London.

Machiavelli, Niccolo. 1512. *On Principalities*, Florence, Harmondsworth: Penguin Classics, 1975.

Makemie, Francis. 1705. *A Persuasive to Towns and Cohabitation*, Virginia Magazine of History and Biography, vol. iv (1896–1897), pp. 252–271.

Martin, R. M. 1838. *History, Statistics and Geography of Upper and Lower Canada*, London.

Martyn, Benjamin. 1733. *Reasons for Establishing the Colony of Georgia*, Reprint: Georgia Historical Society, Collections, vol. i, pp. 203–238, Savannah, 1840.

Merivale, Herman. 1841. *Lectures on Colonization and Colonies*. London.

Mill, John Stuart. 1861. *Consideration on Representative Government*. London.

Montgomery, Sir Robert. 1717. *A Discourse Concerning the Designed Establishment of a New Colony*, Reprinted: Washington, 1835.

Petty, William. 1899. *Economic Writings*, Charles H. Hull, ed., 2 vols., Cambridge.

———. 1927. *Some Unpublished Writings*, The Marquis of Landsdowne, ed., 2 vols., London.

R. G. 1662. *Virginia's Cure: An Advisive Narrative Concerning Virginia*, London: W. Godbid and Henry Brome.

Robert E. Leader, ed. 1897. *Life and Letters of John Arthur Roebuck*. London.

Roebuck, John Arthur. 1849. *The Colonies of England: A Plan for the Government of Some Portion of Our Colonial Possessions*, London.

Smith, Adam. 1763. *Lectures on Justice, Police, Revenue and Arms*, E. Cannan, ed., London, 1896.

———. 1776. *An Inquiry into the Nature and Causes of Wealth*, 2 vols., reprint, London: Oxford University Press, 1979.

Smith, David William. 1813. *A Short Topographical Description of Upper Canada in North America*, London: W. Faden, Geographer to His Majesty.

Stow, John. 1598. *A Survey of London*, 2 vols., London.

Wakefield, Edward Gibbon. 1829. *A Letter From Sydney*, London.

———. 1833. *England and America*, London.

———. 1849. *A View of the Art of Colonization*, London.

Other References

On State and Corporations

Anderson, Perry. 1974. *Lineages of the Absolutist State*, London: New Left Books.

Anderson, James, ed. 1986. *The Rise of the Modern State*, Atlantic Highlands, NJ: Humanities Press.

Aston, T., ed. 1965. *Crisis in Europe, 1560–1660*, London.

Barber, Benjamin R. 1974. *The Death of Communal Liberty*, Princeton, New Jersey: Princeton University Press.

Bateson, Mary. 1903. *Medieval England, 1066–1350*, London: Unwin.

Berman, Harold J. 1983. *Law and Revolution: The Formation of Western Legal Tradition*, Cambridge, MA: Harvard University Press.

Black, Antony. 1984. *Guilds and Civil Society in European Political Thought from the Twelfth Century to the Present*, London: Methuen.

Bloch, Marc. 1961. *Feudal Society*, London: Routledge and Kegan Paul.

Braudel, Fernand. 1979. *Civilization and Capitalism, 15th–18th Century*, vol. i: *The Structures of Everyday Life: The Limits of the Possible*, London, 1981; vol. ii: *The Wheels of Commerce*, London, 1982; vol. iii: *The Perspective of the World*, London, 1984.

Breisach, Ernst. 1983. *Historiography: Ancient, Medieval, and Modern*, Chicago: University of Chicago Press.

Brooks, Nicholas. 1971. "The Development of Military Obligations in Eighth and Ninth Century England" in P. Clemeos and K. Hughes, ed., *England Before the Conquest*, Cambridge: Cambridge University Press, pp. 69–84.

Burns, J. H., ed. 1988. *The Cambridge History of Medieval Political Thought, 350–1450*, Cambridge: Cambridge University Press.

Cam, Helen M. 1940. "The Decline and Fall of English Feudalism," *Liberties and Communities in Medieval England*, Cambridge: Cambridge University Press, 1944, pp. 205–222.

———. 1950. "The Community of the Vill," Helen M. Cam, *Law-Finders and Law-Makers in Medieval England*, London: Merlin Press, 1962, pp. 71–84.

———. 1962. "The Quality of English Feudalism," Helen M. Cam, *Law-Finders and Law-Makers in Medieval England*, London: Merlin Press, pp. 44–58.

Canning, Joseph P. 1981. "The Corporation in the Thought of Thirteenth and Fourteenth Century Jurists," *History of Political Thought*, vol. i, pp. 9–32.

———. 1987. *The Political Thought of Baldus de Ubaldis*, Cambridge, Cambridge University Press.

Cantor, Norman F. 1958. *Church, Kingship and Lay Investiture in England, 1089–1135*, Princeton, NJ: Princeton University Press.

———. 1968. *The English: A History of Politics and Society to 1760*, London: George Allen and Unwin.

———. 1969. *Medieval History*, 2nd ed., London: Macmillan.

Cawson, Alan. 1986. *Corporatism and Political Theory*, London: Blackwell.

Cheyette, Fredric L., ed. 1968. *Lordship and Community in Medieval Europe*, New York: Holt, Rinehart, and Winston.

Chroust, Anton-Hermann. 1947. "The Corporate Idea and the Body Politic in the Middle Ages," *The Review of Politics*, vol. ix, pp. 423–452.

Clarke, M. V. 1936. *Medieval Representation and Consent*, New York: Russell and Russell.

Clarke, Helen. 1984. *The Archaeology of Medieval England*, London: British Museum Publications.

Cole, C. W. 1939. *Colbert and a Century of French Mercantilism*, 2 vols., New York: Columbia University Press.

Coleby, Andrew M. 1987. *Central Government and Localities: Hampshire, 1649–1689*, Cambridge: Cambridge University Press.

Davies, R. G. and J. H. Denton, eds. 1981. *The English Parliament in the Middle Ages*, Manchester: Manchester University Press.

Elias, Norbert. 1939. *Power and Civility*, vol. ii of *The Civilizing Process*, London.

Elton, G. R. 1969. "The Body of the Whole Realm: Parliament and Representation in Medieval and Tudor England," in G. R. Elton, *Studies in Tudor and Stuart Politics and Government*, Cambridge: Cambridge University Press, pp. 19–61.

———. *Policy and Police*, Cambridge: Cambridge University Press.

Fourquin, Guy. 1976. *Lordship and Feudalism in the Middle Ages*, London: George Allen and Unwin.

Frantzen, Allen J. 1983. "The Tradition of Penitentials in Anglo-Saxon England, in P. Clemeos, ed., *Anglo-Saxon England*, vol. xi, Cambridge: Cambridge University Press, pp. 23–56.

Ganshof, F. L. 1952. *Feudalism*, trans. Philip Grierson, New York: Longman.

Giddens, Anthony. 1987. *The Nation-State and Violence*, Berkeley and Los Angeles: University of California Press.

Gierke, Otto. 1900. *Political Theories of the Middle Age*, trans. with an introduction by Frederic W. Maitland, Cambridge: Cambridge University Press.

———. 1934. *Natural Law and the Theory of Society, 1500–1800*, Cambridge: Cambridge University Press.

———. 1939. *The Development of Political Theory*, London: George Allen and Unwin.

———. 1977. *Associations and Law*, trans. George Heiman, Toronto: University of Toronto Press.

———. 1990. *Community in Historical Perspective: A Translation of Selections From* Das Deutsche Genossenschaftsrecht *(The German Law Of Fellowship)* Deutsche Genossenschaftsrecht. *English Selections*, New York, NY: Cambridge University Press.

Gomme, George L. 1907. *The Governance of London*, London: Unwin.

Greenleaf, W. H. 1964. *Order, Empiricism and Politics*, London: Oxford University Press.

Guenee, Bernard. 1985. *States and Rulers in Later Medieval Europe*, Oxford: Basil Blackwell.

Hilton, Rodney, ed. 1976. *The Transition from Feudalism to Capitalism*, London: Verso.

———. 1985. *Class Conflict and the Crisis of Capitalism: Essays in Medieval Social History*, London: The Hambledon Press.

Hinsley, F. H. 1986. *Sovereignty*, 2nd ed., Cambridge: Cambridge University Press.

Hintze, Otto. 1975. *The Historical Essays of Otto Hintze*, New York: Oxford University Press.

Holton, R. J. 1985. *The Transition from Feudalism to Capitalism*, London: Methuen.

Hoyt, Robert S. 1968. *The Royal Demesne in English Constitutional History,* 1066–1272, New York: Greenwood Press.

Huppert, George. 1986. *After the Black Death: A Social History of Early Modern Europe,* Indianapolis: Indiana University Press.

Jewell, Helen M. 1972. *English Local Administration in the Middle Ages,* New York: Barnes and Noble Books.

Jolliffe, J. E. A. 1937. *The Constitutional History of Medieval England,* 4th ed., London: Adam and Charles Black, 1961.

Kantorowicz, Ernst H. 1957. *The King's Two Bodies,* Princeton, N.J.: Princeton University Press.

Kelley, Donald R. 1970. *Foundations of Modern Historical Scholarship: Language, Law, and History in the French Renaissance,* New York: Columbia University Press.

———. 1984. *History, Law and the Human Sciences: Medieval and Renaissance Perspectives,* London: Variorum Reprints.

Keohane, N. O. 1980. *Philosophy and the State in France,* Princeton: Princeton University Press.

Loyn, Henry. 1962. *Anglo-Saxon England and the Norman Conquest,* London.

Lyon, Bryce. 1974. *Henri Pirenne: A Biographical and Intellectual Study,* Ghent: Scientia.

Maitland, Frederic W. 1897. *Domesday Book and Beyond,* Cambridge: Cambridge University Press.

———. 1908. *The Constitutional History of England,* Cambridge: Cambridge University Press.

———. 1936. *Selected Essays,* H. D. Hazeltine, G. Lapsley and P. H. Winfield, eds., New York.

McRee, Ben R. 1987. "Religious Gilds and Regulation of Behavior in Late Medieval Towns," *People, Politics and the Community in the Later Middle Ages,* Joel Rosenthal and Colin Richmond, eds., New York: St. Martin's, pp. 108–122.

Mitteis, Heinrich. 1975. *The State in the Middle Ages,* Amsterdam: North-Holland Publishing Company.

Monahan, Arthur P. 1987. *Consent, Coercion, and Limit: The Medieval Origins of Parliamentary Democracy,* Ottawa: McGill-Queen's University Press.

Morall, John B. 1958. *Political Thought in Medieval Times,* London: Hutchinson.

Nelson, Benjamin. 1981. *On the Roads to Modernity,* Totowa, NJ.

Painter S. 1951. *The Rise of Feudal Monarchies*, Ithaca, New York: Cornell University Press.

Palmer, R. Liddesdale. 1934. *English Social History in the Making*, London: Ivor Nicholson and Watson.

Petit-Dutaillis, Charles. 1908. *Studies and Notes Supplementary to Stubbs' Constitutional History*, Manchester: Manchester University Press.

———. 1936. *The Feudal Monarchy in France and England from the Tenth to the Thirteenth Century*, London: Routledge and Kegan Paul, 1964.

Pirenne, Henri. 1933. *Economic and Social History of Medieval Europe*, New York: Harvest Books, 1937.

———. 1936. *A History of Europe: From the Invasions to the XVI Century*, New York: University Books, 1955.

Poggi, Gianfranco. 1978. *The Development of the Modern State*, London: Hutchinson.

Pollard, A. F. 1926. *The Evolution of Parliament*, London: Longmans, Green and Co.

Pollock, Frederick and Frederic W. Maitland. 1895. *The History of English Law before the Time of Edward I*, 2nd ed., Cambridge: Cambridge University Press, 1898.

Powicke, Michael R. 1973. *The Community of the Realm*, New York: Alfred A. Knopf.

Rabb, T. K. 1975. *The Struggle for Stability in the Early Europe*, New York.

Reynolds, Susan. 1984. *Kingdoms and Communities in Western Europe, 900–1300*, Oxford: Clarendon Press.

Rosen, George. 1958. *A History of Public Health*, New York: MD Publications.

———. 1974. *From Medical Police to Social Medicine*, New York: Science History Publications.

Shennan, J. H. 1974. *The Origins of the Modern European State, 1450–1725*, London: Hutchinson University Library.

———. 1986. *Liberty and Order in the Early Modern Europe*, London.

Slack, Paul. 1990. *The English Poor Law, 1531–1782*, Basingstoke: Macmillan Education.

Stenton, F. M. 1932. *The First Century of English Feudalism*, Oxford: Oxford University Press.

———. *Anglo-Saxon England*, 2nd ed., Oxford: Oxford University Press.

Strayer, Joseph A. 1970. *On the Medieval Origins of the Modern State*, Princeton, NJ: Princeton University Press.

Stubbs, W. 1874–1878. *The Constitutional History of England*, 3 vols., Oxford: Oxford University Press.

Tierney, Brian. 1955. *Foundations of the Conciliar Theory: The Contribution of the Medieval Canonists from Gratian to the Great Schism*, Cambridge: Cambridge University Press.

———. 1959. *Medieval Poor Law: A Sketch of Canonical Theory and Its Application in England*, Berkeley: University of California Press.

———. 1982. *Religion, Law, and the Growth of Constitutional Thought, 1150–1650*, Cambridge: Cambridge University Press.

Tierney, Brian and Sidney Painter. 1983. *Western Europe in the Middle Ages, 300–1475*, New York: Alfred A. Knopf.

Tilly, Charles. 1975. "Reflections on the History of European State-Making," in C. Tilly, ed., *The Formation of National States in Europe*, Princeton: Princeton University Press.

———. 1990. *Coercion, Capital and European States, AD 990–1990*.

Trevor-Roper, H. 1967. *Religion, the Reformation and Social Change*, London.

Ullmann, Walter. 1965. *Medieval Political Thought*, Harmondsworth: Penguin.

———. 1968. "Juristic Obstacles to the Emergence of the Concept of State in the Middle Ages," *Annali di Storia diritto*, vols. xii–xiii (1968-1969), pp. 43–64.

———. 1975. *Law and Politics in the Middle Ages*, Ithaca, NY: Cornell University Press.

———. 1988. *Law and Jurisdiction in the Middle Ages*, London: Variorum Reprints.

Wallerstein, Immanuel. 1984. *The Politics of the World-Economy: The States, the Movements, and the Civilizations*, Cambridge: Cambridge University Press.

Wang, H. Ke Chin "The Corporate Entity Concept (or Fiction Theory) in the Yearbook Period," *Law Quarterly Review*, lviii, 1942, pp. 498–511; lix, 1943, pp. 72–86.

Weber, Max. 1922. *Economy and Society*, 2 vols., Berkeley: University of California Press, 1978.

White, Albert B. 1933. *Self-Government at the King's Command*, Minneapolis: University of Minnesota Press.

On Cities

Abrams, Philip. 1978. "Towns and Economic Growth: Some Theories and Problems," in P. Abrams and E. A. Wrigley, eds., *Towns in Societies*, Cambridge.

Bairoch, Paul. 1988. *Cities and Economic Development: From the Dawn of History to the Present*, Chicago: University of Chicago Press.

Barley, M. W. 1976. "Town Defences in England and Wales after 1066," *The Plans and Topography of Medieval Towns in England and Wales*, M. W. Barley, ed., Council for British Archaeology Research Report no. 14, pp. 57–70.

Benevolo, L. 1967. *The Origins of Modern Town Planning*, Cambridge, Mass.

————. 1980. *The History of the City*, Cambridge: MIT Press.

Benton, Johm F., ed. 1968. *Town Origins: The Evidence from Medieval England*, Boston: D.C. Heath.

Beresford, Maurice W. 1967. *New Towns of the Middle Ages: Town Plantation in England, Wales, and Gascony*, New York: Frederick A. Praeger.

Beresford, Maurice W. and H. P. R. Finberg. 1973. *Medieval English Boroughs: A Handlist*, London: David Charles.

Biddle, Martin. 1976. "The Evolution of Towns: Planned Towns before 1066," *The Plans and Topography of Medieval Towns in England and Wales*, M. W. Barley, ed., Council for British Archaeology Research Report no. 14, pp. 19–31.

————. 1976. "Towns," David M. Wilson, ed., *The Archeology of Anglo-Saxon England*, London: Methuen.

Biddle, Martin and David Hill. 1971. "Late Saxon Planned Towns," *Antiquaries Journal*, li, pp. 70–85.

Blumenfeld, Hans. 1967. *The Modern Metropolis*, Cambridge: MIT Press.

Bookchin, Murray. 1987. *The Rise of Urbanization and the Decline of Citizenship*, San Francisco: Sierra Club Books.

Bookchin, Murray. 1992. *Urbanization Without Cities: The Rise and Decline of Citizenship*, rev. ed., Montréal: Black Rose Books.

Boyer, Paul. 1978. *Urban Masses and Moral Order in America*, 1820–1920, Cambridge: Harvard University Press.

Boyer, Christine. 1983. *Dreaming the Rational City: The Myth of American City Planning*, Cambridge: MIT Press.

Butler, Lawrence. 1976. "The Evolution of Towns: Planted Towns after 1066," *The Plans and Topography of Medieval Towns in England and Wales*, M. W. Barley, ed., Council for British Archaeology Research Report no. 14, pp. 32–47.

Clark, Peter. 1972. *Crisis and Order in English Towns 1500–1700: Essays in Urban History*, Toronto: University of Toronto Press.

Coleman, B. I. 1973. *The Idea of the City in Nineteenth-Century Britain*, London: Routledge and Kegan Paul.

DeVries, J. 1984. *European Urbanization, 1500–1800*, Cambridge: Harvard University Press.

Diamond, William. 1941. "On the Dangers of an Urban Interpretation of History," in E. F. Goldman, ed., *Historiography and Urbanization*, Baltimore.

Fairlie, John A. 1901. *Municipal Administration*, London: Macmillan.

Gillette, Howard. 1987. "The City in American Culture," in H. Gillette and Z. L. Miller, eds., *American Urbanism: A Historiographical Review*, New York.

Green, J. R. 1894. *Town Life in the Fifteenth Century*, London: Macmillan.

Gross, Charles. 1890. *The Guild Merchant: A Contribution to British Municipal History*, 2 vols., Oxford: Clarendon Press.

———. 1907. "Mortmain in Medieval Boroughs," *American Historical Review*, vol. xii, no. 4, pp. 733–742.

Hemmeon, Morley DeWolf. 1914. *Burgage Tenure in Medieval England*, Cambridge: Harvard University Press.

Hill, David. 1969. "The Burghal Hidage: The Establishment of a Text," *Medieval Archaeology*, vol. xiii, pp. 84–92.

———. 1981. *An Atlas of Anglo-Saxon England*, Toronto: University of Toronto Press.

Hilton, Rodney. 1982. "Towns in Societies—Medieval England," *Urban History Yearbook*, David Reeder, ed., Leicester: Leicester University Press, pp. 7–13.

———. 1985. "Towns in English Feudal Society," *Class Conflict and the Crisis of Capitalism: Essays in Medieval Social History*, London: The Hambledon Press, pp. 175–186.

Hohenberg, P. M. and L. H. Lees. 1985. *The Making of Urban Europe 1000–1950*, Cambridge: Harvard University Press.

Holton, R. J. 1986. *Cities, Capitalism and Civilization*, London: Allen and Unwin.

Jacobs, Jane. 1969. *The Economy of Cities*, New York: Random House.

Le Goff, Jacques. 1972. "The Town as an Agent of Civilisation, c.1200–c.1500," in C. M. Cipolla, ed., *The Fontana Economic History of Europe*, London: Fontana Press.

Lees, A. 1985. *Cities Perceived*, New York: Columbia University Press.

Loyn, Henry. 1971. "Towns in Late Anglo-Saxon England: The Evidence and Some Possible Lines of Enquiry," in P. Clemeos and K. Hughes, eds., *England Before the Conquest*, Cambridge: Cambridge University Press.

Maitland, Frederic W. 1898. *Township and Borough*, Cambridge: Cambridge University Press.

McInnes, Angus. 1980. *The English Town, 1660–1760*, London: Historical Association.

Merewether, H. A. and A. J. Stephens. 1835. *The History of the Boroughs and Municipal Corporations of the United Kingdom*, 3 vols., reprint. London: Harvester Press, 1972.

Mohl, R. A. 1985. *The New City: Urban America in the Industrial Age, 1860–1920*, Arlington Heights, Illinois: Harlan Davidson.

Morris, A. E. J. 1972. *History of Urban Form*, London: George Godwin.

Mumford, Lewis. 1938. *The Culture of Cities*, New York: Harcourt and Brace.

———. 1961. *The City in History*, New York: Harcourt, Brace and Jovanovich.

Munro, William Bennett. 1912. *The Government of American Cities*, New York: Macmillan.

———. 1916. *Principles and Methods of Municipal Administration*, New York: Macmillan.

———. 1923. *The Government of European Cities*, New York: Macmillan.

Page, Edward. 1985. *Political Authority and Bureaucratic Power: A Comparative Analysis*, Brighton, England: Wheatsheaf Books.

———. 1987. *Central and Local Government Relations: A Comparative Analysis of West European Unitary States*, London, Beverly Hills: SAGE Publications.

Pirenne, Henri. 1925. *Medieval Cities: Their Origins and the Revival of Trade*, Princeton: Princeton University Press.

Platt, Colin. 1976. "The Evolution of Towns: Natural Growth," *The Plans and Topography of Medieval Towns in England and Wales*, M. W. Barley, ed., Council for British Archaeology Research Report no. 14, pp. 48–56.

———. 1979. *The English Medieval Town*, London: Granada.

Reclus, Elise. 1895. "Evolution of Cities," *Contemporary Review*, vol. lxvii (February), pp. 246–264.

Reynolds, Susan. 1977. *An Introduction to the History of English Medieval Towns,* Oxford: Clarendon Press.

————. 1982. *Medieval Urban History and the History of Political Thought,* Urban History Yearbook, David Reeder, ed., Leicester: Leicester University Press, pp. 14–23.

————. 1984. "The Idea of the Corporation in Western Christendom Before 1300," in J. A. Guy and H. G. Beale, eds., *Law and Social Change in British History,* London: Royal Historical Society.

Rorig, Fritz. 1932. *The Medieval Town,* London: Batsford.

Schmal, H., ed. 1981. *Patterns of European Urbanization since 1500,* London: Croom Helm.

Sjoberg, Gideon. 1960. *The Preindustrial City,* Glencoe: Free Press.

Slack, Paul, ed. 1976. *The Early Modern Town: A Reader,* New York: Longman, 1976.

————, ed. 1977. *Towns and Townspeople, 1500–1780: A Document Collection,* Milton Keynes: Open University Press.

————, ed. 1984. *The Transformation of English Provincial Towns 1600–1800,* London.

Stephenson, Carl. 1933. *Borough and Town: A Study of Urban Origins in England,* New York: Medieval Academy of America.

Tait, James. 1936. *The Medieval English Borough,* Manchester: Manchester University Press.

Thrupp, Sylvia L. 1941. "Social Control in the Medieval Town," *Journal of Economic History,* Supplement 1, pp. 39–52.

Tout, Thomas Frederick. 1917. *Medieval Town Planning,* Manchester: Manchester University Press.

Turner, Hilary L. 1971. *Town Defences in England and Wales, 900–1500,* London: John Baker.

Vance, James E. 1977. *This Scene of Man,* New York: Harper's College Press.

Weber, Max. 1921. *The City,* Don Martindale and Gertrud Neuwirth, trans. and ed., New York: The Free Press, 1958.

Weinbaum, Martin. 1937. *The Incorporation of Boroughs,* Manchester: Manchester University Press.

Wheatley, P. 1972. "The Concept of Urbanism," in P. J. Ucko, et al, eds., *Man, Settlement and Urbanism,* London, pp. 601–637.

White, M. and L. White. 1962. *The Intellectual versus the City,* Cambridge: MIT Press.

Wickett, S. Morley. 1907. *The Problems of City Government,* Empire Club Speeches, Toronto.

————. 1908. "Municipal Publicity Through Uniformity in Municipal Statistics," *Eighth Annual Convention of the Union of Canadian Municipalities,* Montréal.

————, ed. 1907. *Municipal Government in Canada,* Toronto: University of Toronto Studies in History and Economics, vol. ii.

Wilcox, Delos F. 1897. *The Study of City Government,* New York: Macmillan.

Willard, James F. 1933. "Taxation Boroughs and Parliamentary Boroughs," in *Historical Essays in Honour of James Tait,* Manchester: Manchester University Press.

Williams, Raymond. 1973. *The Country and the City,* New York: Oxford University Press.

Williams, John H. 1984. "A Review of Some Aspects of Late Saxon Urban Origins and Development," in Margaret L. Faull, ed., *Studies in Late Anglo-Saxon Settlement,* Oxford: Oxford University Press.

Wirth, Louis. 1939. "The Urban Society and Civilization," *American Journal of Sociology,* vol. xlv, pp. 743–755.

Young, Charles R. 1961. *The English Borough and Royal Administration, 1130–1307,* Durham, N.C.: Duke University Press.

On British Colonial Apparatus

Andrews, Charles M. 1908. *British Committees, Commissions and Councils of Trade and Plantations,* Baltimore: Johns Hopkins, University Studies in Historical and Political Science.

Basye, Arthur Herbert. 1925. *The Lords Commissioners of Trade and Plantations, 1748–1782,* New Haven: Yale University Press.

Beaglehole, J. C. 1930. "The Royal Instructions to Colonial Governors 1783–1854," *Bulletin of the Institute of Historical Research,* vii, 184f.

————.1941. "The Colonial Office, 1782–1854," *Historical Studies Australia and New Zealand,* vol. i, 170f.

Beer, G. L. 1908. *The Origins of the British Colonial System, 1578–1660,* London.

————. 1913. *The Old Colonial System, 1660–1754,* Part I: *The Establishment of the System, 1660–1688,* 2 vols., London: Macmillan.

Cell, John W. 1970. *British Colonial Administration in the Mid-Nineteenth Century: The Policy-Making Process,* London.

Hartz, Louis. 1964. *The Founding of New Societies,* New York.

Keith, Arthur B. 1935. *The Government of the British Empire*, New York.

Knorr, Klaus E. 1944. *British Colonial Theories, 1570–1850*, Toronto: University of Toronto Press.

Keith, Arthur B. 1930. *Constitutional History of the British Empire*, Oxford.

Labaree, Leonard Woods. 1930. *Royal Government in America: A Study of the British Colonial System before 1783*, London.

Manning, Helen Taft. 1933. *British Colonial Government After the American Revolution, 1782–1820*, Hamden, Connecticut.

———. 1965. "Who Ran the British Empire 1830–1850?," *Journal of British Studies*, vol. v, 88f.

Martin, G. 1972. *The Durham Report and British Policy*, Cambridge.

Steele, I. K. 1968. *Politics of Colonial Policy*, Oxford: Clarendon Press.

Swinfen, D. B. 1970. *Imperial Control of Colonial Legislation, 1813–1865*, Oxford.

Ward, John Manning. 1976. *Colonial Self-Government: The British Experience, 1759–1856*, London.

Winch, Donald. 1965. *Classical Political Economy and Colonies*, Cambridge.

On Colonial America

Adams, Herbert B. 1882. "The Germanic Origins of New England Towns," in Herbert B. Adams, ed., *Johns Hopkins University Studies in Historical and Political Science*, Baltimore.

Akagi, Roy Hidemich. 1924. *The Town Proprietors of the New England Colonies, 1620–1770*, Philadelphia, University of Pennsylvania Press.

Andrews, Charles M. 1908. *British Committees, Commissions and Councils of Trade and Plantations*, Baltimore: Johns Hopkins, University Studies in Historical and Political Science.

———. 1934–1938. *The Colonial Period of American History*, 4 vols., New Haven: Yale University Press.

———. 1944. "On the Writing of Colonial History," *William and Mary Quarterly*, 3rd Series I, pp. 27–48.

Bailyn, Bernard. 1968. *The Origins of American Politics*, New York.

Channing, Edward. 1884. "Town and Country Government in the English Colonies of North America," in Herbert B. Adams, ed., *Johns Hopkins University Studies in Historical and Political Science*, Baltimore.

Basye, Arthur Herbert. 1925. *The Lords Commissioners of Trade and Plantations, 1748–1782*, New Haven: Yale University Press.

Beer, G. L. 1908. *The Origins of the British Colonial System, 1578–1660,* London: Macmillan.

————. 1913. *The Old Colonial System, 1660–1754,* Part I: *The Establishment of the System, 1660–1688,* 2 vols., London: Macmillan.

Bond, Beverley W. 1919. *The Quitrent System in the American Colonies,* London: Oxford University Press.

Bridenbaugh, Carl. 1938. *Cities in the Wilderness,* New York: Ronald Press.

————. 1955. *Cities in Revolt: Urban Life in America, 1743–1776,* New York: Alfred A. Knopf.

Daniels, Bruce C. 1979. *The Connecticut Town: Growth and Development, 1635–1790,* Middletown, Connecticut: Wesleyan University Press.

Davis, Joseph Stancliffe. 1917. *Essays in the Earlier History of American Corporations,* 2 vols., Cambridge: Harvard University Press.

Dickerson, Oliver M. 1912. *American Colonial Government, 1696–1765,* Cleveland, Ohio: Arthur H. Clark.

Earle, C. E. 1977. "The First English Towns of North America," *The Geographical Review,* vol. lxvii, no. 1, pp. 34–50.

Egleston, Melville. 1886. *The Land System of New England Colonies,* Baltimore: Johns Hopkins University.

Fairlie, John A. 1898. "Municipal Corporations in the Colonies," *Municipal Affairs,* vol. ii, September, no. 3.

————. 1904. "American Municipal Councils," *Political Science Quarterly,* vol. xix, no. 2, pp. 234–251.

Fries, Sylvia D. 1977. *The Urban Idea in Colonial America,* Philadelphia: Temple University Press.

Griffith, Ernest F. 1938. *History of American City Government: Colonial Period,* New York: Oxford University Press.

Griffith, Ernest F. and Charles R. Adrian. 1976. *A History of American City Government: The Formation of Traditions, 1775–1870,* New York.

Haller, William. 1951. *The Puritan Frontier: Town Planting in New England,* New York: Columbia University Press.

Harris, Marshall. 1953. *Origins of the Land Tenure System in the United States,* Ames: Iowa State College Press.

Howard, George E. 1889. *An Introduction to the Local Constitutional History of the United States,* Baltimore: Johns Hopkins University.

Johnson, Hildegard Binder. 1976. *Order Upon the Land,* New York: Oxford University Press.

Johnston, Alexander. 1883. "The Genesis of a New England State," in Herbert B. Adams, ed., *Johns Hopkins University Studies in Historical and Political Science*. Baltimore.

Knorr, Klaus E. 1944. *British Colonial Theories, 1570–1850*, Toronto: University of Toronto Press.

Labaree, Leonard Woods. 1930. *Royal Government in America: A Study of the British Colonial System before 1783*, London: Oxford University Press.

Leach, Douglas Edward. 1966. *The Northern Colonial Frontier*, New York: Holt, Rinehart and Winston.

Lemon, James T. 1972. *The Best Poor Man's Country: A Geographical Study of Early Southeastern Pennsylvania*, New York: W. W. Norton.

———. 1984. "Spatial Order: Households in Local Communities and Regions," in J. P. Greene and J. R. Pole, *Colonial British America*, Baltimore.

Lingelbach, William E. 1944. "William Penn and City Planning," *The Pennsylvania Magazine of History and Biography*, vol. lxviii, no. 4, pp. 398–418.

Lockridge, Kenneth A. 1985. *A New England Town: The First Hundred Years*, 2nd ed., New York.

McBain, Howard Lee. 1925. "The Legal Status of the American Colonial City," *Political Science Quarterly*, vol. xl, June, no. 2.

McIlwain, C. H. 1923. *The American Revolution: A Constitutional Interpretation*, New York.

Mohl, Raymond A., ed. 1988. *The Making of Urban America*, Wilmington, Delaware: Scholarly Resources Imprint.

Nettels, Curtis P. 1952. "British Mercantilism and the Economic Development of the Thirteen Colonies," *Journal of Economic History*, vol. xii, pp. 105–114.

Nettels, Curtis P. 1933. "England's Trade with New England and New York, 1685–1720," *Publications of the Colonial Society of Massachusetts*, vol. xxviii (February), pp. 322–350.

Osgood, Herbert L. 1896. "The Corporation as a Form of Colonial Government," *Political Science Quarterly*, vol. xi, pp. 259–277; pp. 502–533; pp. 694–715.

———. 1898. "The Proprietary Province as a Form of Colonial Government," *The American Historical Review*, vol. ii, pp. 644–664; vol. iii, pp. 31–55; vol. iii, pp. 244–265.

———. 1926. *The American Colonies in the Seventeenth Century*, London.

Porter, Kirk H. 1922. *County and Township Government in the United States*, New York: Macmillan.

Reps, John W. 1956. "William Penn and the Planning of Philadelphia," *Town Planning Review*, vol. xxvii, no. 1, pp. 27–39.

———. 1960. "Town Planning in Colonial Georgia," *The Town Planning Review*, vol. xxx, no. 4, pp. 272–285.

———. 1965. *The Making of Urban America*, Princeton: Princeton University Press.

———. 1969. *Town Planning in Frontier America*, Princeton: Princeton University Press.

Riley, Edward M. 1950. "The Town Acts of Colonial Virginia," *The Journal of Southern History*, vol. xvi (August), pp. 306–323.

Rogers, Henry Wade. 1901. "Municipal Corporations, 1701–1901," in *Two Centuries" Growth of American Law*, New York: Yale Law School Collective.

Sakolski, Aaron M. 1957. *Land Tenure and Land Taxation in America*, New York: Robert Schalkenbach Foundation.

Sato, Shosuke. 1886. *History of the Land Question in the United States*, Baltimore: Johns Hopkins University Press.

Steele, I. K. 1968. *Politics of Colonial Policy*, Oxford: Clarendon Press.

Glaab, C. N. and A. T. Brown. 1983. *A History of Urban America*, New York: Macmillan.

Teaford, Jon C. 1973. "The City versus State: The Struggle for Legal Ascendancy," *The American Journal of Legal History*, vol. xvii, pp. 51–65.

———. 1975. *The Municipal Revolution in America: Origins of Modern Urban Government, 1650–1825*, Chicago: University of Chicago Press.

———. 1981. "State Administrative Agencies and the Cities, 1890–1920," *The American Journal of Legal History*, vol. xxv, pp. 225–248.

Winch, Donald. 1965. *Classical Political Economy and Colonies*, Cambridge: Harvard University Press.

Zagarri, Rosemarie. 1987. *The Politics of Size*, Ithaca and London: Cornell University Press.

On British North America

Aitchison, J. H. 1949. "The Municipal Corporations Act of 1849," *Canadian Historical Review*, vol. xxx, pp. 107–122.

———. 1953. "Development of Local Government in Upper Canada," Ph.D. Thesis, University of Toronto.

Akins, T. B. 1895. *History of Halifax City*, Halifax: Nova Scotia Historical Society.

Anderson, R. M. 1936. "Development of Township Surveys in Ontario," *Canadian Surveyor*, vol. v, no. 8.

Armstrong, F. H. et. al, eds. 1974. *Aspects of Nineteenth Century Ontario*, Toronto: University of Toronto Press.

Basevi, Vincent. 1912. "The Evolution of Municipal Government," *Canadian Magazine*, vol. xxxix, pp. 367–372.

Beck, J. M. 1973. *The Evolution of Municipal Government in Nova Scotia, 1749–1973*, Halifax: Study prepared for the Nova Scotia Royal Commission on Education, Public Services and Provincial-Municipal Relations.

Berger, Carl. 1986. *The Writing of Canadian History: Aspects of English-Canadian Historical Writing since 1900*, 2nd ed., Toronto: University of Toronto Press.

Betts, George M. 1976. "Municipal Government and Politics," G. J. J. Tulchinski, ed., *To Preserve and Defend: Essays on the Nineteenth-Century Kingston*, Montréal.

Bourinot, John George. 1887. *Local Government in Canada: An Historical Study*, Johns Hopkins University Studies, Herbert B. Adams, ed., Series 5. Baltimore.

———. 1901. *A Manual of the Constitutional History of Canada*, Toronto: Copp Clark.

———. 1928. *How Canada is Governed*, Toronto: Copp Clark.

Bradshaw, F. 1903. *Self-Government in Canada and How it was Achieved*, London: P. S. King and Son.

Brittain, Horace L. 1951. *Local Government in Canada*, Toronto.

Buckner, Phillip A. 1985. *The Transition to Responsible Government: British Policy in British North America, 1815–1850*, London.

———. 1985. "The Colonial Office and British North America, 1801–1850," *Dictionary of Canadian Biography*, vol. viii, 1851–1860, Toronto: University of Toronto Press.

Burroughs, P. 1971. *British Attitudes Towards Canada, 1822–1849*, Scarborough, Ontario.

———. 1972. *The Canadian Crisis and British Colonial Policy, 1828–1841*, London.

Burt, A. L. 1940. *The United States, Great Britain and British North America*, New Haven.

Careless, J. M. S. 1974. "Some Aspects of Urbanization in Nineteenth-Century Ontario," Armstrong, F. H. et. al, eds., *Aspects of Nineteenth Century Ontario*, Toronto: University of Toronto Press.

————. 1978. *The Rise of Cities in Canada before 1914*, The Canadian Historical Association Booklets, no. 32, Ottawa.

————. 1989. *Frontier and Metropolis: Regions, Cities, and Identities in Canada before 1914*, Toronto: University of Toronto Press.

Crawford, Kenneth Grant. 1954. *Canadian Municipal Government*, Toronto.

Cruikshank, E. A. 1929. "An Experiment in Colonization in Upper Canada," *Ontario Historical Society, Papers and Records*, vol. xxv, pp. 32–77.

Feldman, Lionel D., ed. 1981. *Politics and Government of Urban Canada*, 4th ed., Toronto: Methuen.

Fergusson, C. B. 1961. *Local Government in Nova Scotia*, Halifax: Institute of Public Affairs of Dalhousie University.

Gates, Lillian F. 1968. *Land Policies of Upper Canada*, Toronto.

Gentilcore, Louis. 1963. "The Beginnings of Settlement in the Niagara Peninsula, 1782-1792," *Canadian Geographer*, vol. vii, no. 2, pp. 72-82.

Gentilcore, L. and K. Donkin. 1973. *Land Surveys of Southern Ontario*, Cartographica, Monograph no. 8.

Glazebrook, G. T. 1974. "The Origins of Local Government," F. H. Armstrong, et. al, eds., *Aspects of Nineteenth Century Ontario*, Toronto: University of Toronto Press.

Graham, G. S. 1930. *British Policy and Canada, 1774–1791*, London.

Harris, R. C. and J. Warkentin. 1974. *Canada before Confederation: A Study in Historical Geography*, New York: Oxford University Press.

Higgins, Donald J. H. 1986. *Local and Urban Politics in Canada*, Toronto.

Kennedy, W. P. M. 1938. *The Constitution of Canada, 1534–1937: An Introduction to its Development Law and Custom*, 2nd ed., Oxford.

Knaplund, Paul. 1953. *James Stephen and the British Colonial System, 1813–1847*, Madison.

Macdonald, Norman. 1939. *Canada, 1763–1841: Immigration and Settlement*, London: Longmans.

Martin, Chester. 1929. *Empire and Commonwealth: Studies in Governance and Self-Government in Canada*, Oxford: Clarendon Press.

McEvoy, J. M. 1889. *The Ontario Township*, University of Toronto Studies in Political Science, W. J. Ashley, ed., Toronto: Warwick and Sons.

Mills, David. 1988. *The Idea of Loyalty in Upper Canada, 1784–1850*, Kingston: McGill-Queen's University Press.

Morison, J. L. 1919. *British Supremacy and Canadian Self-Government, 1839–1854*, Glasgow.

Morrison, H. M. 1933. "The Principle of Free Grants in the Land Act of 1841," *Canadian Historical Review*, vol. xiv, pp. 392–407.

Murphy, Joseph J. 1889. "Documentary History of the First Surveys in the Province of Ontario," Paper read before the Association of Ontario Land Surveyors, Archives of Ontario.

Ormsby, W. 1969. *The Emergence of the Federal Concept in Canada*, 1839–1845, Toronto.

Paterson, Gilbert Clarence. 1921. *Land Settlement in Upper Canada 1783–1840*, Report no. 16, Toronto: Archives of Ontario.

Riddell, R. G. 1937. "A Study in the Land Policy of the Colonial Office, 1763–1855," *Canadian Historical Review*, vol. xviii, pp. 385–405.

Ross, Romaine K. 1962. *Local Government in Ontario*, 2nd ed., Toronto.

Schott, Carl. 1936. *Landnahme und Kolonisation in Kanada*, Kiel.

Shortt, Adam. 1902. "The Beginning of Municipal Government in Ontario," *Transactions of the Canadian Institute*, vol. vii, pp. 409–524.

————. 1907. "Municipal Government in Ontario: A Historical Sketch," Morley S. Wickett, ed., *Municipal Government in Canada*, Toronto: University of Toronto Studies in History and Economics.

Spelt, J. 1955. *The Urban Development in South-Central Ontario*, Assen: Netherlands.

Stelter, G. A. 1975. "The Urban Frontier in Canadian History," in *Cities in the West*, A. R. McCormack and I. Macpherson, eds., Ottawa: National Museum of Civilization.

————. 1980. "Urban Planning and Development in Upper Canada," in W. Borah, J. Hardoy, and G. A. Stelter, eds., *Urbanization in the Americas*, Ottawa: National Museum of Man.

————. 1984. "The Classical Ideal: Cultural and Urban Form in Eighteenth-Century Britain and America," *Journal of Urban History*, vol. x, no. 4, pp. 351–382.

Stelter, G. A., ed. 1975. "The Canadian City in the Nineteenth Century," *Urban Historical Review*, pp. 1–75.

Stelter, G. A. and A. Artibise, eds. 1982. *Shaping the Urban Landscape: Aspects of the Canadian City Building Process*, Ottawa: Carleton University Press.

————. 1984. *The Canadian City: Essays in Urban and Social History*, Ottawa: Carleton University Press.

Stewart, Gordon T. 1986. *The Origins of Canadian Politics*, Vancouver.

Taylor, John H. 1984. "Urban Autonomy in Canada: Its Evolution and Decline," in G. A. Stelter and A. Artibise, eds., *The Canadian City: Essays in Urban and Social History*, Ottawa: Carleton University Press.

Teeple, Gary. 1972. "Land, Labour, and Capital in Pre-Confederation Canada," in G. Teeple, ed., *Capitalism and the National Question in Canada*, Toronto.

Thomson, Don W. 1966. *Men and Meridians: The History of Surveying and Mapping in Canada*, 2 vols., Ottawa: Information Canada, Department of Mines and Technical Surveys.

Tindal, C. R. and S. Nobes Tindal. 1984. *Local Government in Canada*, 2nd ed., Toronto: McGraw-Hill Ryerson.

Weaver, W. F. 1962. *Crown Surveys in Ontario*, Ontario: Department of Lands and Forests.

Whalen, Hugh J. 1960. "Democracy and Local Government," *Canadian Public Administration*, vol. iii, pp. 1–13.

———. 1963. *The Development of Local Government in New Brunswick*, Fredericton.

Whebell, C. F. J. 1974. "Robert Baldwin and Decentralization, 1841–1849," F. H. Armstrong, et. al, eds., *Aspects of Nineteenth Century Ontario*, Toronto: University of Toronto Press.

———. 1989. "The Upper Canada District Councils Act of 1841 and British Colonial Policy," *The Journal of Imperial and Commonwealth History*, vol. xvii, number 2, pp. 185–209.

Wilson, A. 1968. *The Clergy Reserves of Upper Canada*, Toronto: University of Toronto Press.

Wood, David J. 1982. "Grand Design on the Fringes of Empire: New Towns for British North, America," *Canadian Geographer*, vol. xxvi, pp. 243–255.

———. 1988. "Population Change on an Agricultural Frontier: Upper Canada, 1796–1841," R. Hall, W. Westfall and L. S. MacDowell, eds., *Patterns of the Past: Interpreting Ontario's History*, Toronto: Dundurn Press.

———, ed. 1975. *Perspectives on Landscape and Settlement in 19th Century Ontario*, Toronto.

INDEX

POLITICAL ARRANGEMENTS
Power and the City

Henri Lustiger-Thaler, editor

In *Political Arrangements: Power and the City* urban sociologist Henri Lustiger-Thaler presents a timely collection of writings which puncture, once and for all, the curious Canadian myth that meaningful politics somehow only occurs on the Provincial and Federal levels of the state.

This book examines the age-old question of democracy in light of the specificity of the Canadian urban experience. It soberly assesses the failure of the mainstream 'democratic' imagination by developing much needed linkages within the current round of nation-state building to the activities of social movements, the growing and contradictory terrain of contemporary urban politics, aboriginal self-government and Canadian cities, women and municipalities, the relationship between global concerns and local politics, and the movement to entrench municipalities in provincial and federal charters.

Political Arrangements: Power and the City offers the inquisitive and critical reader some early traces of the "other Canadian constitution."

Henri Lustiger-Thaler holds a Ph.D. from the Université de Montréal. He has taught and researched at the University of Cambridge, and is currently teaching urban sociology and social theory at Concordia University in Montréal.

210 pages
Paperback ISBN: 1-895431-54-9 $19.95
Hardcover ISBN: 1-895431-55-7 $38.95

THE *CANADIAN* CITY

Kent Gerecke, editor

Based on a belief that a healthy city life is possible, Kent Gerecke collected articles, stories and histories about the city and its people—a collection and summary of various radical viewpoints on urban planning methods and priorities.

…this book makes for refreshing and often illuminating reading…it is honest and intelligent, and it is wide open to new ideas.
Books In Canada

…entertaining and informative reading, and will be of interest to anyone concerned with the many challenges facing today's urban environment.
Canadian Dimension

…an eclectic fare…written by advocates rather than dispassionate analysts.
Environment and Planning

220 pages
Paperback ISBN: 0-921689-92-6 $19.95
Hardcover ISBN: 0-921689-93-4 $38.95

PEOPLE, POTHOLES AND CITY POLITICS
Karen Herland

On the premise that 'knowledge is power,' here is a kind of handbook, the result of nearly a year of research, that will give the tools to understand how the city works and how you can make it work for you. This guide is intended for those who don't know where to begin, or who understand one aspect of the city, but want to know more about the big picture and how everything fits together.

The book is divided into three parts, each providing a thumbnail sketch of the demographics, quality of life, resources and problems to be found in the neighbour-hoods, some general tips on how to go about getting on the agenda at City Hall, or how to react once an issue is on the agenda and you have something to say about it—data that can be helpful when organizing. Knowing who you are trying to reach and what the local concerns are go a long way towards getting people organized. This guide is dedicated to anyone who wants to exercise power and make a difference.

200 pages
Paperback ISBN: 1-895431-52-2 $16.95
Hardcover ISBN: 1-895431-53-0 $35.95

MONTRÉAL
A Citizen's Guide to City Politics
Jean-Hugues Roy and Brendan Weston, editors

This citizen's guide attempts to critically inform the reader of what has happened to Montréal since the demise of the Jean Drapeau era. Some of the city's best known jour-nalists, community activists, urbanists, politicians and academics guide the reader through the maze of local politics. Montréal is scrutinized from every angle: housing and urban planning, ecology, public transportation, public health, its governing institu-tions and democracy, economic development relations between ethnic groups, and crime. What emerges is a clear picture of the policies and actions that influence the development of Montréal, with a vision of what the future could be like given the will and the imagination.

...[this] work should be interesting to a wider readership than the citizens of Montreal, for all our urban centres suffer from many of the same problems. We can all learn from Montreal's problems and intended solutions...we should be thankful to the editors.
Canadian Book Review Annual

Montréal is more than worthwhile...the writing is high calibre...visible minorities speak for themselves, just as women, tenants and even the MCM were permitted to do.
McGill Daily

250 pages
Paperback ISBN: 0-921689-70-5 $14.95
Hardcover ISBN: 0-921689-71-3 $33.95
L.C. No. 90-81637

URBANIZATION WITHOUT CITIES
The Rise and Decline of Citizenship
revised edition

Murray Bookchin

In this original work, Murray Bookchin introduces provocative ideas about the nature of community, and what it means to be a fully empowered citizen.

The city was once conceived as a nurturing environment that educated the individual while creating a rich legacy of popular, democratic, and participatory institutions. By uncovering this "hidden" history, Bookchin helps us to understand how cities can achieve a harmonious relationship with the natural world and what we must do to reaffirm the grassroots democratic traditions that have guided generations. What is envisaged is an environmentally oriented politics, a new ecological ethics and a citizenry that will restore the balance between city and country and, ultimately, between humanity and nature.

Murray Bookchin has been a pioneering thinker, writer, and activist in the environmental movement for more than thirty years and widely regarded by the international community as one whose ideas are decades ahead of his time. He is a teacher, lecturer, and keynote speaker throughout Europe and North America, and Professor Emeritus at the School of Environmental Studies, Ramapo College of New Jersey and Director Emeritus of the Institute for Social Ecology at Plainfield, Vermont, as well as author of more than a dozen major books.

340 pages
Paperback ISBN: 1-895431-00-X $19.95
Hardcover ISBN: 1-895431-01-8 $38.95

THE LIMITS OF THE CITY
2nd revised edition

Murray Bookchin

"City air makes people free." With this medieval adage, Bookchin begins a remarkable book on the evolution and dialectics of urbanism. Convincingly, he argues that there was once a human and progressive tradition of urban life and that this heritage has reached its "ultimate negation in the modern metropolis."

Bookchin's study is valuable for its historical perspective and its discussion of the effects on the individual of the modern city.
The Humanist in Canada

Limits of the City *is an antidote to superficial thinking...Bookchin — whose previous work has dealt with ecology, nature, anarchism and activism in a nuclear age — brings together 30 years of thinking...*
Toronto Star

194 pages, index
Paperback ISBN: 0-920057-64-0 $16.95
Hardcover ISBN: 0-920057-34-9 $35.95

THE CITY AND RADICAL SOCIAL CHANGE
Dimitrios Roussopoulos, editor

Intriguing new essays on the role of the city and city-based movements in the evolution of society. The authors take a fresh approach to urban activism, using specific examples from Toronto, Ottawa and the active community in Montréal. They present the perspectives of those who fight to improve transport, housing and public health, and trace the development of democracy, neighbourhood control and decentralization.

A most provocative and engaging proposal.
The Kingston Whig Standard

344 pages
Paperback ISBN: 0-929618-82-0 $12.95
Hardcover ISBN: 0-919618-83-9 $22.95

THE POLITICS OF URBAN LIBERATION
Stephen Schecter

A wide-ranging study dealing with political economy in an urban context and underlining the importance of the city in the history of social revolution. From France to Chile, the larger upheavals have been parallelled by insurgency from below over issues of daily life such as housing and transportation. Professor Schecter provides a libertairan evaluation of such questions as monopoly capital and the transformation of social life, the fiscal crisis of the State, and strategic implications of urban struggles, and relates them to our immediate situation with a chapter on the Montréal Citizens' Movement.

203 pages
Hardcover ISBN: 0-919618-79-0 $19.95

MONTRÉAL AFTER DRAPEAU
Jean François Léonard and Jacques Léveillée

In 1986, Montréal witnessed an election in which the Civic Party, after ruling the city for more than twenty years, was defeated by the reformist Montréal Citizens' Movement. The authors examine both political formations to determine their differences, the state of affairs in Montréal at the moment of the election, and what the future holds for the only bilingual city in North America.

134 pages
Paperback ISBN: 0-920057-88-8 $9.95
Hardcover ISBN: 0-920057-89-6 $19.95